Contributions to Economics

More information about this series at http://www.springer.com/series/1262

Aswini Kumar Mishra • Vairam Arunachalam
Debasis Patnaik
Editors

Critical Perspectives on Emerging Economies

An International Assessment

Springer

Editors
Aswini Kumar Mishra
Department of Economics and Finance
BITS Pilani, K K Birla Goa Campus
Sancoale, Goa, India

Vairam Arunachalam
Trulaske College of Business
University of Missouri
Columbia, MO, USA

Debasis Patnaik
Department of Economics and Finance
BITS Pilani, K K Birla Goa Campus
Sancoale, Goa, India

ISSN 1431-1933 ISSN 2197-7178 (electronic)
Contributions to Economics
ISBN 978-3-030-59780-1 ISBN 978-3-030-59781-8 (eBook)
https://doi.org/10.1007/978-3-030-59781-8

This Springer imprint is published by the registered company Springer Nature Switzerland AG
The registered company address is: Gewerbestrasse 11, 6330 Cham, Switzerland

Preface

The International Monetary Fund (IMF)'s recent ***World Economic Outlook Update*** (*June 2020: A Crisis Like No Other, An Uncertain Recovery June 24, 2020*), projects the global growth at −4.9% in 2020, 1.9 percentage points below the April 2020, World Economic Outlook (WEO) forecast. The COVID-19 pandemic has had a more adverse impact on activity in the first half of 2020 than expected, and the recovery is projected to be more gradual than previously forecast. In 2021, global growth is projected at 5.4%. Overall, this would leave 2021 GDP some 6½ percentage points lower than in the pre-COVID-19 projections of January 2020. While the ultimate growth outcome is still uncertain, and an even worse scenario is possible if it takes longer to bring the health crisis under control, the pandemic will result in output contractions across the vast majority of emerging market and developing economies (EMDEs). The adverse impact on low-income households is particularly acute, imperilling the significant progress made in reducing extreme poverty in the world since the 1990s. Thus, the immediate policy urgencies are to alleviate the human costs and attenuate the near-term economic losses. Further, to make future economies more resilient, many countries will need systems that can build and retain more human and physical capital during the recovery.

Against this backdrop, this volume comprises chapters by leading academicians, scholars, and practitioners from India and abroad on current topics that are relevant to emerging economies. The chapters have been a mix of qualitative and quantitative approaches to socio-economic and institutional issues that are relevant to the current world struggling for happiness and efficiency in uncertain times. The chapters are theoretically strong and largely tested through primary and secondary data.

The first chapter 'Does Globalization Lead to Happiness? Experience from Asian Lower-Middle Income Countries Using Pooled Mean Group (PMG) Model' by Neha Kumari, Naresh Chandra Sahu, and Pushp Kumar examines the impact of globalization on happiness in Asian lower-middle income countries (LMICs) from the period 2006 to 2016. The empirical results show that globalization has a positive impact on happiness in the long run though in the short run, it affects happiness negatively. Apart from globalization, economic growth, inflation, and unemployment are used as independent variables. The study reveals that happiness increases with the rise in economic growth. The effect of inflation on happiness is found unfavourable. This finding implies that inflation is an important determinant of happiness in lower-middle income countries. In this sample, people are happier when there is a low rate of inflation. Unemployment is seen as a negative determinant of happiness. The study suggests utilizing the fruits of globalization in promoting inclusive and sustainable economic growth for happiness in selected LMICs.

Our second chapter, by Elora Sil Roy, Rittu Susan Varkey, and Prasant Kumar Panda on 'Pattern of Carbon Dioxide Emission, Economic Growth and Energy Consumption in South-Asian Countries: An Empirical Analysis' analyses the pattern of environmental pollution as represented by percapita carbon dioxide emission ($PCCO_2$), per capita gross domestic product (PCGDP), and per capita energy consumption (PCEC) and their nexus in case of South-Asian countries for the time period 1991–2014. Results show a positive significant relationship that has been observed between PCGDP and $PCCO_2$ emission. In addition, an increase in PCEC also has a positively significant impact on $PCCO_2$ emission. The chapter suggests that economies in South-Asian region should underline sustainable economic activities by balancing growth of economy with clean environment.

The third chapter by Pushp Kumar, Naresh Chandra Sahu, and Siddharth Kumar on 'Natural Disasters and Income Inequality in South Asia: An FGLS Panel Analysis' focuses on the effects of natural disasters on income inequality in selected South-Asian countries during 1967–2014. The selected South-Asian countries for the study include India, Bangladesh, Nepal, Pakistan, and Sri Lanka. The study uses the feasible generalized least squares (FGLS) panel model to address the first-order serial correlation and panel group-wise heteroscedasticity problem. The frequencies of natural disasters have been used as proxies for natural disasters. We use Gini coefficients, Palma ratio, and Atkinson index as the proxies for income inequality. The results of the study show that natural disasters occurred in the same year, one-year lag, two-year lag, and three-year lag have a positive impact on income inequality in South-Asian countries. But the effect of natural disasters with the four-year lag and five-year lag on income inequality is not observed.

The next chapter on 'Factors Influencing Inflationary Condition in Sri Lanka: Orthodox Streamlining of Influential Factors' by E.A. Indunil, N. Ediriweera, and N. P. Thilini Deshika attempts to streamline most significant variables which were impacted to create a volatility in the general price level of the country. Money supply, foreign exchange rates, treasury bill rate, gold prices, oil prices, and gross domestic production were considered. The data was collected for 213 months for all the macroeconomic indicators and analysed based on the descriptive and inferential statistics. The trend analysis of inflation shows a high variation of price level within the Sri Lankan economy while foreign exchange rate, Gross domestic production, and money supply show a smooth trend with least shocks. Oil prices, gold prices, and treasury bill rate have structural breaks for both intercept and trend. Once the augmented Dickey–Fuller test result confirmed the stationarity of the data at level and first difference level, with the availability of the co-integration among the variables, it was concluded to develop an error correction model (ECM) to analyse the long-run relationship between the variables while eliminating the spurious effect of ordinary least square method. ECM confirmed that short-run coefficients of ECM are not significant and emphasizes that the system corrects the disequilibrium of its previous period at a speed of 7.82% monthly.

The fifth chapter on 'Information, Policy, and Market Disorder Under Democracy: Evidences from the United States' by Purbash Nayak, Mayank Sharma, and Harshit Shandilya studies how financial markets are perplexed by economic functioning especially policies determined by changing governments and election cycles. Noise through civilian interactions creates bias impacting portfolio valuation. This chapter takes the stand against the possibility of efficient market system while the system interacts socially. Reactions of investors are modelled. These reactions are used by big market players to control the masses and hold the levers of the game. Information for the market is generated in three dimensions—phase (path dependency), economic strength, and existing globalization processes with the undercurrents of election cycle. The chapter finds that the failure of Republicans is partially related to their taxation anomaly. The convolution of politics, economics, and financial markets is illustrated through a bipolar lens of both political exogeneity and endogeneity. Further, analysis suggests that financial market is in disorder following its denial towards development. Evidence shows that civil expenditure favours opulence but gains are more for the politically endorsed system. In order to reach a favourable state, one needs to first identify the broader aspects of developmental processes.

The sixth chapter, by Aswini Kumar Mishra, Pratyush Pradhan, and Divya Satish Revankar on 'Eliciting Time, Risk, and Social Preferences: Experimental Evidence from India' is based on a survey on 614 subjects in India. The chapter reveals the correlations of positive reciprocity and time preferences, trust and cognitive ability, and negative reciprocity and risk preferences. With reference to literature outside India, the results suggest that Indians have different preferences. Results based on principal component analysis (PCA) confirm that age, highest education, and cognitive ability play an important role in determining these preferences. Moreover, results also reveal that the regional diversities in these preferences indicate the need for unique implementation strategies in different regions for various governmental policies.

Our next chapter on 'Inflation Targeting and Exchange Rate Pass-Through in India: An Empirical Investigation' by Arshid Hussain Peer and Mirza Allim Baig examines the exchange rate pass-through (ERPT) to consumer prices under inflation targeting (IT) framework in India. The chapter uses monthly data from the period January 2011 to October 2019 for the empirical investigation. The vector autoregression (VAR) model is employed with variables on exchange rate, oil price, output, policy interest rate, and consumer prices index for the empirical analysis. The study finds that there is a significant decline of exchange rate pass-through under inflation targeting regime as compared to its previous regime, i.e. the multiple indicator approach regime. The chapter suggests that the decline in exchange rate pass-through via imported inflation may be helpful for monetary policy to achieve the target of inflation in India. The chapter suggests that the decline in ERPT through imported inflation is helpful for monetary policy to achieve the target of inflation in India.

The eighth chapter, by Sabitri Dutta on 'Indoor Fuel Choice and Women Empowerment: A Demand-Side Analysis', relates women's empowerment to fuel choice and calculates Women Empowerment Index (WEI) by applying structural equation modelling (SEM) technique. The structural model finds that WEI has a positive significant impact on the fuel choice made by the household, after controlling for other associated variables including per capita income and education of a woman and her spouse. The data used here is IHDS-II data (2011–2012) for rural women of India. This study reveals that empowerment of women is a crucial determinant of demand for clean fuel by the household. Thus, the chapter suggests that policies are needed to empower women like well-structured education system and financial inclusion of women and create an environment that would enable them to make larger participation in the society as well as to make them confident to take part in household decision.

The ninth and final chapter of this volume, by Bishnu Prasad Mishra on 'Smart City and Urban Poor: Can They Coexist?' uses a demographic profile of Bhubaneswar, Capital city of Odisha, India and applies survey technique to answer questions on relocation: basic needs? In a planned (so-called) locality on the city fringes, are these people not segregated to a world thrust upon them? What are the support systems provided to continue with the same lifestyle enjoyed by them earlier? In respect of people forcefully uprooted, is there life for rebuilding?

We are grateful to the authors for making their studies available for this edited volume. We sincerely hope that the studies included in this volume will stimulate academic debates and lead to further analytical advances in the domains of critical issues pertaining to emerging economies.

Goa, India — Aswini Kumar Mishra
Columbia, MO, USA — Vairam Arunachalam
Goa, India — Debasis Patnaik

Acknowledgments

This volume in Springer Series contains nine selected chapters presented or accepted at the Second International Conference on Economics and Finance (ICEF-2020) held at Birla Institute of Technology and Science, Pilani-K K Birla Goa Campus, Goa, India during January 23–25, 2020, especially the critical perspectives on emerging economies. The event aimed at stimulating critical thinking and sharing knowledge across emerging themes towards sustainable development, finance and trade, business and innovation, and related fields.

Eminent speakers like Jeffrey C. Thomson, President and CEO of IMA® (Institute of Management Accountants); Prof. Avanidhar (Subra) Subrahmanyam, Distinguished Professor of Finance, Goldyne and Irwin Hearsh Chair in Money and Banking, The John E. Anderson Graduate School of Management, University of California at Los Angeles (UCLA); Dr. Hamza Ali Malik, Director, Macroeconomic Policy and Financing for Development Division, United Nations Economic and Social Commission for Asia and the Pacific (United Nations ESCAP); Dr. Sweta Chaman Saxena, Chief, Macroeconomic Policy and Analysis, Macroeconomic Policy and Financing for Development, UN Economic and Social Commission for Asia and the Pacific (UN-ESCAP); Prof. Sanket Mohapatra, Economics Area Chairperson, IIM Ahmedabad; Prof. Sujeet K. Sharma, Associate Professor, Information System and Analytics, IIM Trichy; Dr. Joyojeet Pal, Principal Researcher, Microsoft Research India; Prof. Prakash Singh, Professor in Finance and Accounting, IIM Lucknow; and Mr. Jaywardhan Semwal, Vice President, Corporate Financial Accounting, Hewlett Packard Enterprise delivered distinguished lectures on this occasion. The event was supported by National Bank for Agriculture and Rural Development (NABARD) and Institute of Management Accountants (IMA®) provided an avenue for disseminating information on contemporary research and future practices in economics.

An edited book such as this also required the cooperation and dedication of its many contributing authors. Apart from penning excellent chapters, the authors were always prompt in their responses. We are also indebted to the anonymous referees and members of scientific committee for providing insightful reviews with many useful comments and suggestions.

This book deserves mentioning of a few colleagues and research scholars whose indefatigable efforts helped us in compiling this book. We would particularly like to thank (in no particular order) for the help and cooperation received from Dr. Arfat Ahmad Sofi, Dr. Sukumar Vellakkal, Dr. Rajorshi Sen Gupta, and Mr. Abhishek Kumar Sinha. We would also like to acknowledge the support we received from Prof. Raghurama G, Director, BITS Pilani-K K Birla Goa Campus in organizing the above-mentioned event and this book is an outcome of it.

Most importantly, we would like to thank Springer editor, Nitza Jones Sepulveda and Assistant Editor, Faith Su for their enthusiasm, advice, and encouragement.

Aswini Kumar Mishra

Department of Economics and Finance, BITS Pilani, K K Birla Goa Campus, Sancoale, Goa, India

Vairam Arunachalam

Trulaske, Sr. College of Business, University of Missouri, Columbia, MO, USA

Debasis Patnaik

Department of Economics and Finance, BITS Pilani, K K Birla Goa Campus, Sancoale, Goa, India

Contents

About the Editors

Aswini Kumar Mishra presently serves as the Head in the Department of Economics and Finance and an Associate Professor at BITS, Pilani-K K Birla Goa Campus, India. His research and teaching interests relate to applied econometrics, behavioral and applied development economics, and financial risk management. Dr. Mishra has published related articles in most leading scholarly journals including *International Journal of Finance & Economics*, *Journal of Quantitative Economics*, *International Economic Journal*, *Journal of Economic Studies*, *Economic Change and Restructuring*, etc.

Vairam Arunachalam serves as Director of the School of Accountancy and PricewaterhouseCoopers Distinguished Professor at the University of Missouri. His research and teaching interests pertain to forensic accounting, data analytics, and information systems. He is a member of the Accountancy Advisory Board at the University of Illinois at Urbana-Champaign. He is also a member of the Research Foundation of the Institute of Management Accountants (IMA). He has chaired several AACSB accounting accreditation review teams. His research has been published in several leading journals.

Debasis Patnaik serves as Associate Professor at BITS, Pilani-K K Birla Goa Campus, India, and was Past Head of the Department of Economics and Finance in Goa Campus. He has conducted many workshops and undertakes Consultancy and Management Development Program (MDP) for Insurance cum Assurance cum Banking Organizations. Dr. Patnaik has published over 80 papers in reputed national and international journals. He has been awarded and felicitated by different organizations and universities for his commitment to academic pedagogical approaches.

Contributors

Mirza Allim Baig Department of Economics, Jamia Millia Islamia (Central University), New Delhi, India

N. P. Thilini Deshika Department of Accountancy, Faculty of Business Studies and Finance, Wayamba University of Sri Lanka, Kuliyapitiya, Sri Lanka

Sabitri Dutta DumDum Motijheel Rabindra Mahavidyalaya, Kolkata, India

E. A. Indunil N. Ediriweera Department of Accountancy, Faculty of Business Studies and Finance, Wayamba University of Sri Lanka, Kuliyapitiya, Sri Lanka

Neha Kumari School of Humanities, Social Sciences and Management, Indian Institute of Technology, Bhubaneswar, India

Pushp Kumar School of Humanities, Social Sciences and Management, Indian Institute of Technology, Bhubaneswar, Odisha, India

Siddharth Kumar School of Humanities, Social Sciences and Management, Indian Institute of Technology, Bhubaneswar, Odisha, India

Aswini Kumar Mishra Department of Economics and Finance, BITS Pilani, K K Birla Goa Campus, Sancoale, Goa, India

Bishnu Prasad Mishra XIMB, Xavier University, Bhubaneswar, Odisha, India

Purbash Nayak Research Faculty, Gokhale Institute of Politics and Economics, Pune, India

Prasant Kumar Panda Department of Economics, Central University of Tamil Nadu, Thiruvarur, Tamil Nadu, India

Arshid Hussain Peer Department of Economics, Jamia Millia Islamia (Central University), New Delhi, India

Pratyush Pradhan Department of Economics, BITS Pilani, K K Birla Goa Campus, Sancoale, Goa, India

Divya Satish Revankar Department of Economics, BITS Pilani, K K Birla Goa Campus, Sancoale, Goa, India

Elora Sil Roy Deloitte, Salt Lake City, West Bengal, India

Naresh Chandra Sahu School of Humanities, Social Sciences and Management, Indian Institute of Technology, Bhubaneswar, Odisha, India

Harshit Shandilya Postgraduate, Gokhale Institute of Politics and Economics, Pune, India

Mayank Sharma Postgraduate, Gokhale Institute of Politics and Economics, Pune, India

Rittu Susan Varkey Department of Economics, CHRIST (Deemed to be University), Bengaluru, Karnataka, India

Chapter 1
Does Globalization Lead to Happiness? Experience from Asian Lower-Middle Income Countries Using Pooled Mean Group (PMG) Model

Neha Kumari, Naresh Chandra Sahu, and Pushp Kumar

1.1 Introduction

Earlier happiness studies were only confined to the area of Psychology, Sociology, and Philosophy. From the past few decades, economics of happiness became the emerging field of research that facilitates multidisciplinary research. Happiness[1] is increasingly recognized as "a fundamental human goal for achieving inclusive and balanced economic growth which could promote the wellbeing of people of the world" (UN 2013). Veenhoven (2008) has defined happiness as "an overall appreciation of one's life or how much one likes the life one lives". Everywhere people prefer desirable than undesirable and pleasant over unpleasant (Veenhoven 1991).

The measurement of happiness always remained in the discussion by various scholars across the globe. Broadly, the happiness of a person can be divided into objective and subjective measures. On the one hand, objective measures state about the physiological condition of a person, while on the other hand, subjective measures directly assess the well-being of the person (Frey et al. 2002). Economic and social factors of happiness can be divided into micro and macro (Welsch and Kuhling 2009). Micro determinants include personal and demographic factors, e.g. education, health, urbanization, household size and structure, marital status, and age. While macro factors are democracy, unemployment, inflation, economic growth, corruption, political freedom, civil war, environmental services, the rule of law, and terrorism.

[1] In this chapter, life satisfaction, subjective well-being, and happiness are used interchangeably.

N. Kumari (✉) · N. C. Sahu · P. Kumar
School of Humanities, Social Sciences and Management, Indian Institute of Technology, Bhubaneswar, India
e-mail: nk24@iitbbs.ac.in; naresh@iitbbs.ac.in; pk27@iitbbs.ac.in

A. K. Mishra et al. (eds.), *Critical Perspectives on Emerging Economies*, Contributions to Economics, https://doi.org/10.1007/978-3-030-59781-8_1

Several studies are undertaken to investigate the impact of macro factors on happiness. However, many studies are based on the nexus between economic growth and happiness. Apart from income, the other factors which influence happiness are political freedom (Fitoussi and Stiglitz 2012). Unemployment significantly reduces subjective well-being, both at the micro-level and macro-level (Frey et al. 2002; Oswald 1997; Tella et al. 2003). Eger and Maridal (2015) found that the standard of living, peace, health status, and security are major determinants of life satisfaction. In another study, Helliwell (2007) reports that social capital and trust are correlated with lower suicides across the countries. Blanchflower and Oswald (2005) found that friendship, crime, health, divorce rate, and traffic jams affect the happiness of the people. Also, Blanchflower and Oswald (2005) argued that the Human Development Index is unable to measure the mental well-being of the person. Thus, it cannot be a measure of happiness. Despite having the third rank in HDI, Australia has not performed well in terms of happiness indicators. Ram (2009) found a positive association between happiness and government spending.

Among different macro determinants, globalization plays a significant role in determining the happiness of people. Dreher (2006) has defined "Globalization is a process that erodes national boundaries, integrates national economies, cultures, technologies, and governance, and produces complex relations of mutual interdependence". There are many studies based on globalization and welfare. Wright (2000) reported that developing countries are more benefitted from globalization than developed economies. Afia and Harbi (2017) found that the export of goods and services have a positive impact on happiness. Tsai et al. (2012) found that achieving global language proficiency gives a feeling of accomplishment, happiness, and job satisfaction to the individuals. In contrast to this, Xin and Smyth (2010) found that globalized Chinese cities reported lower subjective well-being than less exposed cities. Beng (2012) found that globalization, frequent business cycles, and break up of families have resulted in a weak social protection system in globalized Singapore.

There is the inadequacy of empirical research focusing especially on the relationship between globalization and happiness. Only a few studies examined the relationship between happiness and globalization (Lin et al. 2016; Hessami 2011). Lin et al. (2016) examined the impact of globalization on happiness in 145 countries. They applied the spatial econometrics model to estimate the impact. Hessami (2011) also inquired about the impact of globalization on happiness in 15 European countries. He used an ordered probit model. Both studies applied a different methodology and econometric methods. Therefore, this chapter set out to explore the impact of globalization on happiness in lower-middle income countries (LMICs) of Asia during 2006–2016. This study differs from other studies from the perspective of methods and sampled areas. In this chapter, economic growth, inflation, and unemployment along with globalization are used as the independent variables. This study applied the latest econometric techniques, namely Westerlund (2007) cointegration test; CADF and CIPS unit root tests; and pooled mean group (PMG) model. This study provides new insights into the impact of globalization on happiness.

The remaining of the chapter is organized as follows: Sect. 1.2 reviews the studies related to the relationship between happiness and macroeconomic variables, i.e. globalization, economic growth, unemployment, and inflation. Section 1.3 discusses the description of the objective of the study, database, and econometric methods adopted in the study. Section 1.4 deals with results and discussion. Lastly, Sect. 1.5 provides the conclusion.

1.2 Literature Review

1.2.1 Globalization and Happiness

Globalization, directly and indirectly, influences the human well-being. Sen (2002) said that it is not the western countries which are responsible for globalization. Around AD 1000, there was an inverse flow of knowledge and technology from east to west. China invented high technology products and India educated the world by developing a decimal system. No country has achieved a high rate of growth without globalization. Only due to globalization, India and China reduced the poverty level in their country (Bhagwati and Srinivasan 2016). Afia and Harbi (2017) studied the impact of trade openness on happiness among 45 sample countries during 2000–2013. They found that trade openness affects happiness positively. Lin et al. (2016) examined the impact of globalization on happiness in 145 countries by using World Gallup poll data. The findings of the study reveal that globalization has a positive effect on happiness. Moreover, they showed that there exists an inverted U-shaped association between average happiness and happiness inequality. They justified this relation by arguing that initially due to the spillover effect of globalization, happiness inequality increases among countries due to fear and insecurity and after reaching the threshold level, the government implements various reforms that reduce the inequality.

In many parts of the world, mass disappointment against globalization has been seen. It has been argued by protectionists that globalization has created fear, insecurity, inequality, and dependency, especially in poor economies. Munck (2008) found that people living in other countries feel a sense of refusal, insecurity, starvation, social exclusion, and lack of peace.

The increasing stress on the environment has resulted in global warming, deforestation, climate change, and pollution, which is ultimately increasing the health cost (Costanza et al. 2014). Wanie and Tanyi (2013) studied agro-based industries in Cameroon. They found that due the globalization there are huge capital movements from developed countries to developing countries but simultaneously there is the extinction of local products, loss of natural vegetation; increased pollution; and highly competitive market. In the same line, Krishnakumar and Sarti (2013) found that economic globalization affects happiness negatively. This may be due to fear of job losses or takeover of ownership by foreign companies. A study by Bran et al. (2015) revealed that developing countries had not utilized the advantages of globalization. In another study, Freeman and Jackson (2012) evaluated the role of globalization on happiness in Bhutan. They found that due to globalization, positive changes have been seen like access to improved technology, transport facilities, and better job opportunities. On the contrary, people are negatively affected due to pollution, migration, habitat conservation, Buddhist heritage preservation, and recurring floods by the melting of glaciers. Wright (2000) found that once a developed country attains a certain level of standard of living like good food, clean shelter, medicines, transport, and communication along with democratic and human rights, globalization will not increase the happiness of people.

1.2.2 Happiness and Economic Growth

From the beginning of economics of happiness, the link between economic growth and happiness remained the burning topic of discussion. In a study, Easterlin (1974) tried to determine the level of happiness in the United States. He found that initially, happiness increases, with an increase in income. However, over the period, i.e. 1946–1966, it was found that happiness remained unaltered with the growth of income. This idea is popularly known as Easterlin Paradox.

Hagerty and Veenhoven (2003) challenged Easterlin's statement that an increase in income will not increase happiness. They found that in cross-sectional studies, income affects happiness positively. In another study, Easterlin (2009) again justified that the rise in income does not lead to an increased level of happiness. By supporting Easterlin (1974), Oswald (1997) found that happiness increases with the rise in income but at a marginal rate.

Tella et al. (2003) examined the association between macroeconomic indicators and happiness in Europe and America. It was found that GDP and happiness have a positive relationship. However, due to adaptive behaviour and habitual effect, GDP has a strong effect on happiness in the long run as compared to the short run. A positive relationship is found between subjective well-being and GDP (Stevenson and Wolfers 2008). According to them, relative income plays an insignificant role in determining happiness. Bran et al. (2015) found that income, quality of work conditions, availability of jobs, social capital, and health are the significant drivers of happiness. For the developed countries, it has been found that after the fulfilment of material consumption, there is no change in happiness

1.2.3 Unemployment, Inflation, and Happiness

For the country England, Clark and Oswald (1994) explored the association between happiness and unemployment. British household panel survey was used to examine this relationship. It was found that unemployment is a driving force of unhappiness. Lin et al. (2016) found unemployment as a negative determinant of happiness.

Similarly, happiness was found negatively associated with unemployment and inflation in 45 countries during the period 2000–2013 (Afia and Harbi 2017).

Blanchflower et al. (2014) analysed the impact of inflation and unemployment on happiness across European countries. It was found from their study that inflation and unemployment have a negative impact on happiness. Sanfey and Teksoz (2007) examined the impact of micro- and macroeconomic variables on life satisfaction from 1999 to 2002 for transition and non-transition countries. The negative association is found between unemployment and happiness. While in contrast to this, inflation has a positive impact on happiness. Perovic and Golem (2010) investigated the impact of macroeconomic variables on subjective well-being during 1991–1998 for 13 transition countries. An inverted U-shaped relation between inflation and unemployment on happiness was found.

1.3 Objective, Database, and Econometric Techniques

1.3.1 Objective

The above literature provides important insights regarding the role of globalization, inflation, economic growth, and unemployment on happiness. While reviewing the literature, the researchers have focused mainly on developed countries. So the objective of the chapter is as follows:

(a) To investigate the short-run and long-run impact of globalization on happiness in the lower-middle income countries of Asia.
(b) To examine the impact of economic variables like inflation, unemployment, and economic growth on happiness in these selected countries.

1.3.2 Database

The chapter uses the secondary data for the period of 2006–2016 for nine lower-middle income countries (LMICs) of Asia. The World Bank classification is used for choosing LMICs. According to these criteria, the countries whose GDP lie between \$1026 and \$3995 are called as LMICs. The selected countries are Bangladesh, Cambodia, Georgia, India, Indonesia, Pakistan, Philippines, Sri Lanka, and Vietnam. Economic globalization, economic growth, inflation, and unemployment are used as the independent variables for the study.

There are different measures of globalization, i.e. KOF index (2002), Maastricht globalization index (MGI) 2006, KFP index (2007), Centre for the Study of Globalization and regionalization (CSGR index), New globalization index or NGI (2009), and Randolph J G-index (2001). In this chapter, the KOF index of globalization has been used because it measures all types of foreign capital and the trade level along with restrictions. For measuring the globalization, the KOF economic globalization

Table 1.1 Variable descriptions

Variable	Symbol	Description	Units	Source
Happiness	HAPPI	Cantril life ladder ranging from 0 to 10	Scale	World Gallup poll
Economic growth	EG	GDP per capita growth (annual percentage) constant 2010 US dollars	Dollar	World development indicators
Inflation	INF	GDP deflator (annual percentage)	Percent units	World development Indicators
Unemployment	UNEMP	Percentage of unemployed persons out of total labour force	Percent units	World development indicators
Economic globalization	EGLB	Includes indicators of trade and financial globalization like trade flows, restrictions, taxes, and foreign investments	Index	Dreher (2006)

Table 1.2 Descriptive statistics

Statistics	HAPPI	EG	INF	UNEM	EGLB
Mean	4.746	4.597	7.073	4.555	52.337
Median	4.724	4.806	6.216	3.566	53.214
Maximum	5.786	13.168	22.799	18.300	80.353
Minimum	3.569	−2.791	−2.136	0.398	28.160
Std. dev.	0.540	2.345	5.304	4.383	13.115
Observations	99	99	99	99	99

Source Author's calculation

index is used. Economic growth is measured in terms of GDP per capita growth. The unemployment rate is used as the proxy for unemployment. Inflation is measured in terms of the GDP deflator (annual %). Earlier GDP deflator is used as a proxy for inflation by many studies (Tsai 2008; Alem and Köhlin 2014).

The variable happiness is used from the World Gallup poll survey. This survey reports happiness in terms of the Cantril ladder: "it asks respondents to think of a ladder, with the best possible life for them being 10, and worst possible life being 0". Other studies also used the Cantril ladder as a proxy for happiness (Abounoori and Asgarizadeh 2013; Degutis et al. 2010; Lew and Arvin 2012; Kuzu et al. 2019). The detailed description and descriptive statistics of the variables are presented in Tables 1.1 and 1.2 respectively.

To investigate the impact of globalization on happiness, the following functional relationship is used.

$$\text{HAPPI} = f(\text{EGLB}, \text{EG}, \text{UNEMP}, \text{INF}) \qquad (1.1)$$

$$HAPPI_{it} = \alpha_0 + \alpha_1 EGLB_{it} + \alpha_2 EG_{it} + \alpha_3 UNEMP_{it} + \alpha_4 INF_{it} + \mu_{it} \quad (1.2)$$

where, i, t, and μ represent the country, time, and error term, respectively.

The symbols α_1 to α_4 indicate estimated coefficients.

HAPPI indicates life satisfaction.

EGLB is KOF index of economic globalization.

EG denotes GDP per capita annual growth (%), and UNEMP is unemployment (% of the total labour force). INF indicates GDP deflator (annual %).

1.3.3 Econometric Techniques

Different econometric techniques are used to investigate the impact of globalization on happiness. These techniques are explained in the following subsections.

1.3.3.1 Cross-Section Dependence

Firstly, the study uses tests for the presence of cross-section dependence (CD) in the data. Because, in the presence of cross-section dependence, results may be spurious. So, this chapter used Breusch-Pagan LM, Pesaran Scaled LM, and Pesaran CD tests to test the presence of CD.

1.3.3.2 Unit Root Tests

To specify the stationarity of the variables, different panel unit root tests are used. For the establishment of the long run relationship among the variables, variables should be stationary either at a level or at first difference. In this chapter, we used second-generation unit root tests along with traditional panel unit root tests. Traditional panel unit root tests are Levin et al. (2002), Fisher-Augmented Dickey–Fuller (Fisher-ADF), and Fisher-Phillip Perron (Fisher-PP). While second-generation unit root tests are cross-sectionally augmented IPS (CIPS) and cross-sectionally augmented ADF (CADF) test developed by Pesaran (2007). Second-generation unit root tests have advantages over the traditional panel unit root tests. Second-generation unit roots have accounted for the issues of cross-section dependence in panel data (Ahmed et al. 2020). While traditional unit root tests do not account for the issue of cross-section dependence. In the traditional unit root tests, the null hypothesis states that there is a unit root against the alternative hypothesis that there is an absence of unit root in each series. CADF test is based on the following regression.

$$\Delta y_{it} = \alpha_i + \rho_i y_{it-1} + c_i \bar{y}_{t-1} + \sum_{j=0}^{n} d_{ij} \Delta \bar{y}_{it-1} + \sum_{j=0}^{n} \beta_{ij} \Delta y_{it} + \mu_{it} \tag{1.3}$$

where, y_{it} represents the variables. α is the intercept. μ_{it} represents error term. $\bar{y}$ is the mean. CIPS test can be obtained in the following equation:

$$\text{CIPS} = \frac{1}{N} \sum_{i=1}^{N} t_i(N, T) \tag{1.4}$$

1.3.3.3 Cointegration Tests

Pedroni (1999) and Westerlund (2007) cointegration tests are used for empirical analysis in this chapter. Researchers extensively used these tests for establishing the cointegration among the variables. Pedroni test is based on two statistics, namely panel-based statistics and group-based statistic. There are four panel-based statistics, and three group-based statistics. Panel-based statistic is also called *within dimension tests*. On the other hand, group-based statistic is called *between dimension tests*. ADF, rho panel-v, and PP statistics are the part of within dimension tests while between dimension tests include group-rho, ADF, and PP.

Along with the Pedroni test, we have used the Westerlund (2007) cointegration test to control the cross-section dependence. This test is used to produce robust results. Westerlund test is based on group mean statistics and pooled panel statistics. Group mean statistics are G_t and G_a. Pooled panel statistics are P_t and P_a.

1.3.3.4 Panel PMG Model

The objective of the chapter is to investigate the impact of globalization on happiness. To estimate the short-term and long-term impact of globalization on happiness, Pooled mean group (PMG) is used. This model is developed by Pesaran et al. (1999). The ARDL model equation for estimating the short-term and long-term impact is as follows:

$$\begin{aligned}\Delta \text{HAPPI}_{it} &= \alpha_{1i} + \gamma_{1i}\text{HAPPI}_{it-1} + \gamma_{2i}\text{EG}_{it-1} + \gamma_{3i}\text{EGLB}_{it-1} + \gamma_{4i}\text{INF}_{it-1} \\ &+ \gamma_{5i}\text{UNEMP}_{it-1} + \sum_{j=1}^{p} \delta_{1i}\Delta\text{HAPPI}_{it-j} + \sum_{i=0}^{q} \delta_{2i}\Delta\text{EG}_{it-j} \\ &+ \sum_{i=0}^{q} \delta_{3i}\Delta\text{EGLB}_{it-j} + \sum_{i=0}^{q} \delta_{4i}\Delta\text{INF}_{it-1} \\ &+ \sum_{i=0}^{q} \delta_{5i}\Delta\text{UNEMP}_{it-j} + \varepsilon_{1it}\end{aligned} \tag{1.5}$$

where Δ denotes the first difference operator. i and t stand for cross-sections and time.

ARDL, as mentioned in Eq. (1.5) is estimated through the PMG model. This model accounts the individual characteristics, i.e. country and region. According to Pesaran et al. (1999), the estimator obtained by the PMG model is asymptotically and normally distributed.

1.4 Results and Discussion

In panel data, estimation of the existence of the cross-section dependence is a key focus of the study in the recent literature (Hasan 2019; Zafar et al. 2019; Aydin 2019). The presence of cross-section dependence (CD) may give rise to biased results. So Breusch-Pagan LM, Pesaran scaled LM, and Pesaran CD tests are applied. The results of CD test are presented in Table 1.3. The null hypothesis of the absence of CD is rejected against the alternative hypothesis (Table 1.3). This result implies that there is a presence of CD in the data. Therefore, second-generation unit root tests are used. Second-generation unit root tests are CADF and CIPS. LLC, ADF, and PP unit root tests are also employed to test the stationarity of the variables along with second-generation unit root tests. The results of these tests are reported in Table 1.4. Some variables are stationary at level, while some are at first difference. It

Table 1.3 Cross-section dependence tests

Tests	EGLB	INF	HAPPI	EG	UNEM
Breusch-pagan LM	132.477***	129.348***	44.628	85.330***	68.005**
	(0.000)	(0.000)	(0.1530)	(0.000)	(0.001)
Pesaran scaled LM	10.309***	9.940***	−0.044	4.753***	2.711**
	(0.000)	(0.000)	(0.965)	0.000	(0.007)
Pesaran CD	1.132	10.658***	−1.103	6.927***	−0.956
	(0.258)	(0.000)	(0.270)	0.000	(0.339)

Source Author's calculation
Note *P*-values are given in the parentheses. ***, **, and * denotes significance at 1%, 5%, and 10% level, respectively

Table 1.4 Unit root test results

Variables	LLC		ADF		PP		CIPS		CADF	
	Level	First difference	Level	First difference	Level	First difference	Level	First difference	Level	First difference
EGLB	−5.584***	−7.235***	23.931	40.210**	11.031	64.244***	−1.400	−2.861*	−2.394	−3.187**
	(0.000)	(0.000)	(0.157)	(0.002)	(0.893)	(0.000)			(0.349)	(0.035)
INF	−9.117***	−24.060***	53.010***	74.455***	65.732***	114.342***	−3.318***	−3.077***	−2.803*	−3.077*
	(0.000)	(0.000)	(0.000)	(0.000)	(0.000)	(0.000)			(0.068)	(0.055)
HAPPI	−6.576***	−9.609***	37.607**	48.011**	62.373***	109.219***	−3.248**	−4.520***	−2.290	−4.520**
	(0.000)	(0.000)	(0.004)	(0.000)	(0.000)	(0.000)			(0.457)	(0.000)
EG	−13.613***	−16.144***	59.740***	58.144***	40.077**	74.905***	−2.661	−3.974***	−2.951**	−3.974***
	(0.000)	(0.000)	(0.000)	(0.000)	(0.002)	(0.000)			(0.029)	(0.000)
UNEM	−2.894**	−11.719***	13.485	49.960***	21.079	97.835***	−1.299	−3.288**	−1.370	−3.288**
	(0.002)	(0.000)	(0.762)	(0.000)	(0.276)	(0.000)			(0.991)	(0.023)

Source Author's calculation
Note *P*-values are given in the parentheses. ***, **, and * denotes significance at 1%, 5%, and 10% level, respectively

Table 1.5 Pedroni cointegration test

	Statistics	Weighted statistics
Common AR coefficients (within dimension)		
Panel v-statistic	−2.691	−2.580
	(0.996)	(0.995)
Panel rho-statistic	3.157	2.978
	(0.999)	(0.999)
Panel PP-statistic	−9.171***	−10.559***
	(0.000)	(0.000)0
Panel ADF-statistic	−4.013***	−4.785***
	(0.000)	(0.000)
Individual AR coefficients (between dimension)		
Group rho-statistic	3.970	
	(1.000)	
Group PP-statistic	−12.263***	
	(0.000)	
Group ADF-statistic	−5.539***	
	(0.000)	

Source Author's calculation
Note *P*-values are given in the parentheses. ***, **, and * denotes significance at 1%, 5%, and 10% level, respectively

Table 1.6 Westerlund panel cointegration test

Statistic	Value	*Z*-value	*P*-value
Gt	−4.006***	5.913	0.000
Ga	−0.398	4.000	1.000
Pt	−3.987	0.681	0.752
Pa	−0.403	2.344	0.991

Source Author's calculation
Note *P*-values are given in the parentheses. ***, **, and * denotes significance at 1%, 5%, and 10% level, respectively

is found that all variable is stationary either at level or at first difference. This indicates the possibility of a long-run relationship among the variables.

To establish the cointegration among the variables, Pedroni (1999) and Westerlund (2007) cointegration tests are used. These tests are called as second-generation cointegration tests. Results of the Pedroni and Westerlund cointegration test are reported in Tables 1.5 and 1.6. Pedroni cointegration tests show that out of seven statistics, four are significant at 5% level of significance (Table 1.5). In the same way, the Westerlund test reveals that out of four statistics, one statistics is significant at 1% level of significance (Table 1.6). Thus, these two tests confirm the existence of cointegration among the variables.

To analyse the long-run and short-run impact of globalization on happiness, PMG model is applied. The outcomes of the model are reported in Table 1.7. Table 1.7 reveals the short-run and long-run elasticities of happiness in relation to globalization, economic growth, inflation, and unemployment. The coefficient of error

Table 1.7 PMG long-run estimation (LNHAPPI is dependent variable)

Variable	Coefficient	*t*-statistic	Probability
Long-run equation			
EGLB	0.130***	8.230	0.000
INF	−0.012**	−2.300	0.022
EG	0.062**	3.300	0.001
UNEM	−0.843***	−9.930	0.000
ECM equation			
ECT(-1)	−0.493***	−3.960	0.000
Δ EGLB	−0.066*	−1.740	0.083
Δ INF	−0.011	−1.050	0.294
Δ EG	0.003	0.050	0.957
Δ UNEM	−0.132	−0.680	0.498
C	3.660	1.810	0.071

Source Author's calculation
Note *P*-values are given in the parentheses. ***, **, and * denotes significance at 1%, 5%, and 10% level, respectively

correction term (ECT) is found to be significant with a negative sign. The result of ECT shows that the process converges over the long run.

In Table 1.7, economic globalization is found to be statistically significant at 1% level of significance with a positive sign in the long run. Also, in the short run, economic globalization is found to be significant at 10% level and has a negative relationship with happiness. It reveals that economic globalization has a positive impact on happiness in the long run. However, it has a negative impact in the short run. A negative result may be supported by the fact that in the early stages of globalization, there may be insecurity among people due to fear of loss and the spread of monopoly by foreigners. While a positive result, in the long run, can be explained in three ways. Firstly, people get benefitted from access to varieties of the basket of commodities at cheaper rates. Secondly, people get adjusted to the MNC's and foreign trade and thus, adversely affected people from globalization have either shifted their occupation or way of living to tackle the situation. Thirdly, the government has implemented different socio-economic policies to compensate the affected people so that the fruits of globalization and growth can be distributed equally. These results agree with the findings of other studies, i.e. (Lin et al. 2016; Kalmijn and Veenhoven 2005; Veenhoven 2005), in which globalization is found to have a positive impact on happiness.

Another variable, economic growth is also found as significant at 1% level with a positive sign in the long run. But in the short run, it is found to be insignificant. It shows that with a rise in economic growth, there will be a rise in happiness in the long run. This finding is supported by other studies (Stevenson and Wolfers 2008; Hagerty and Veenhoven 2003; Tella et al. 2003).

In the long run, unemployment is found as statistically significant with the negative sign at 1% level of significance. It means that happiness is negatively affected by unemployment. The level of happiness will be high if there is a low level of unemployment rate in the economy. Other studies (Chang et al. 2013; Afia and Harbi 2017; Tella et al. 2003) found that unemployment reduces happiness.

Lastly, the coefficient of inflation is found as significant with the negative sign at 5% level of significance in the long run. It implies that in the long run, happiness is negatively determined by inflation. The level of happiness will be high when there is a low rate of inflation in the economy in the long run. This result is supported by other studies in the literature (Graham and Pettinato 2001; Frey and Stutzer 2000). In summary, our results found that economic globalization leads to happiness in the sampled country.

1.5 Conclusion

The chapter aims to investigate the impact of globalization on happiness in LMICs of Asia during 2006–2016. To estimate this impact, we have used second-generation unit root tests and the Westerlund cointegration test. Through PMG, we examined the long-term and short-term impact of globalization on happiness.

Results of the study show that globalization has a positive impact on happiness. In the long run, with the rise in the degree of globalization, happiness increases in the sample lower-middle income countries of Asia. However, in the short run, with the rise in the degree of globalization, happiness diminishes. Other than globalization, economic growth, inflation, and unemployment are used as independent variables. The study reveals that happiness increases with the rise in economic growth. This can be understood that economic growth matters for happiness in sampled countries.

The effect of inflation on happiness is found as unfavourable. This finding implies that inflation is an important determinant of happiness in lower-middle income countries. In these countries, people are happier when there is a low rate of inflation. Lastly, unemployment is seen as a negative determinant of happiness. It implies that people will be happier when there is a low rate of unemployment in sampled countries.

In light of these results, it can be said that the opening of boundaries is giving a plethora of opportunities to the people. At the same time, the government should take care of the adversely affected people from the globalization. The different socio-economic policy is required to make a balance between labour-intensive areas, i.e. small-scale industries and agriculture and capital-intensive industries. In this way, more employment opportunities can be availed with efficient technology use. Furthermore, human resource development can be one step ahead of where people can cope with the challenging situation aroused by globalization and maintain their current level of happiness.

Suitable monetary and fiscal policies are also required to keep inflation at a tolerable level, simultaneously giving opportunities to the producers to invest. For the lower-middle countries, economic growth and globalization is a necessary condition for uplifting people from the poverty trap and enhancing their happiness. Thus, maintaining a sustainable and inclusive growth must be the objective of the governments of these countries to enhance happiness among their citizens.

References

Abounoori, E., & Asgarizadeh, D. (2013). Macroeconomic factors affecting happiness. *International Journal of Business and Development Studies, 5*(1), 5–22.

Afia, N. B., & Harbi, S. (2017). Empirical analysis of the relationship between military endeavor, economic growth and happiness. *Journal of Economic Development, 42*(2), 51–66. https://doi.org/10.35866/caujed.2017.42.2.004.

Ahmed, Z., Zafar, M. W., & Ali, S. (2020). Linking urbanization, human capital, and the ecological footprint in G7 countries: An empirical analysis. *Sustainable Cities and Society, 55*, 102064. https://doi.org/10.1016/j.scs.2020.102064.

Alem, Y., & Köhlin, G. (2014). The impact of food price inflation on subjective well-being: Evidence from urban Ethiopia. *Social Indicators Research, 11*(3), 853–868. https://doi.org/10.1007/s11205-013-0318-7.

Aydin, M. (2019). The effect of biomass energy consumption on economic growth in BRICS countries: A country-specific panel data analysis. *Renewable Energy, 138*, 620–627. https://doi.org/10.1016/j.renene.2019.02.001.

Beng, C. S. (2012). Employment-based social protection in Singapore: Issues and prospects. *ASEAN Economic Bulletin, 29*(3), 218–229. https://doi.org/10.1355/ae29-3d.

Bhagwati, J., & Srinivasan, T. N. (2016). Trade and poverty in the poor countries. *American Economic Association, 92*(2), 180–183. https://doi.org/10.1257/000282802320189212.

Blanchflower, D. G., Bell, D. N. F., Montagnoli, A., & Moro, M. (2014). The happiness trade- off between unemployment and inflation. *Journal of Money, Credit and Banking, 46*(S2), 117–141. https://doi.org/10.1111/jmcb.12154.

Blanchflower, D. G., & Oswald, A. J. (2005). Happiness and the human development index: The paradox of Australia. *Australian Economic Review, 38*, 307–318. https://doi.org/10.1111/j.1467-8462.2005.00377.x.

Bran, F., Radulescu, C. V., & Ioan, I. (2015). Globalization, economic growth and happiness: The perspectives of an economy based on non-material values. *Journal of Knowledge Management, Economics and Information Technology, 5*(6), 1–14.

Chang, S. S., Stuckler, D., Yip, P., & Gunnell, D. (2013). Impact of 2008 global economic crisis on suicide: Time trend study in 54 countries. *BMJ (Online), 347*(7925), 1–15. https://doi.org/10.1136/bmj.f5239.

Clark, A. E., & Oswald, A. J. (1994). Unhappiness and unemployment. *The Economic Journal, 104*(424), 648–659. https://doi.org/10.2307/2234639.

Costanza, R., Cumberland, J. H., Daly, H., Goodland, R., Norgaard, R. B., Kubiszewski, I., & Franco, C. (2014). *An introduction to ecological economics*. Boca Raton: CRC Press. https://doi.org/10.1201/b17829.

Degutis, M., Urbonavičius, S., & Gaižutis, A. (2010). Relation between GDP and life satisfaction in the European Union. *Ekonomika, 89*(1), 9–21. https://doi.org/10.15388/Ekon.2010.0.997.

Dreher, A. (2006). Does globalization affect growth? Evidence from a new index of globalization. *Applied Economics, 38*, 1091–1110. https://doi.org/10.1080/00036840500392078.

Easterlin, R. A. (1974). Does economic growth improve the human lot? Some empirical evidence. In P. A. David & M. W. Reder (Eds.), *Nations and households in economic growth essays in honor of Moses Abramovitz* (pp. 89–125). New York: Academic Press. https://doi.org/10.1016/B978-0-12-205050-3.50008-7.

Easterlin, R. A. (2009). Happiness and growth the world over: Time series evidence on the happiness-income paradox. *IZA Discussion Paper, 4060*.

Eger, R. J., & Maridal, J. H. (2015). A statistical meta-analysis of the wellbeing literature. *International Journal of Wellbeing, 5*(2), 45–74. https://doi.org/10.5502/ijw.v5i2.4.

Fitoussi, J., & Stiglitz, J. E. (2012). On the measurement on social progress and wellbeing: Some further thoughts. In *The global macro economy and finance* (pp. 13–24). London: Palgrave Macmillan.

Freeman, K. A., & Jackson, K. C. (2012). In pursuit of happiness, Bhutan opens to globalization and business. *International Journal of Business and Social Research, 2*(2), 132–143. https://doi.org/10.18533/ijbsr.v2i5.104.

Frey, B. S., & Stutzer, A. (2000). Happiness, economy and institutions. *The Economic Journol, 110* (15), 918–938.

Frey, B. S., Stutzer, A., Di Tella, R., & Macculloch, R. (2002). What can economists learn from happiness research? *Journol of Economic Literature, 40*(2), 402–435. https://doi.org/10.1257/jel.40.2.402.

Graham, C., & Pettinato, S. (2001). Happiness, markets, and democracy: Latin america in comparative perspective. *Journal of Happiness Studies, 2*, 237–268. https://doi.org/10.1023/A:1011860027447.

Hagerty, M. R., & Veenhoven, R. (2003). Wealth and happiness revisited – Growing national income does go with greater happiness. *Social Indicators Research, 64*(1), 1–27. https://doi.org/10.1023/A:1024790530822.

Hasan, M. A. (2019). Does globalization accelerate economic growth? South Asian experience using panel data. *Journal of Economic Structures, 8*(1), 26. https://doi.org/10.1186/s40008-019-0159-x.

Helliwell, J. (2007). Well-being and social capital: Does suicide pose a puzzle? *Social Indicators Research, 81*(3), 455. https://doi.org/10.1007/s11205-006-0022-y.

Hessami, Z. (2011). Globalization's winners and losers—Evidence from life satisfaction data, 1975–2001. *Economics Letters, 112*, 250–253. https://doi.org/10.1016/j.econlet.2011.05.016.

Kalmijn, W., & Veenhoven, R. (2005). Measuring inequality of happiness in nations: In search for proper statistics. *Journal of Happiness Studies, 6*(4), 357–396. https://doi.org/10.1007/s10902-005-8855-7.

Krishnakumar, J., & Sarti, E. (2013). The impact of globalization on work capability. *International Journal of Sustainable Human Development, 1*(4), 146–153. https://doi.org/10.1108/01435120010693988.

Kuzu, S., Elmas-Atay, S., & Gerçek, M. (2019). The analysis of unemployment, happiness and demographic factors using log-linear models. *International Journal of Economics and Business Research, 17*(1), 87–105. https://doi.org/10.1504/IJEBR.2019.096588.

Levin, A., Lin, C. F., & Chu, C. S. J. (2002). Unit root tests in panel data: Asymptotic and finite-sample properties. *Journal of Econometrics, 108*(1), 1–24. https://doi.org/10.1016/S0304-4076(01)00098-7.

Lew, B., & Arvin, B. M. (2012). Happiness and air pollution: Evidence from 14 European countries. *International Journal of Green Economics, 6*(4), 331–345. https://doi.org/10.1504/IJGE.2012.051492.

Lin, C. A., Lahiri, S., & Hsu, C. (2016). Happiness and globalization: A spatial econometric approach happiness and globalization: A spatial econometric approach. *Journal of Happiness Studies, 18*, 1841–1857. https://doi.org/10.1007/s10902-016-9793-2.

Munck, R. (2008). Globalisation, governance and migration: An introduction. *Third World Quarterly, 29*(7), 1227–1246. https://doi.org/10.1080/01436590802386252.

Oswald, A. J. (1997). Happiness and economic performance. *The Economic Journal, 107*(445), 1815–1831. Retrieved from https://www.andrewoswald.com/docs/happecperf.pdf.

Pedroni, P. (1999). Critical values for cointegration tests in heterogeneous panels with multiple regressors. *Oxford Bulletin of Economics and Statistics, 61*(S1), 653–670. https://doi.org/10.1111/1468-0084.0610s1653.

Perovic, L. M., & Golem, S. (2010). Investigating macroeconomic determinants of happiness in transition countries. *Eastern European Economics, 48*(4), 59–75. https://doi.org/10.2753/eee0012-8775480403.

Pesaran, M. H. (2007). A simple panel unit root test in the presence of cross-section dependence. *Journal of Applied Econometrics, 22*(2), 265–312. https://doi.org/10.1002/jae.951.

Pesaran, M. H., Shin, Y., & Smith, R. P. (1999). Pooled mean group estimation of dynamic heterogeneous panels. *Journal of the American Statistical Association, 94*(446), 621–634. https://doi.org/10.1080/01621459.1999.10474156.

Ram, R. (2009). Government spending and happiness of the population: Additional evidence from large cross-country samples. *Public Choice, 138*, 483–490. https://doi.org/10.1007/s11127-008-9372-0.
Sen, A. (2002). How to judge globalism. *The American Prospect, 13*(1), 1–14.
Stevenson, B., & Wolfers, J. (2008). Economic growth and subjective well-being: Reassessing the Easterlin paradox. *Brookings Papers on Economic Activity*, (1), 102.
Sanfey, P. & Teksoz, U. (2007). Does transition make you happy? *The Economics of Transition, 15* (4), 707–731. https://doi.org/10.1111/j.1468-0351.2007.00309.x.
Tella, R. D., MacCulloch, R. J., & Oswald, A. J. (2003). The macroeconomics of happiness. *Review of Economics and Statistics, 85*(4), 809–827. https://doi.org/10.1162/003465303772815745.
Tsai, K. S. (2008). Factions and finance in China: Elite conflict and inflation. By Victor C. Shih. New York: Cambridge University Press, 2008. 264p. $85.00. *Perspectives on Politics, 6*(4), 851–852. https://doi.org/10.1017/S153759270808225X.
Tsai, M. C., Chang, H. H., & Chen, W. c. (2012). Globally happy: Individual globalization, expanded capacities, and subjective wellbeing. *Social Indicators Research, 108*(3), 509–524. https://doi.org/10.1007/s11205-011-9890-x.
UN. (2013). Happiness: Towards a holistic approach to development. In *UN dag repository*. https://unstats.un.org/unsd/broaderprogress/pdf/Happiness towards a holistic approach to development (A-67-697).pdf
Veenhoven, R. (1991). Is happiness relative? *Social Indicators Research, 24*(1), 1–34. https://doi.org/10.1007/BF00292648.
Veenhoven, R. (2005). Return of inequality in modern society? Test by dispersion of life-satisfaction across time and nations. *Journal of Happiness Studies, 6*(4), 457–487. https://doi.org/10.1007/s10902-005-8858-4.
Veenhoven, R. (2008). Healthy happiness: Effects of happiness on physical health and the consequences for preventive health care. *Journal of Happiness Studies, 9*, 449–469. https://doi.org/10.1007/s10902-006-9042-1.
Wanie, C. M., & Tanyi, F. O. (2013). The impact of globalisation on agro-based corporations in Cameroon: The case of the Cameroon development Corporation in the South West Region. *International Journal of Business and Globalisation, 11*(2), 136–148. https://doi.org/10.1504/IJBG.2013.055599.
Welsch, H., & Kuhling, J. (2009). Using happiness data for environmental valuation: Issues and applications. *Journal of Economic Surveys, 23*(2), 385–406. https://doi.org/10.1111/j.1467-6419.2008.00566.x.
Westerlund, J. (2007). Testing for error correction in panel data. *Oxford Bulletin of Economics and Statistics, 69*(6), 709–748. https://doi.org/10.1111/j.1468-0084.2007.00477.x.
Wright, R. (2000). Will globalization make you happy? *Foreign Policy*, (120), 54–64. https://doi.org/10.2307/1149713.
Xin, W., & Smyth, R. (2010). Economic openness and subjective well-being in China. *China and World Economy, 18*(2), 22–40. https://doi.org/10.1111/j.1749-124X.2010.01187.x.
Zafar, M. W., Saud, S., & Hou, F. (2019). The impact of globalization and financial development on environmental quality: Evidence from selected countries in the Organization for Economic Co-operation and Development (OECD). *Environmental Science and Pollution Research, 26* (13), 13246–13262. https://doi.org/10.1007/s11356-019-04761-7.

Chapter 2
Pattern of Carbon Dioxide Emission, Economic Growth and Energy Consumption in South-Asian Countries: An Empirical Analysis

Elora Sil Roy, Rittu Susan Varkey, and Prasant Kumar Panda

2.1 Introduction

In the changing development paradigm, the problem of increasing carbon dioxide has become a great challenge. Besides, it is equally challenging to ensure strict enforcement of carbon dioxide emissions to ensure clean environment, sustainable development and welfare of the society. Carbon dioxide level in the atmosphere has been increasing substantially over the years. In the Kyoto protocol in 1997, governments around the world have come to a common consensus to reduce the national emissions of greenhouses gases to 5% by the period 2008–2012. Among all the greenhouse gases, the contribution of CO_2 occupies a major role. It is ever-increasing over the year which is aggravating the situation including temperature and climate change. In the future, companies have to provide reliable information regarding carbon footprint and its contribution in reducing the emission of the gas. A majority of the major energy users have supported the decision of governments to reduce the carbon dioxide emission.

Economic growth is a crucial element for the economy, as it creates high wage jobs and facilitates improvement in standards of living. As employment and income increase, demand for various goods and services also increases. To match the increased demand and at the same time be competitive in the international market,

E. S. Roy
Deloitte, Salt Lake City, West Bengal, India

R. S. Varkey
Department of Economics, CHRIST (Deemed to be University), Bengaluru, Karnataka, India
e-mail: rittususan.varkey@christuniversity.in

P. K. Panda (✉)
Department of Economics, Central University of Tamil Nadu, Thiruvarur, Tamil Nadu, India
e-mail: prasantkumar@cutn.ac.in

A. K. Mishra et al. (eds.), *Critical Perspectives on Emerging Economies*,
Contributions to Economics, https://doi.org/10.1007/978-3-030-59781-8_2

industries should be growing at a rapid rate to be able to produce while experiencing economies of scale. More industries might also have to be set up to tend to the domestic and world market separately. As industries grow, demand for energy mainly from conventional sources also increases, leading to high energy consumption and it may have an impact on increased carbon emission. With economic growth, countries may experience a rising demand for use of energy and simultaneous emission of carbon dioxide.

Climate change has become an issue for both developed and developing world. In South Asia that constitutes of Maldives, India, Bangladesh, Pakistan, Sri Lanka, Nepal and Bhutan, energy consumption has been considered as the major factor influencing environmental degradation. The Environmental Kuznets Curve suggests that as an economy develops, the environment first degrades but eventually improves. This means that developing countries have a higher level of environmental degradation while environmental degradation is lower for developed countries. It has been observed that countries that have rapid growth are countries with higher rates of energy consumption (Dunkerley 1982). In the context of rising global warming and climate change, how CO_2 emissions can be reduced should be a concern and solution to these and is essential for economic and environmental sustainability.

As we shall see in this chapter, carbon dioxide emission has been steadily increasing over the years, simultaneously with economic growth mainly due to the rising demand of energy for consumption. It is only in 2020 when the entire world is hit with the COVID-19 pandemic, we are experiencing a sharp decline in the levels of carbon dioxide emission. Demand for energy has declined due to the policies taken by the governments across the world as many international borders are closed and people are restricted to their homes with minimal outdoor activities. Economies are locked down and most economic activities are suspended. India's carbon dioxide emission fell and China's carbon dioxide emission reduced 200 m tonnes (Myllyvirta 2020). However, when the country-wide lockdowns are lifted and the economy normalises, carbon dioxide levels will once again soar and it may become worse than the pre-pandemic levels. As history has it, the decline in carbon dioxide emissions of 1.4% in 2009 due to the Global Financial Crisis was more than offset by an increase in the carbon dioxide emissions of 5.9% in 2010 (Peters et al.). Hence, even though the pandemic has helped to reduce the carbon dioxide level in the atmosphere to some extent but it is not permanent.

The main objective of this chapter is to analyse the pattern of environmental pollution as represented by per capita carbon dioxide emission ($PCCO_2$), per capita gross domestic product (PCGDP) and per capita energy consumption (PCEC) and their nexus in case of South-Asian countries. The rest of the chapter is structured as follows. While Sect. 2.2 critically looks at the related literature, methodological framework of the study is given in Sect. 2.3. Section 2.4 provides empirical results of analysis and discussion, and Sect. 2.5 concludes the study.

2.2 Literature Survey

There is extensive research in analysing the association between energy consumption (EC), CO_2 emission (CO_2) and economic growth (GGDP). Masih and Masih (1996) have observed that there is a positive impact of EC on GDP for Indonesia Pakistan. Adjaye (2000) has observed a unidirectional causality between EC and GDP for Indonesia and India and a bi-directional causality for Thailand and Philippines. Soyta and Sari (2003) have studied the association between EC, CO_2 emission and GDP for G7 countries and emerging economies. Results suggest that the direction of the causality was bi-directional for Argentina, whereas unidirectional causality between GDP and EC for countries such as Korea and Italy. The relationship was unidirectional for countries like Japan, Germany, France and Turkey. Wei et al. (2008) have observed association between GDP growth and EC for industrialised countries. Choi et al. (2010) have analysed whether the Kuznets curve applies for CO2 emissions and GDGP for Korea, China and Japan and using vector auto-regressive model. The countries showed different patterns. In addition, an analysis has also been performed with regard to trade openness and CO_2 emissions. Korea and Japan showed an inverted U shape type of association whereas in china it was a U-shaped curve.

Salahuddin and Khan (2013) did not find long-run association between EC, GDP growth and CO_2 emission for Australia, while Hussain et al. (2012) found it for Pakistan. Akram (2012) has analysed association between climate change and GDP for Asian countries. The results show a negative relationship between temperature, urbanisation, population, precipitation and human development on economic growth.

Saidi and Hammami (2015) have examined the influence of variables like GDP growth and CO_2 on the EC. Generalised method of moments has been used for estimation for regional panels that include Middle Eastern, North Asia, Sub-Saharan, Caribbean, Latin America and North African. The findings show that these variables have a positive and significant impact on energy consumption.

Farhani (2015) has observed short-run association between renewable EC, CO_2 and GDP growth. A study on the nexus among EC, air pollution and GDP growth for the USA and China has been conducted using ARDL test by Koondhar et al. (2018). The results obtained show that in China air pollution can increase when consumption of energy increases but not for the USA.

Peng et al. (2016) have analysed the direction of the causality between GGDP, CO_2 and FDI for Chinese provinces. The results show that GDP causes CO_2 in Gansu Hubei Guangxi and Neimenggu. In addition, the variables GDP and CO_2 show a bi-directional causality in Shanxi. A unidirectional causality was observed between FDI and CO_2 emissions in Shanxi, Beijing, Guizhou and Henan. Tiwari (2012) and Inumula and Deeppa (2017) have studied the nexus among CO_2, EC and GDP using time series techniques like VAR and VECM. In a dynamic framework, they found that energy consumption better explains CO_2 emission than GDP.

It is observed that though a number of works have already been done using variables CO_2, EC and GDP, sparse studies have analysed the issue for South-Asian region. It is crucial to analyse South-Asian region because it consists of developing countries with more population and fast-growing nations. Besides, the study also attempts to analyse the pattern of EC and CO_2 emissions in South-Asian countries.

2.3 Data and Methodology

The necessary data pertaining to environmental pollution, EC and GDP per capita are collected from secondary source such as the World Bank Database. The per capita CO_2 emission ($PCCO_2$) is used as proxy for the environmental indicator, per capita the energy consumption (PCEC) and per capita gross domestic product (PCGDP) are other variables used for analysis. The study mainly focuses on the analysis of how carbon emission and energy consumption are being affected by economic growth. Due to discontinuity of data, out of the eight South-Asian countries, Maldives, Afghanistan and Bhutan have not been taken into consideration in this study. Again, 2015 and 2016 data were not available so they have been eliminated from the period of study. Considering this, the study considers panel data for five countries, namely India, Pakistan, Bangladesh, Nepal and Sri Lanka for the period 1991–2014.

Panel unit root test by Im, Pesaran and Shin is used to find stationarity of variables. As the variables are integrating and order of integration are I(0) Pedroni panel co-integration test has been to verify long-run association between the variables. To study short-term dynamics, vector error correction model (VECM) has been applied. Finally, fully modified ordinary least squares (FMOLS) has been used in order to estimate long-run coefficients.

A general model of the following form has been constructed to analyse the association between variables:

$$\mathrm{PCCO}_{2it} = \alpha + \beta_1 \mathrm{PCGDP}_{it} + \beta_2 \mathrm{PCEC}_{it} + e_{it}, \tag{2.1}$$

where

$PCCO_2$ = Carbon emission per capita
PCGDP = Gross domestic product per capita
PCEC = Energy consumption per capita
e = error term
t = time period
i = country

2.4 Data Analysis and Interpretation

In this section, the pattern of CO_2 emissions and its association with economic variables have been explained. Besides, an attempt is made for empirical verification of long-run equilibrium relationship between CO_2 emission and its associated variables.

2.4.1 *Pattern of GDP Per Capita, CO_2 Emission and Energy Consumption*

Figure 2.1 shows the variations of GDP per capita across different South-Asian countries for three different time periods 1991–1993, 2001–2003 and 2012–2014. Three yearly average figures are used to check yearly fluctuations.

As we can see in Fig. 2.1, throughout the period of analysis, the per capita GDP of all South-Asian countries has increased. Among these countries, Sri Lanka is at the top position in terms of per capita GDP followed by India and Pakistan. Sri Lanka and India have witnessed a significant increase in per capita national income in the last decade in comparison to the same with the previous period. However, Nepal and Pakistan could not show such progress. Several factors may be attributed to these including internal investment, flow of foreign funds, internal geopolitical situation and economic reforms.

Figure 2.2 shows the trend of CO_2 emissions in per capita metric tons for the South-Asian countries during three different time periods 1991–93, 2001–03 and 2012–14.

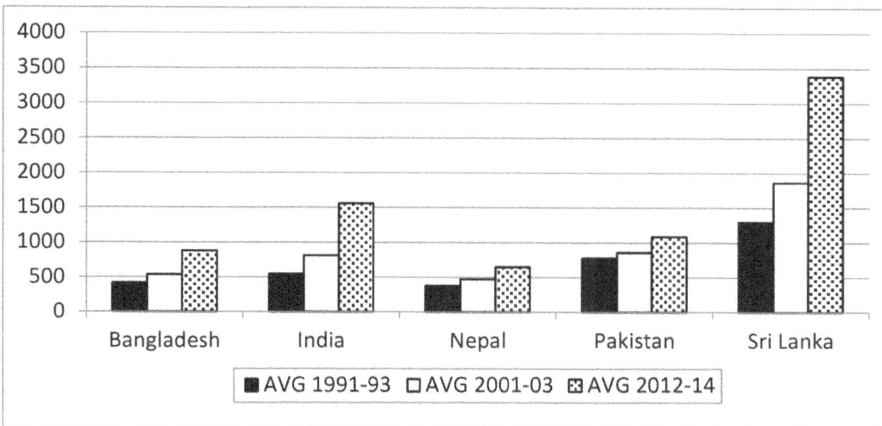

Fig. 2.1 GDP per capita (constant 2010 US$)

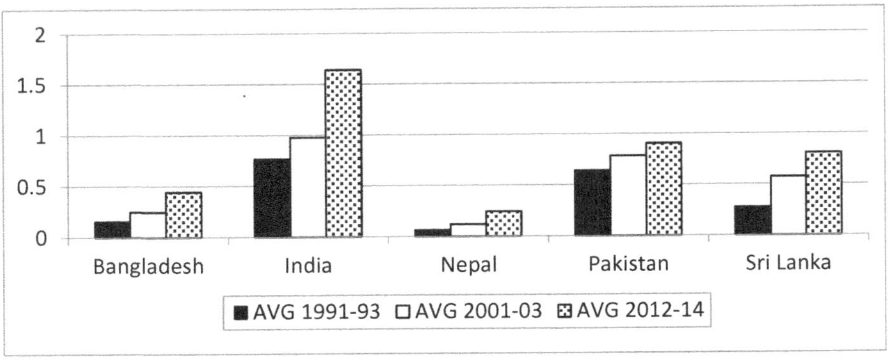

Fig. 2.2 CO_2 emissions (metric tons per capita)

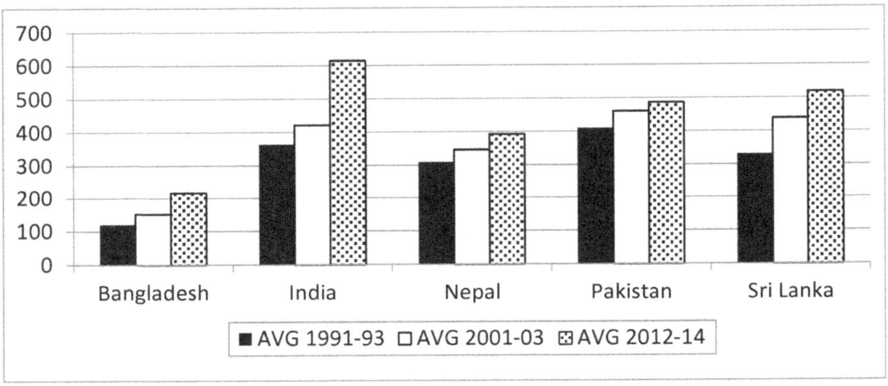

Fig. 2.3 Energy use (kg of oil equivalent per capita)

From Fig. 2.2 it is observed that CO_2 emission has increased across countries over the years. It shows that India has witnessed a significant increase during 2012–2014 in comparison to the same in 2001–2003. While during the same period, an increase in CO_2 emission for South-Asian countries is moderate. Though Sri Lanka has increased its per capita GDP during 2012–2014, but it managed to check its CO_2 emission. India remained at the top position and Pakistan was at the second among this group of South-Asian countries, in regard to CO_2 emission.

Figure 2.3 shows the use of energy in South-Asian countries during 1991–1993, 2001–2003 and 2012–2014.

From Fig. 2.3, it can be clearly observed that these countries have been very aggressive in regard to energy consumption. The increasing trend of energy consumption by all the South-Asian countries correlates with the increased economic growth for the period 1991–2014. Among these countries, India remained at top in terms of energy consumption and Sri Lanka occupied the second position. India has

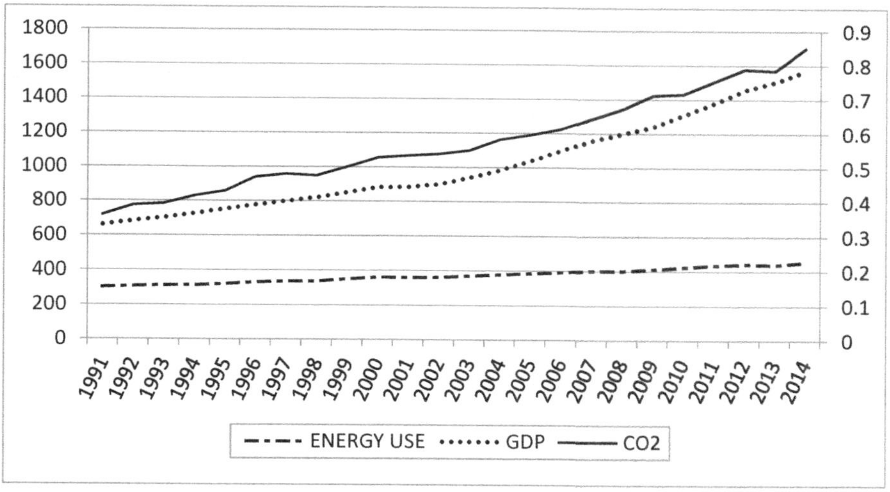

Fig. 2.4 Trend of energy consumption, economic growth and carbon emission

Table 2.1 Panel unit root test

Variable	Im, Pesaran and Shin W-stat*
$\Delta PLNPCO_2$	−2.43844*
Δ(LN_PCGDP)	−2.84130*
Δ(LNPCEC)	−3.28946*

Source: Authors' calculations using EViews
*at 1% level of significance

witnessed a significant increase in energy consumption during the period of 2012–2014 in comparison to the same in previous period that is 2001–2003.

Figure 2.4 shows the pattern of energy consumption, per capita GDP and carbon emission for entire South-Asian average during the time period 1991–2014.

As we can see in Fig. 2.4, energy consumption, per capita income and carbon emission have been seeing an increasing trend in the entire South-Asian region. As GDP increases, energy consumption also closely follows. The carbon emission in the region also grows steadily. It is evident from the pattern that there is association between these variables in South-Asian countries.

2.4.2 Long-Run Relationship

Table 2.1 shows the results for stationarity test (IPS). It can be observed that the null hypothesis of nonstationary is rejected at first difference. However, the variables were nonstationary at level. Thus, variables such as $PCCO_2$, PCGDP and PCEC are stationary at first difference. The order of integrated of these variables is I(1) and variables are suitable for verification of co-integration.

Table 2.2 Pedroni panel co-integration

Alternative hypothesis: common AR coefficients. (within-dimension)				
	Statistic	Prob.	Weighted statistic	Prob.
Panel v-statistic	1.930553	0.0268**	1.289448	0.0986***
Panel rho-statistic	−1.519128	0.0644***	−1.364845	0.0862***
Panel PP-statistic	−2.253725	0.0121*	−2.750522	0.0030*
Panel ADF-statistic	−1.262054	0.1035	−1.943475	0.0260**

Alternative hypothesis: individual AR coefficients. (between-dimension)		
	Statistic	Prob.
Group rho-statistic	−0.425394	0.3353
Group PP-statistic	−2.346067	0.0095*
Group ADF-statistic	−1.805947	0.0355**

Source: Authors' calculations using EViews
*at 1% level of significance, **at 5% level of significance, ***at 10% level of significance

Table 2.3 Vector error correction

Error correction	$D(CO_2)$
CointEq1	0.004553
$D(LNPCO_2(-1))$	−0.149026
$D(LNPCO_2(-2))$	0.135941
D(LN_PCGDP(−1))	0.218512
D(LN_PCGDP(−2))	0.688535
D(LNPCEC(−1))	−0.045670
D(LNPCEC(−2))	−0.182854
C	−0.004768*
R-squared	0.260504
Adj. R-squared	0.207138
F-statistic	4.881479

Source: Authors' calculations using EViews

Table 2.2 shows the results of Pedroni panel co-integration test. The results suggest that five out of seven test statistics confirm the existence of a long-run co-integrating relationship. As a robustness checking, we have also performed the Kao and Fischer co-integration test. Results are similar. This suggests that in the long run these variables like per capita CO_2 emission, GDP per capita and per capita energy consumption are tending towards equilibrium relationship.

Once the long-run dynamics has been established the next step is to see whether there exists any short-run relationship. This has been done by examining the vector error correction model (VECM) results. Table 2.3 shows the estimates and we can see that the error correction coefficient is not statistically significant which suggests that equilibrium error is not adjusting in the short run. Besides, non-significance of short-run coefficients confirms that there is no existence of a short-run relationship.

Co-integration results suggest that there is a long-run equilibrium relationship among the variables. Fully modified ordinary least squares (FMOLS) is used to find the long-run coefficients (Table 2.4). Table 2.4 shows long-run relationship between

Table 2.4 Dependent variable: $PCCO_2$

Variable	FMOLS co-efficient	t-statistic
PCGDP	0.507686	4.186549
PCEC	0.980694	9.144146

Source: Authors' calculations using EViews

PCGDP, PCEC and $PCCO_2$ emissions. The results confirm that per capita income and per capita energy consumption positively and significantly affect per capita CO_2 emission. For a percentage change in the PCGDP the CO_2 emission increases by 0.50%, and for a one percentage in the PCEC, the $PCCO_2$ emission increases by 0.98%. Our findings are in lines with previous studies. Energy consumption and economic growth both have a positively significant impact on the amount of carbon dioxide emitted (Khan et al. 2020). In the process of achieving economic growth countries counties emit a lot of CO_2. The carbon dioxide is a major contributor in global warming thereby leading to the degradation of the environment (Aye and Edoja 2017). The short-run dynamics has been established using vector error correction model which is not significant. Therefore, even if there are any deviations in the short run it does not eventually converge.

2.5 Conclusion

This study shows the nature of relationship between energy consumption, economic growth and CO_2 emissions for five South-Asian countries during the period 1991–2014. It is observed that there is a constant increase in energy consumption in the region. Average CO_2 emission per capita in South-Asian countries closely follows the per capita GDP. Panel co-integration test reveals the existence of a long-run relationship between per capita energy consumption, real per capita income and the per capita CO_2 emission. The results indicate that an increase in energy consumption and per capita income leads to an increase in CO_2 emission. However, the empirical results suggest no evidence of short-run relationship.

The governments of all the countries need to come together and should take steps to curb the rising carbon emission since neither the problem nor the responsibility is restricted to one country alone. With the expansion of economic activities and rising energy consumption through conventional sources, CO_2 emission rises. As South-Asian countries are developing economies and economic growth is important for expansion of economy and creation of employment, countries cannot afford for reduction of their economic activities. Rather they need to explore the sources of alternate and clean energy. Adoption of advanced technology is critical for reducing CO_2 emission. Countries in South-Asian region need to expand the use of renewable energy and reduce dependency on coal and other fossil fuels. Placing limits on the amount of carbon emission and proper sustainable development policy for the region are required. More investment should be made in energy-efficient technologies and industries. Government should take initiative in growing green belts and take steps to reduce deforestation and implement widespread afforestation policies.

References

Adjaye, J. A. (2000). The relationship between energy consumption, energy prices and economic growth: Time series evidence from Asian developing countries. *Energy Economics, Elsevier, 22* (6), 615–625.

Akram, N. (2012). Is climate change hindering economic growth of Asian economies? *Asia-Pacific Development Journal, 19*(2), 1–18.

Aye, G. C., & Edoja, P. E. (2017). Effect of economic growth on CO2 emission in developing countries: Evidence from a dynamic panel threshold model. *Cogent Economics & Finance, 5*(1), 1379239.

Choi E., Heshmati A., & Cho Y. (2010). An empirical study of the relationships between CO2 emissions, economic growth and openness, Discussion paper No. 5304, IZA, November 2010.

Dunkerley, J. (1982). Estimation of energy demand: The developing countries. *Energy Journal, 3*, 79–99.

Farhani S. (2015). Renewable energy consumption, economic growth and CO2 emissions: Evidence from selected MENA countries. Working paper 2015-612, Ipag Business School.

Hussain, M., Javaid, M. I., & Drake, P. R. (2012). An econometric study of carbon dioxide (CO2) emissions, energy consumption, and economic growth of Pakistan. *International Journal of Energy Sector Management, 6*(4), 518–533.

Inumula, K. M., & Deeppa, K. (2017). Cointegration between energy consumption, CO2 emissions, and GDP in India. *Jindal Journal of Business Research, 6*(1), 1–13.

Khan, M. K., Khan, M. I., & Rehan, M. (2020). The relationship between energy consumption, economic growth and carbon dioxide emissions in Pakistan. *Financial Innovation, 6*, 1. https://doi.org/10.1186/s40854-019-0162-0.

Koondhar, M. A., Qiu, L., Li, H., Liu, W., & He, G. (2018). A nexus between air pollution, energy consumption and growth of economy: A comparative study between the USA and China-based on the ARDL bound testing approach. *Agricultural Economics – Czech, 64*, 265–276.

Masih, A. M. M., & Masih, R. (1996). Energy consumption, real income and temporal causality: Results from a multi-country study based on cointegration and error-correction modelling techniques. *Energy Economics, Elsevier, 18*(3), 165–183.

Myllyvirta, L. (2020). Analysis: Coronavirus has temporarily reduced China's CO2 emissions by a quarter, Carbon Brief Clear on Climate.

Peng, H., Tan, X., Li, Y., & Hu, L. (2016). Economic growth, foreign direct investment and CO_2 emissions in China: A panel granger causality analysis. *Sustainability, 8*(3), 233.

Saidi, K., & Hammami, S. (2015). The impact of CO2 emissions and economic growth on energy consumption in 58 countries. *Energy Reports, Elsevier, 1*, 62–70.

Salahuddin, M., & Khan, S. (2013). Empirical link between economic growth, energy consumption and CO_2 emission in Australia. *The Journal of Developing Areas, 47*(2), 81–92.

Soyta, U., & Sari, R. (2003). Energy consumption and GDP: Causality relationship in G-7 countries and emerging markets. *Energy Economics, Elsevier, 25*(1), 33–37.

Tiwari, A. K. (2012). On the dynamics of energy consumption, CO_2 emissions and economic growth: Evidence from India. *Indian Economic Review, 47*(1), 57–87.

Wei, S. Z., Chu, C., & Zhu, Z. (2008). Economic growth and energy consumption revisited - evidence from linear and non-linear granger causality. *Energy Economics, Elsevier, 30*(6), 3063–3076.

Chapter 3
Natural Disasters and Income Inequality in South Asia: An FGLS Panel Analysis

Pushp Kumar, Naresh Chandra Sahu, and Siddharth Kumar

3.1 Introduction

Natural disasters have serious economic and social implications which affect human life, livelihood, property, public infrastructure as well as social and human capital in the long run. It is revealed that natural disasters affect economic growth through direct and indirect effects (Hochrainer 2009). Natural disasters affect economic activities in two folds: firstly, loss of labor in terms of deaths of human and injuries; and secondly, loss of physical assets in terms of damage to infrastructure, houses, and factories. Consequently, these direct effect results in decline of wages and a fall in the expected production output. This may result in affecting economic growth indirectly of a nation. Because if disasters had not happened, then the wage would have been added to the GDP of the country (Noy and Nualsri 2007).

South Asia is a region that is vulnerable to the risk of natural disasters. This region is also marked by high inequalities in income, health, and education. The geography of the region makes it prone to natural disasters. As per the World Risk Report (2011), countries such as Bangladesh, India, Nepal, and Pakistan have demonstrated a high degree of vulnerability as demonstrated by their ability and lack of adaptive capabilities. From 2004–2005 onwards, South Asia became a neighborhood of disasters. Apart from the recurrence of floods and drought, it also suffered from the tsunami in 2004. There was an earthquake in Pakistan in 2008, and a flood in 2010. Also, Uttarakhand state of India and Nepal have experienced floods due to cloudburst.

Over a period of time, South Asian countries are affected by a number of natural disasters. Asia reported a total of 5906 natural disasters between 1900 and 2018. Out

P. Kumar (✉) · N. C. Sahu · S. Kumar
School of Humanities, Social Sciences and Management, Indian Institute of Technology, Bhubaneswar, Odisha, India
e-mail: pk27@iitbbs.ac.in; naresh@iitbbs.ac.in; sk52@iitbbs.ac.in

A. K. Mishra et al. (eds.), *Critical Perspectives on Emerging Economies*, Contributions to Economics, https://doi.org/10.1007/978-3-030-59781-8_3

of these, South Asia accounts for 1920 natural disasters which are 32.51% of total natural disasters occurred in Asia (EM-DAT 2018). According to Clark et al. (1998), it is widely accepted that household income and expenditure are adversely affected by natural disasters. The effect of natural disasters varies from country to country. As per studies taken by Peacock et al. (1997), Wisner et al. (1994), and Krueger and Perri (2010), economically weaker populace is more vulnerable to the disasters resulting in higher poverty and inequality. The poor households are more exposed to the negative effects of natural disasters than rich households. Since poor households are often socially, politically and geographically marginalized.

There are a large number of published studies (e.g., Skidmore and Toya 2002; Raddatz 2007; Noy 2009) which examined the effects of disasters on economic growth. But inconclusive results are revealed from these studies regarding how economic growth gets impacted by natural disasters. Skidmore and Toya (2002) found that natural disasters have a positive impact on economic growth. While studies by Raddatz (2007) and Noy (2009) found that natural disasters have a negative impact on economic growth. So far it is found from the existing literature that there has been couple of studies which has investigated the association between the natural disasters and income inequality. Previous published studies (e.g., Yamamura 2015; Keerthiratne and Tol 2018) are limited to a group of countries or a single country.

But, when we analyze the impact post-natural disasters, the issue of income inequality becomes an important matter. A comparative analysis can be made in between affected area and non-affected area in terms of income redistribution pattern to get a clear picture about the impact of natural disasters on income inequality. Therefore, the empirical analysis of the effects of natural disasters on income inequality is crucial and warranted. Against this backdrop, the aim of this chapter is to analyze the effects of natural disasters on income inequality in South Asian countries for the period 1967–2014. The study uses the Parks' (1967) robust feasible generalized least squares (FGLS) panel data model.

The structure of the chapter is as follows. Section 3.2 presents the brief review of literature related to the effects of natural disasters. In Sect. 3.3, database and econometrics methods are described. Section 3.4 analyzes the results of the study. Lastly, Sect. 3.5 presents the conclusion and the policy implications of the study.

3.2 Brief Review of Literature

Most of the current literature (e.g., Shabnam 2014; Albala-Bertrand 1993; Skidmore and Toya 2002; Loayza et al. 2012) on natural disasters pays particular attention to the relationship between natural disasters and economic growth. These studies provide the inconclusive results regarding the impact of natural disasters on economic growth. But, till date, there is a scarcity of the literature which estimates the effects of natural disasters on income inequality.

A study by Yamamura (2015) examined the association between the natural disasters and income inequality. He examined this relationship for 86 countries of world during 1970–2004. Gini coefficient is used for income inequality over other measures, e.g., Theil index, Palma ratio, and Atkinson index. To accomplish this relationship, he used the panel fixed effect model. It is found from the study that in the short-run, natural disasters lead to a rise in income inequality. But, in the long term, the effects of disasters on income inequality is not found. From the methodological perspective, the study has not used the robust methods for estimating the effects of disasters on inequality. Moreover this study has not incorporated the tests for the presence of serial correlation, panel group-wise heteroscedasticity and associated remedial measures.

Keerthiratne and Tol (2018) investigated the effect of natural disasters on income inequality in Sri Lanka for the period 1990–2013. This study was based on the primary survey of 25 districts of Sri Lanka. They used the Theil index instead of Gini coefficients for income inequality. In their study, it was found that household expenditure inequality is not affected by natural disasters. They also observed that inequality in non-agriculture and non-seasonal agriculture is decreased due to natural disasters in Sri Lanka.

Abdullah et al. (2016) estimated the impact of Cyclone Alia on the Sundarbans region of Bangladesh in 2009. The finding of this study revealed that aftermath of Cyclone Alia, income inequality has diminished. Feng et al. (2016) studied the effects of the Wenchuan earthquake on Sichuan region of China in 2008. They found that household income fell by 14% due the earthquake.

Karim and Noy (2016) surveyed the literature on the direct and indirect effects of natural disasters on the income distribution of poor peoples. They will bear the high costs of natural disasters as compared to rich households (Kim 2012). Bui et al. (2014) analyzed the impact of natural disasters on household income, expenditure, poverty, and inequality in Vietnam using the Vietnam Household Living Standard Survey of 2008. It is found that due to natural disasters, household per capita income and expenditure decreased by 6.9% and 7.1%, respectively, in Vietnam. In other words, income inequality at household level increased due to the natural disasters in Vietnam.

From the above literature, it can be concluded that a very few studies have concentrated on the direct link between natural disasters and income inequality. Some studies have estimated the impact of natural disasters on income inequality in a particular country or a panel. But no research has focused on a specific region, e.g., South Asia. Also, most of the studies are based on the primary survey. Moreover, there are some methodological drawbacks, as they used only a simple regression model to estimate the effects of disasters on inequality. With this research gap, this study tries to fill the gap by assessing the effects of natural disasters on income inequality in South Asian countries during 1967–2014.

3.3 Database and Econometric Methodology

3.3.1 Data

The present study is based on the secondary data of South Asian countries. The secondary data have been collected for six South Asian countries for the period 1967–2014. Due to the paucity of data pertaining to all South Asian countries for the study period, only selected countries, namely Bangladesh, India, Nepal, Sri Lanka, and Pakistan have been taken into account. Natural disasters data have been taken from the Emergency Events Database (EM-DAT) maintained by the Centre for Research on the Epidemiology of Disaster (CRED). EM-DAT reports the natural disasters in mainly three types following: frequency of natural disasters, total number of affected population, and total economic losses. Following the literature review, frequency of natural disasters has been taken as a proxy of natural disasters (Yamamura 2015; Hochrainer 2009; Skidmore and Toya 2002; Klomp and Valckx 2014).

The frequency of natural disasters in selected South Asian countries during the period 1967–2014 are shown in Fig. 3.1. EM-DAT provides different types of disasters data. Studies taken by Bakkensen and Mendelsohn (2016), Noy (2015), Gignoux and Menéndez (2016) were based on single type of disasters. While study by Schumacher and Strobl (2011) was based on multiple. However, in this study, we have considered only aggregate natural disasters which include droughts, earthquakes, epidemics, storms, floods, landslides, extreme temperature, wildfires, mass movement, insect infestation, wave action, fog, volcanic activities, animal accidents (see, https://www.emdat.be/classification).

In the study, Gini coefficient, Palma ratio, and Atkinson index are used as the proxies for income inequality which serve as the dependent variable. Gini coefficient lies between 0 and 1. The value of 0 and 1 indicate perfect income equality and perfect income inequality. In perfect equality, every person in the society has same

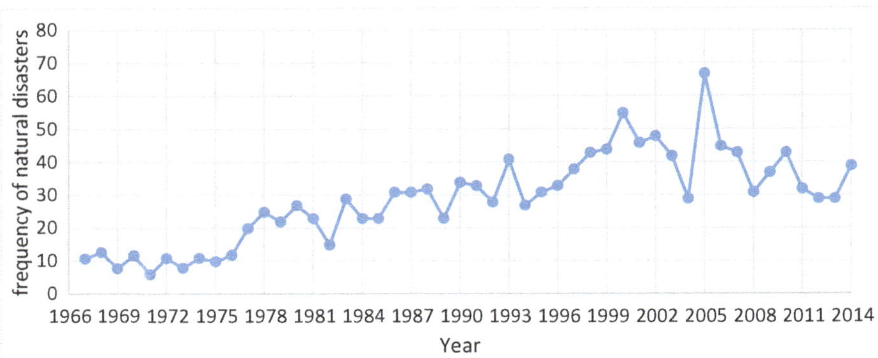

Fig. 3.1 Natural disasters in selected South Asian countries. Source: Emergency Events Database (EM-DAT)

income level. On the other hand, a single person holding the complete income pie denotes perfect income inequality. According to Zhang and Naceur (2019), the Gini coefficient does not capture the low-income strata's welfare, it manifests the income distribution up to some extent. So, the chapter utilizes other supplementary measures of income inequality, namely the Atkinson index and Palma ratio. The Atkinson index counts how much of total income of a society must be passed for increasing income equality amongst its citizens. The Palma ratio represents the ratio of income of top 10% to the income of bottom 40% in a society.

A major limitation of the study is paucity of income inequality data for the countries selected for the analysis of this study. From the review of literature, it is found that Lahoti et al. (2016) have developed an income inequality database in the Global Consumption and Income Project (GCIP). The database comprises various secondary sources including but not limited to, UNU-WIDER World Income Inequality Database (WIID), the Luxembourg Income Study (LIS), and the World Bank's Povcalnet database. Recently, the GCIP income inequality database has been used by several scholars in their studies (Meniago and Asongu 2018; Tchamyou et al. 2019). The frequency of natural disasters is the key independent variable. We have used lag value of natural disasters as natural disasters may last long effect on income inequality. Five-year lag value of natural disasters along with current value of natural disaster is used. Trade openness (% of GDP) and per capita real GDP are used as the control variables as in the prevailing literature (Yamamura 2015). These control variables have been compiled from World Development Indicators (WDI) of World Bank (2018).

3.3.2 Econometric Methods

A number of estimation techniques are available in the literature to estimate the panel data. But these estimation techniques depend on the nature of panel data based on cross-sectional dependence or independence. According to Hausman specification, one can use fixed or random effect model if panel cross-sections are independent. The panel estimation is inconsistent in the presence of cross-sectional dependence and requires new methodologies for estimation (Bataka 2019). To address the problem of serial correlation and panel group-wise heteroscedasticity in panel data, feasible generalized least squares (FGLS) method has been proposed by Parks (1967).

For applying the FGLS model, number of cross-sections (i) should be more than the time period (t). If number of cross-sections are less than the time period, Panel Corrected Standard Error (PCSE) is the appropriate estimation technique (Reed and Ye 2011). So, this study employs the FGLS model for removing cross-sectional dependence, panel group-wise heteroscedasticity, and serial autocorrelation problems. Therefore, the results being based on Park's FGLS model are least influenced by outliers. Moreover, other existing techniques do not remove serial correlation and panel group-wise heteroscedasticity problem, which is a concern in this chapter. The panel estimation equation is specified as follows:

$$\begin{aligned}\text{Gini}_{it} = {} & \alpha_0 + \alpha_1\text{Dis}_{it} + \alpha_2\text{Dis}_{i,t-1} + \alpha_3\text{Dis}_{i,t-2} + \alpha_4\text{Dis}_{i,t-3} + \alpha_5\text{Dis}_{i,t-4} \\ & + \alpha_6\text{Dis}_{i,t-5} + \alpha_7\text{Top}_{it} + \alpha_8\text{Lnpcgdp}_{it} + u_{it}\end{aligned} \tag{3.1}$$

$$\begin{aligned}\text{Pratio}_{it} = {} & \alpha_0 + \alpha_1\text{Dis}_{it} + \alpha_2\text{Dis}_{i,t-1} + \alpha_3\text{Dis}_{i,t-2} + \alpha_4\text{Dis}_{i,t-3} + \alpha_5\text{Dis}_{i,t-4} \\ & + \alpha_6\text{Dis}_{i,t-5} + \alpha_7\text{Top}_{it} + \alpha_8\text{Lnpcgdp}_{it} + u_{it}\end{aligned} \tag{3.2}$$

$$\begin{aligned}\text{Aindex}_{it} = {} & \alpha_0 + \alpha_1\text{Dis}_{it} + \alpha_2\text{Dis}_{i,t-1} + \alpha_3\text{Dis}_{i,t-2} + \alpha_4\text{Dis}_{i,t-3} + \alpha_5\text{Dis}_{i,t-4} \\ & + \alpha_6\text{Dis}_{i,t-5} + \alpha_7\text{Top}_{it} + \alpha_8\text{Lnpcgdp}_{it} + u_{it}\end{aligned} \tag{3.3}$$

where

$i =$ India, Sri Lanka, Pakistan, Nepal, and Bangladesh
$t =$ 1967, 1968, 1969,…, 2014
Gini: Gini coefficient
Pratio: Palma ratio
Aindex: Atkinson index
Dis_t: Frequency of natural disasters at time t
Dis_{t-1}: Frequency of natural disasters at time $t-1$
Dis_{t-2}: Frequency of natural disasters at time $t-2$
Dis_{t-3}: Frequency of natural disasters at time $t-3$
Dis_{t-4}: Frequency of natural disasters at time $t-4$
Dis_{t-5}: Frequency of natural disasters at time $t-5$
Top: Trade openness
Lnpcgdp: Natural log of per capita GDP

In the short run, it is found that natural disasters impact economic growth negatively (Noy 2009). On the other hand, it is found that in the long run, natural disasters have a positive impact on economic growth (Skidmore and Toya 2002). So this proposes that there is a difference in impact of natural disasters on growth rate in short run and long run. This leads to an empirical question about the effects of natural disasters on income distribution depending on their time of occurrence.

3.4 Empirical Results

To investigate how natural disasters affect the income inequality in South Asian countries, we have applied panel data models. Firstly, we have estimated fixed effect and random effects. Hausman (1978) test is used to selecting between the fixed effect model and random effect model. The null hypothesis in Hausman test states that random effect is appropriate against the alternative hypothesis. After performing the Hausman test, heteroscedasticity and serial correlation is tested on the fixed effect (FE) or random effect (RE) model. The modified Wald test is performed for group-wise heteroscedasticity. Afterwards, Wooldridge (2010) test is applied to check first-order autocorrelation. The regression results are biased having inaccurate standard deviation in the presence of serial correlation and heteroscedasticity. Thus, heteroscedasticity and serial correlation problems must be solved (Petersen 2009).

In Tables 3.2, 3.3, and 3.4, fixed effect (FE), and random effect (RE) models are investigated. Hausman test results in Tables 3.2 and 3.4 indicate that random effect model is appropriate. In the next step, the results presented in Tables 3.2, 3.3, and 3.4 confirms the presence of heteroscedasticity and first-order serial correlation problems. Thus, to resolve these problems and estimate the relationship between natural disasters and income inequality, feasible generalized least squares (FGLS) method is applied. The results of FGLS models are reported in Tables 3.2, 3.3, and 3.4.

In Tables 3.2, 3.3, and 3.4, impact of natural disasters on different income inequalities, i.e., Gini coefficients, Palma ratio, and Atkinson index is investigated. In Table 3.2, coefficients of dis (*t*) are positive and significant at 5% level of significance, while statistical significance of dis (*t*) disappears in Tables 3.3 and 3.4. It implies that increase of current frequency of natural disaster by one percentage point would increase Gini coefficient by 0.0008 points, ceteris paribus.

Furthermore, in Tables 3.2, 3.3, and 3.4, the coefficients of dis ($t-1$) are positive and statistical significant at 1% level of significance. One year previous value of natural disasters have positive impact of income inequality. These results show that increase of dis ($t-1$) by one percentage point would increase *Gini, Pratio*, and *Aindex* by 0.0012, 0.011, and 0.0013 points, respectively, ceteris paribus.

Similarly, the coefficients of dis ($t-2$) are positive and statistical significant at 1% percent level of significance in Tables 3.2, 3.3, and 3.4. The coefficients show that increase of dis ($t-2$) by one percentage point would increase *Gini, Pratio*, and *Aindex* by 0.0008, 0.0123, and 0.0012 points, respectively, ceteris paribus. In Tables 3.2 and 3.4, the coefficient of dis ($t-3$) are positive and statistical significant. This implies that 3-year lag period of disasters have a positive impact on inequality measured by Gini coefficient and Palma ratio.

The results show that dis ($t-4$) and dis ($t-5$) have insignificant impact of income inequality measured by Gini coefficients, Palma ratio, and Atkinson index in Tables 3.1, 3.2, and 3.3. Also, the coefficient of control variable, i.e., *lngdp* is positive and statistical significant at 1% level of significance in Tables 3.2, 3.3, and 3.4. This shows that economic growth has a positive impact on income inequality.

Taken together, these results suggest that natural disasters occurred in one-, two-, and 3-year lag period increase income inequality. But after 4- and 5-year lag period, the effects of disasters on income inequality is disappeared. Therefore, these findings reveal that natural disasters have an adverse effect on income inequality aftermath of natural disasters in the lag of 1-, 2-, and 3-year lag period. However, with the passage of time, natural disasters have no impact on income inequality. In the long run, the government vigorously pursues various income enhancing and redistributive

Table 3.1 Descriptive statistics of the variables

Variable		Mean	Std. Dev.	Min	Max	Observations
Gini coefficient	Overall	0.402	0.072	0.172	0.572	$N = 240$
	Between		0.038	0.367	0.449	$n = 5$
	Within		0.063	0.205	0.573	$T = 48$
Palma ratio	Overall	2.199	0.756	0.600	5.609	$N = 240$
	Between		0.390	1.781	2.617	$n = 5$
	Within		0.671	0.916	5.195	$T = 48$
Atkinson index	Overall	0.402	0.117	0.081	0.708	$N = 240$
	Between		0.061	0.342	0.475	$n = 5$
	Within		0.103	0.133	0.738	$T = 48$
GDP per capita	Overall	764.158	562.421	270.947	3505.551	$N = 240$
	Between		433.035	395.547	1496.521	$n = 5$
	Within		407.030	−88.166	2773.187	$T = 48$
Trade openness	Overall	36.871	19.207	7.662	88.636	$N = 240$
	Between		16.984	23.475	65.735	$n = 5$
	Within		11.713	13.224	69.191	$T = 48$
Natural disasters	Overall	5.063	4.963	0.000	31.000	$N = 240$
	Between		4.043	1.896	11.688	$n = 5$
	Within		3.391	−4.625	24.375	$T = 48$

programs and policies in the aftermath of the natural disasters in the affected region for a long period. This may contribute to falling income inequality in selected South Asian countries aftermath of natural disaster in the affected region.

3.5 Conclusion

In the twenty-first century, studies on natural disasters have found adequate focus in economics. Though several studies have attempted to investigate the relationship between natural disasters and economic growth, the literature on the effects of natural disasters on income inequality is scarce. This study is expected to fill this gap in comprehending how natural disasters affect income inequality in selected South Asian countries. Previous studies have not used diagnostic checking after the estimation of panel model. Here, we use different diagnostic test and used FGLS panel model to resolve the problem of first-order serial correlation and panel group-wise heteroscedasticity. The results show that income inequality is increased by the occurrence of natural disasters in the short run. But in the long run, natural disasters have no impact on income inequality. These findings make contributions to the current literature. We find that income inequality increases significantly rises after the natural disasters.

Table 3.2 Panel regression results (*Dependent variable is Gini coefficient*)

Variables	FEM	REM	FGLS
Dis (*t*)	0.00244*	0.00405***	0.000798**
	(0.00126)	(0.00122)	(0.000345)
Dis (*t*–1)	0.00200	0.00281**	0.00119***
	(0.00125)	(0.00128)	(0.000349)
Dis (*t*–2)	0.000701	0.00118	0.000812**
	(0.00124)	(0.00128)	(0.000340)
Dis (*t*–3)	4.47e-05	0.000795	0.000729**
	(0.00125)	(0.00128)	(0.000342)
Dis (*t*–4)	−0.000858	−0.000607	0.000341
	(0.00123)	(0.00128)	(0.000356)
Dis (*t*–5)	−0.00152	−0.00165	−8.04e-06
	(0.00117)	(0.00121)	(0.000348)
Lngdp	0.0210*	0.0286***	0.0371***
	(0.0124)	(0.00853)	(0.0133)
Lntop	0.0586***	0.0361***	0.00205
	(0.0116)	(0.00885)	(0.00963)
Constant	0.0518	0.0613	0.139*
	(0.0643)	(0.0388)	(0.0732)
Observations	235	235	235
R-squared	0.356		
Number of id	5	5	5
Diagnostic tests			
Tests	Statistic	Value	*P*-value
Hausman specification test	Chi-Square	1.74	0.9879
Modified Wald test for group-wise heteroscedasticity	Chi-Square	42.55	0.0000
Wooldridge test for autocorrelation	*F*	13.820	0.0205

Standard errors in parentheses
***$p < 0.01$; ** $p < 0.05$; * $p < 0.1$

To contain that inequality, the policymakers should strengthen preparedness and develop resilience in the areas which are prone and vulnerable to disasters. The insurance cover, both for life and property, must be broadened for such areas as it will reduce the premium by spreading the insurance costs. The insurance coverage will protect the affected population from falling in the trap of poverty after the occurrence of any disaster and income redistribution will be reduced. The insurance industry will also get benefited from such moves. At both the local and central level, the governments of South Asian countries should undertake capacity building and socio-economic empowerment programs in grassroots disaster-affected areas in collaboration with community-based organizations. This would minimize the

Table 3.3 Panel regression results (*Dependent variable is Palma ratio*)

Variables	FEM	REM	FGLS
Dis (*t*)	0.0237*	0.0411***	0.00548
	(0.0131)	(0.0129)	(0.00384)
Dis (*t*−1)	0.0187	0.0274**	0.0109***
	(0.0130)	(0.0136)	(0.00389)
Dis (*t*−2)	0.00589	0.0120	0.0123***
	(0.0128)	(0.0136)	(0.00383)
Dis (*t*−3)	−0.00292	0.00682	0.00763**
	(0.0130)	(0.0136)	(0.00384)
Dis (*t*−4)	−0.0132	−0.00790	0.00390
	(0.0128)	(0.0135)	(0.00399)
Dis (*t*−5)	−0.0186	−0.0171	0.00125
	(0.0121)	(0.0129)	(0.00387)
Lngdp	0.557***	0.372***	0.602***
	(0.129)	(0.0905)	(0.154)
Lntop	0.574***	0.448***	0.0321
	(0.120)	(0.0939)	(0.101)
Constant	−3.432***	−2.054***	−2.105**
	(0.668)	(0.412)	(0.862)
Observations	235	235	235
R-squared	0.439		
Number of id	5	5	5
Diagnostic tests			
Tests	Statistic	Value	P-value
Hausman specification test	Chi-Square	4.76	0.7831
Modified Wald test for group-wise heteroscedasticity	Chi-Square	116.35	0.0000
Wooldridge test for autocorrelation	*F*	41.018	0.0031

Standard errors in parentheses
***$p < 0.01$; ** $p < 0.05$; * $p < 0.1$

economic loss and the income redistribution of income. Thus, it is recommended to the policymakers to take into account the role of natural disasters and the income distribution in the aftermath of the disasters for sustainable and inclusive economic development of the selected countries.

Table 3.4 Panel regression results (*Dependent variable is Atkinson index*)

Variables	FEM	REM	FGLS
Dis (*t*)	0.00349*	0.00607***	0.000707
	(0.00198)	(0.00194)	(0.000471)
Dis (*t*−1)	0.00264	0.00392*	0.00127***
	(0.00196)	(0.00204)	(0.000482)
Dis (*t*−2)	0.000796	0.00171	0.00122***
	(0.00194)	(0.00204)	(0.000473)
Dis (*t*−3)	−0.000243	0.00119	0.000770
	(0.00196)	(0.00204)	(0.000475)
Dis (*t*−4)	−0.00195	−0.00123	0.000321
	(0.00192)	(0.00203)	(0.000491)
Dis (*t*−5)	−0.00292	−0.00272	7.19e-05
	(0.00183)	(0.00194)	(0.000474)
Lngdp	0.0854***	0.0600***	0.0765***
	(0.0195)	(0.0136)	(0.0188)
Lntop	0.0833***	0.0665***	0.00726
	(0.0182)	(0.0141)	(0.0133)
Constant	−0.443***	−0.257***	−0.135
	(0.101)	(0.0619)	(0.105)
Observations	235	235	235
R-squared	0.431		
Number of id	5	5	5
Diagnostic tests			
Tests	Statistic	Value	P-value
Hausman specification test	Chi-Square	−0.65	–
Modified Wald test for group-wise heteroscedasticity	Chi-Square	65.88	0.0000
Wooldridge test for autocorrelation	*F*	36.894	0.0037

Standard errors in parentheses
$^{***}p < 0.01$; $^{**}p < 0.05$; $^{*}p < 0.1$

References

Albala-Bertrand, J. M. (1993). Natural disaster situations and growth: A macroeconomic model for sudden disaster impacts. *World Development, 21*(9), 1417–1434.

Abdullah, A. N. M., Zander, K. K., Myers, B., Stacey, N., & Garnett, S. T. (2016). A short-term decrease in household income inequality in the Sundarbans, Bangladesh, following cyclone Aila. *Natural Hazards, 83*(2), 1103–1123.

Bakkensen, L. A., & Mendelsohn, R. O. (2016). Risk and adaptation: Evidence from global hurricane damages and fatalities. *Journal of the Association of Environmental and Resource Economists, 3*(3), 555–587.

Bataka, H. (2019). De jure, De facto globalization and economic growth in sub-Saharan Africa. *Journal of Economic Integration, 34*(1), 133–158.

Bui, A. T., Dungey, M., Nguyen, C. V., & Pham, T. P. (2014). The impact of natural disasters on household income, expenditure, poverty and inequality: Evidence from Vietnam. *Applied Economics, 46*(15), 1751–1766.

Clark, G. E., Moser, S. C., Ratick, S. J., Dow, K., Meyer, W. B., Emani, S., et al. (1998). Assessing the vulnerability of coastal communities to extreme storms: The case of Revere, MA., USA. *Mitigation and Adaptation Strategies for Global Change, 3*(1), 59–82.

EM-DAT. (2018). *The OFDA/CRED international disaster database*. Brussels: Universite Catholique de Louvain. Available at: www.emdat.be.

Feng, S., Lu, J., Nolen, P., & Wang, L. (2016). The effect of the Wenchuan earthquake and government aid on rural households. IFPRI book chapters, 11–34.

Gignoux, J., & Menéndez, M. (2016). Benefit in the wake of disaster: Long-run effects of earthquakes on welfare in rural Indonesia. *Journal of Development Economics, 118*, 26–44.

Hausman, J. A. (1978). Specification tests in econometrics. *Econometrica: Journal of the Econometric Society, 46*, 1251–1271.

Hochrainer, S. (2009). *Assessing the macroeconomic impacts of natural disasters: Are there any?* (The World Bank policy research working paper series). Washington, DC: The World Bank. https://doi.org/10.1596/1813-9450-4968.

Karim, A., & Noy, I. (2016). Poverty and natural disasters—A qualitative survey of the empirical literature. *The Singapore Economic Review, 61*(01), 1640001.

Keerthiratne, S., & Tol, R. S. (2018). Impact of natural disasters on income inequality in Sri Lanka. *World Development, 105*, 217–230.

Kim, N. (2012). How much more exposed are the poor to natural disasters? Global and regional measurement. *Disasters, 36*(2), 195–211.

Klomp, J., & Valckx, K. (2014). Natural disasters and economic growth: A meta-analysis. *Global Environmental Change, 26*(1), 183–195. Retrieved from. https://doi.org/10.1016/j.gloenvcha.2014.02.006.

Krueger, D. and Perri, F. (2010) How do households respond to income shocks?, Mimeo, University of Pennsylvania.

Lahoti, R., Jayadev, A., & Reddy, S. (2016). The global consumption and income project (GCIP): An overview. *Journal of Globalization and Development, 7*(1), 61–108.

Loayza, N. V., Olaberria, E., Rigolini, J., & Christiaensen, L. (2012). Natural disasters and growth: Going beyond the averages. *World Development, 40*(7), 1317–1336.

Meniago, C., & Asongu, S. A. (2018). Revisiting the finance-inequality nexus in a panel of African countries. *Research in International Business and Finance, 46*, 399–419.

Noy, I., & Nualsri, A. (2007). What do exogenous shocks tell us about growth theories? (No. 07–16). Working Paper.

Noy, I. (2015). Comparing the direct human impact of natural disasters for two cases in 2011: The Christchurch earthquake and the Bangkok flood. *International Journal of Disaster Risk Reduction, 13*, 61–65.

Noy, I. (2009). The macroeconomic consequences of disasters. *Journal of Development Economics, 88*(2), 221–231.

Parks, R. W. (1967). Efficient estimation of a system of regression equations when disturbances are both serially and contemporaneously correlated. *Journal of the American Statistical Association, 62*(318), 500–509.

Peacock, W. G., Morrow, B. H., & Gladwin, H. (Eds.). (1997). *Hurricane Andrew: Ethnicity, gender, and the sociology of disasters*. London: Psychology Press.

Petersen, M. A. (2009). Estimating standard errors in finance panel data sets: Comparing approaches. *The Review of Financial Studies, 22*(1), 435–480.

Raddatz, C. (2007). Are external shocks responsible for the instability of output in low-income countries? *Journal of Development Economics, 84*(1), 155–187.

Reed, W. R., & Ye, H. (2011). Which panel data estimator should I use? *Applied Economics, 43*(8), 985–1000.

Shabnam, N. (2014). Natural disasters and economic growth: A review. *International Journal of Disaster Risk Science, 5*(2), 157–163.

Schumacher, I., & Strobl, E. (2011). Economic development and losses due to natural disasters: The role of hazard exposure. *Ecological Economics, 72*, 97–105.

Skidmore, M., & Toya, H. (2002). Do natural disasters promote long-run growth? *Economic Inquiry, 40*(4), 664–687.

Tchamyou, V. S., Erreygers, G., & Cassimon, D. (2019). Inequality, ICT and financial access in Africa. *Technological Forecasting and Social Change, 139*, 169–184.

Wisner, B., Blaikie, P., Cannon, T., & Davis, I. (1994). *At risk: Natural hazards, people's vulnerability, and disasters*. London: Routledge.

Wooldridge, J. M. (2010). *Econometric analysis of cross section and panel data*. Cambridge: MIT Press.

World Bank. (2018). *World development indicators 2018*. World Bank: Washington.

Yamamura, E. (2015). The impact of natural disasters on income inequality: Analysis using panel data during the period 1970 to 2004. *International Economic Journal, 29*(3), 359–374.

Zhang, R., & Naceur, S. B. (2019). Financial development, inequality, and poverty: Some international evidence. *International Review of Economics & Finance, 61*(1–16).

Chapter 4
Factors Influencing Inflationary Condition in Sri Lanka: Orthodox Streamlining of Influential Factors

E. A. Indunil N. Ediriweera and N. P. Thilini Deshika

4.1 Introduction

Stability of the general price level of the country is a key macroeconomic variable of any economy. However, in practice the economies generally experience a continuous rise in the general price level. Such sustained rise in the general price level is addressed as inflation (Kihangire and Mugyenyi 2005). Inflation or rise in general price level causes to decrease the purchasing power of the currency unit used by a particular country. Thus, it creates troublesome condition which may causes for many internal issues and ultimately leads to decrease the living standards of the population.

From 1987–1995, Iraq experienced a hyper-inflationary condition which causes to depreciate their domestic currency in a rapid rate (Central Bank of Iraq 2012). Such similar conditions have been affected many economies in history. In such condition, the public acceptance for the domestic currency declines and it causes to erode the economic system rapidly. So that any economy pays keen attention on balancing macroeconomic variables while maintaining the inflation in a mild level.

During the recent past, the trend in inflation is highly volatile and causes to emerge many economic problems and imbalances in many other macroeconomic variables in Sri Lanka. The continuous volatility of general price level creates adverse results to the economy thus it demotivates the reach of investors to the country and it demotivates the existing entrepreneurs in the country (Kesavarajah 2009). Currently, as a percentage of gross domestic product (GDP), Sri Lanka is experiencing 5.5% of fiscal policy deficit and both the direct and portfolio investments have been declined in the country between year 2016, 2017, and 2018 (Central Bank Annual Report 2018).

E. A. I. N. Ediriweera (✉) · N. P. T. Deshika
Department of Accountancy, Faculty of Business Studies and Finance, Wayamba University of Sri Lanka, Kuliyapitiya, Sri Lanka

A. K. Mishra et al. (eds.), *Critical Perspectives on Emerging Economies*, Contributions to Economics, https://doi.org/10.1007/978-3-030-59781-8_4

The import inflation is a highly stressful factor to a country which depends on major proportion of imported goods from the aggregate consumption of the country (Cole 1986). Thus, the Sri Lankan economy is experiencing a trade deficit of USD 9619 million with import volume index of 8.1 in year 2017. Further, the government impose heavy duties on imports to control the level of imports of luxury goods (Central Bank Annual Report 2018). And also, this condition may have led to create a cost push inflation within the economy.

However, such inflationary condition could interrupt exporters by making their exports costly and less competitive in the world market. Ultimately, it leads to widen the gap between foreign currency receipts and payments in the balance of payment.

An uncontrolled inflation causes to decrease the interest income of savings and demotivation of saving could highly influence on the investment flow of the country. Thus, the smooth functioning of the business cycle may have adversely affected by the lack of cash flows in the economy.

The continuous rise in general price index is one of a major factors to the current scenario and it is important to stabilize the general price level of the country to overcome from this economic condition. So, there is a clear practical requirement of identifying the most significant macroeconomic variables which need more attention in terms of managing the inflation within the Sri Lankan economy.

In Sri Lankan setup, the food and non-alcoholic beverages majorly contributes for the high inflation rate (http://ww.ukessays.com). In this research, it was analyzed the open economic model by selecting the factors affecting for the inflation rate in Sri Lanka.

So that, through this research, the variables which affect to incur an inflation within Sri Lankan economy will be identified and will develop a model based on the statistic rationale to identify the highly sensitive factors towards inflation in Sri Lanka.

The research focuses on forecasting the possible future rates based on the existing identified independent variables which are affecting for inflation. Since inflation is a key factor which determines the cost of production, this will be useful for the businesses to make their production decisions.

The forecasted percentages of inflation can be used by the exporters to measure the price fluctuation of the production factors. This will help them to become more competitive within the international market.

The importers can value the profitability of their imports, and it will help them to reduce the competitiveness incur within the local market.

In valuing the net present value (NPV) of the economic decisions, the Sri Lankan economy should be able to use the forecasted percentages of inflation which could optimize its resource allocation.

There were many identified factors which are influencing towards the inflation within the country. The key factors determined by the local and international context are money supply, foreign currency exchange rates, gold prices, oil prices, interest rates, and economic growth rate (Colombage 2005; Jayawardana and Jayasinghe 2016; Kihangire and Mugyenyi 2005; Mosayeb and Rahimi 2009; Weerasekara 1992).

4.2 Literature Review

There are various studies done based on the inflation. However, the relationship between inflation and its key determinants is important basement in macroeconomic theories (Sahadudheen 2012). In many researches, it highlights that the mild inflation is economic friendly and leads to create a long-run economic growth and development (Kihangire and Mugyenyi 2005; Mallik and Chowdhury 2001).

Inflation reduces the real value of money and diminish the purchasing power of the local currency unit. This impacts to create many discrepancies in the economic environment. Fixed income earners, in particular adversely effected by the inflation (Colombage 2005).

Colombage (Colombage 2005) has identified cost push factors such as domestic production shortfalls, exchange rate depreciation, import price increases, and wage increases. While Bashir (Bashir 2011) emphasizes that in addition to the above factors budget deficit and raising taxes also may impact to create the production cost which leads to create an increment in the general price level of the country.

The inflation occurs as a result of expansion of monetary or fiscal policies can be identified as the demand pull inflation (Mosayeb and Rahimi 2009). Such will occur mainly due to the high velocity circulation of money which creates an excess demand for goods and services.

Money supply or money available for circulation within the society impacts to increase the inflation rate. The inflation occurs as a result of money supply is known as "Monetary inflation" which can be controlled by imposing taxes. Ukessays.com explains when money supply rises faster than the rate of economic growth or growth of national income, it would lead to create an inflation within the economy. This has been explained by using the quantity theory of money concept. The lack of fiscal restraint has been a prime factor underlying this monetary expansion (Cooray 2008).

As per Weerasekara (Weerasekara 1992), nominal exchange rate between rupee and US dollar is one another key factor which impacts to determine the inflation within the country. The same research has identified a bilateral causality between money supply and exchange rate changes. Bandara (Bandara 1996) reveals that exchange rate and money supply have a large impact on inflation in the long run, while exchange rate depreciation significantly affects inflation in the short run.

Contradiction to that Kesavarajah (Kesavarajah 2009) states that in long run when the Sri Lankan Rupee depreciates by 1%, inflation will increase by approximately 0.18% which is comparatively a less percentage influence compared to the influence generated by the government expenditure. Thus, both the researches emphasis that volatility of exchange rates is highly significant in short run when determining the inflation rates. According to a case in Sweden, Alexius (Alexius 1997) implies that a small open economy like Sweden even has to consider exchange rates as a central factor which influence the price level of the country.

As per Colombage (Colombage 2005) until the hike in crude oil prices in 1973, inflation had not been a major issue to Sri Lanka. This was a major and adverse supply shock that affects the whole Asian economy (Kumar et al. 2012). Such a bad supply shock triggers a sudden hike in inflation, which could be transformed to a permanent galloping inflation (Chari et al. 1998; Clarida et al. 2000). Prior findings support this by which highlights that both in short run and in long run the oil prices are significantly affecting for the inflation within the Sri Lankan economy which disturbs the aggregate supply (Jayawardana and Jayasinghe 2016). As Sri Lanka is a net importer of crude oil, a temporary shock of oil prices in the international market even will trigger a dominant change in the local price level of the country (Goyal 2011).

The lender may charge an interest from the borrower in order to compensate for the loss of money value, when the borrowed money is repaid (). Colombage (Colombage 2005) introduces the interest rates as the opportunity cost of holding the money. There is a one-for-one relationship between interest rates and expected inflation within the country (Jayawardana and Jayasinghe 2016).

Darrat (Darrat 1985) emphasizes that change in interest rates is a significant factor in determining the inflation of the country. Supporting this findings Bhattacharya (Bhattacharya 2013) identified that, interest rates of Vietnam do not have an impact on headline inflation in the short term or medium term, while it has been identified as a major weakness of their monetary policy.

In contrast, several studies identified that the decrease in interest rates influence increased inflation and the empirical results show that the interest rate has a marginal impact on inflation (DaCosta and Greenidge 2002; Kihangire and Mugyenyi 2005; Laryea and Sumaila 2001).

Economic growth is measured by using the change in real gross domestic production (GDP) in the country limits. As per the quantity theory of money, when the real output of a country increases, the national income also increases and this will increase the aggregate demand for goods. If the aggregate demand surpasses the aggregate supply of the economy, there can be an inflationary situation within the economy. However, it is a key objective of any country to maintain a low level of inflation to promote economic growth (Mubarik 2005).

According to Smyth (Smyth 1992), there is a negative relationship between inflation and growth. Further it has found that inflation does not impact to the real output in the long run, but that in the short run there exists a negative effect from inflation on output (Blanchard and Quah 1989).

4.3 Objective of the Study

This research aims to forecast the possible future inflation rates based on the existing identified independent macroeconomic variables that are affecting inflation.

4.4 Methodology

4.4.1 Research Approach

Based on the data collected, the research objectives have been emphasized by using numerical data and statistical analysis thus, it has been followed the quantitative research methodology.

4.4.2 *Population and Sample*

The economic indicators of the post-liberalization period (from year 1977) were selected as the population to this research. However, monthly data from January 2002 to September 2019 were considered as the sample based on the stratified sampling technique. So that, 213 points of monthly economic indicators has been analyzed. Since GDP is published in quarterly basis, monthly data has been interpolated using SPSS software to continue the research.

The secondary data was collected from the annual reports, publications and website of the Central Bank of Sri Lanka (CBSL).

4.4.3 *Conceptual Framework*

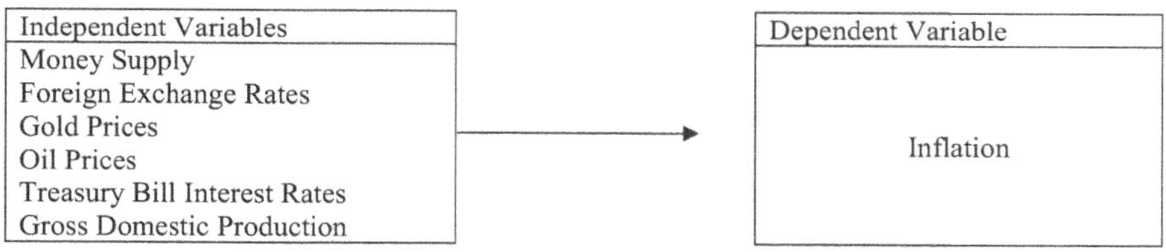

Presentation of variables considered in the study (Source: Author created)

4.4.4 *Operationalization*

The independent variables were measured by using the indicators published by the CBSL. Accordingly, the inflation or change in general price level which is the dependent variable of this study was measured by using the Colombo Consumer Price Index (CCPI). Year-on-year index value published on monthly basis was considered to evaluate the level of inflation within the country.

Money supply (MS), foreign exchange rates (FER), gold prices (GP), oil prices (OP), interest rates (TB), and gross domestic production (GDP) have been identified as the independent variables which impact to incur an inflationary situation within the country. Since all the variables are macroeconomic factors, the circular impact is available in between each mutual independent variable selected to the model. However, in the research only the impact of independent variables towards the dependent variable was analyzed.

In measuring the money supply, the broad money supply (M4) of the country in each month has been considered where M4 is a collection of money held by common public, money in demand deposits owned by common public, money held by common public in the time of deposits and savings deposits, residents' deposits in foreign currency banking units, 50% of time and savings deposits of non-residents' foreign currency units, deposits in licensed special banks, and deposits in registered finance companies (Central Bank Annual Report 2018).

Foreign exchange rate was measured by using the exchange rate between USD and LKR in each month thus the monthly average gold prices per troy oz. has been considered to value the gold price in this research. Further, the price of the crude oil barrel in LKR has been considered to value the oil prices where treasury bill interest rate in each month has been considered in valuing the interest rate. Additionally, the GDP at each month has been considered to value the production level of the economy.

4.5 Empirical Analysis

4.5.1 Descriptive Statistics

The descriptive statistics of the time series macroeconomic variables has been analyzed to identify the behavior of the variables. Mean, standard deviation, skewness, and kurtosis of the distribution have been considered in the basic analysis (Table 4.1).

As per the descriptive statistics presentated in the Table 4.1, mean of CCPI (7.93) has a standard deviation $\pm$ 4.81. CCPI has a positive skewness of 1.28 which means a right tailed distribution, and the kurtosis of 4.55 (kurtosis $>$ 0) illustrates a leptokurtic distribution with considerably heavy tails.

FER has a mean of 122.25 with a standard deviation of $\pm$22.97. The skewness of the data set is 0.78 which means highly right skewed and the kurtosis of the series is 2.93 (Kurtosis $>$ 0) which has a leptokurtic distribution with heavy tails.

GDP has a mean value of 1,747,241 with a standard deviation of $\pm$1,100,819. However, the skewness of the data set is 0.45 which means the distribution is right skewed and the kurtosis of this series is 1.87 (Kurtosis $>$ 0) which illustrate a leptokurtic distribution with light tails.

GP has a mean value of 128,988.10 with a standard deviation of $\pm$67,356.37. Gold prices are fairly symmetrical since the skewness is close to zero ($-$0.08), but the kurtosis of 1.68 (Kurtosis $>$ 0) illustrates a leptokurtic distribution with considerably heavy tails.

Mean value of the MS is 2,791,805.00 with a standard deviation of $\pm$2,048,839.00 which is considerably a high deviation of the data set. Thus, the skewness (0.84) of the data is positive and the data distribution is right skewed with a kurtosis of 2.48 (kurtosis $>$ 0) which illustrates a leptokurtic distribution with heavy tails.

OP have a mean of 8535.52 with a standard deviation of $\pm$3785.84. The skewness ($-$0.06) is a negative value since it is closer to 0 it is possible to conclude that the data set is fairly symmetrical.

Table 4.1 Descriptive statistics

	CCPI	FER	GDP	GP	MS	OP	TB
Mean	7.93	122.25	1,747,241	128988.10	2,791,805	8535.52	9.73
Median	6.60	113.90	1,508,636	150036.10	2,022,307	8166.63	8.71
Std. dev.	4.81	22.97	1,100,819	67356.37	2,048,839	3785.84	3.26
Skewness	1.28	0.78	0.45	−0.08	0.84	0.06	1.45
Kurtosis	4.55	2.93	1.87	1.68	2.48	1.93	4.39
Jarque-Bera	79.462	21.728	18.5547	15.5778	27.3733	10.2994	91.5651
Probability	0.0000	0.0000	0.0001	0.0004	0.0000	0.0058	0.0000

Mean of the TB is 9.73 with a standard deviation of ±3.26. The skewness 1.45 of the data set is positive, and it is a right skewed distribution with a kurtosis of 4.39 (Kurtosis > 0) which illustrate a leptokurtic distribution with considerably heavy tails.

4.5.2 Normality of Distribution of Data

To measure the goodness of fit of the data Jarque-Bera statistic which is a non-negative figure was analyzed. The test results showed distant statistics from zero. Further the below hypothesis were tested to conclude the normality of the data set.

H0 = the data set is normally distributed (*P*-value >0.05).
H1 = the data set is non-normally distributed.

As per the probability values also it can be concluded that the time series data that has been considered in this study is non-normally distributed. So that, to conduct further studies the log transformed data will be used to minimize the effect of normality of the data.

4.5.3 Analysis of Trends of Data

Economic time series data mostly consist of unique characteristics such as clear trend which consists of shocks and high volatility throughout a certain time period (Shrestha and Bhatta 2017).

The Fig. 4.1 illustrates the trends analysis of all dependent and independent variables of this study.

The trend analysis of CCPI shows a high variation of price level within the Sri Lankan economy. There are structural breaks in trend. Such condition may occur disturbances on planning and forecasting of the business sector. However, most of the data is followed by a set of data in the similar range. Thus, there is a possibility of having a relationship between present CCPI and previous CCPI values. Accordingly, the existence of autoregressive character is possible in the general price level of the Sri Lankan economy.

FER, GDP, and MS shows a smooth trend with least shocks. These variables seem to be gradually increasing with the time. However, for OP, GP, and TB there are structural breaks for both intercept and trend. Thus, those variables seem to be highly sensitive to the respective external factors.

However, when analyzing the distribution of data, it can be concluded that there is a possible existence of autoregressive character among all the independent variables defined above. Other than few shocks, most of the data are followed by a series of

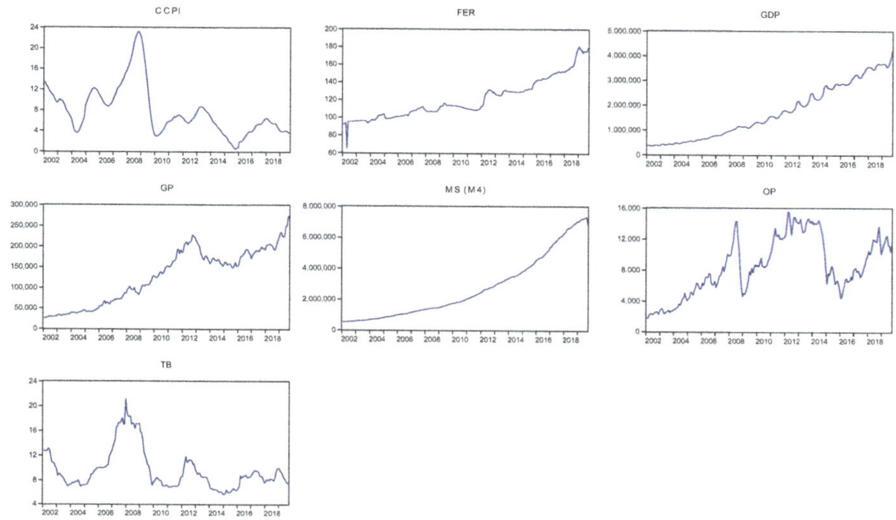

Fig. 4.1 Trend analysis of variables

Table 4.2 Kaiser-Meyer-Olkin (KMO) statistic and Bartlett test

Kaiser-Meyer-Olkin measure of sampling adequacy		0.752
Bartlett's test of sphericity	Approx. chi-square	2681.582
	Df	21
	Sig.	0.000

similar data which is in the same range. So that, it is possible to consider the lagged values of the time series data to conduct this study.

4.5.4 Kaiser-Meyer-Olkin (KMO) Statistic and Bartlett Test to Measure the Sampling Adequacy

The KMO statistic reveals the adequacy of the sample size to conduct the research. The thumb rule of the KMO statistic is 0.6 and since the test results to 0.752, it is possible to conclude that the sample size is adequate to conduct the research (Table 4.2).

Bartlett test is a test that measures whether the "k" samples have equal variances which emphasis the homogeneity of variances. The hypothesis developed to test the homogeneity of variances can be explained as follows.

H0: ${\sigma_1}^2 = {\sigma_2}^2 = \ldots = {\sigma_k}^2$.
H1: ${\sigma_i}^2 \neq {\sigma_j}^2$ for at least one pair (i, j).

As per the result of the Bartlett test illustrated in Table 4.2, which emphasizes that the null hypothesis is being rejected since T = 2681.582 which is greater than the critical value under 0.05 of significance level. Thus, it can be concluded that the $\sigma_i^2 \neq \sigma_j^2$ for at least one pair.

4.5.5 *Unit Root Test*

In the preliminary stage, the research performed the unit root test on each variable in order to examine the stationary or non-stationary level in a time series data set. If both stationary and non-stationary variables were included in an equation and estimated by ordinary least squares (OLS), this will lead to a spurious regression. Thus, differentiate between stationary and non-stationary variables was identified as a critical requirement. There are various alternative tests for testing whether a series is stationary. Commonly used test is augmented Dickey-Fuller (ADF) (Colombage 2005; Kulatunge 2017) (Table 4.3).

To perform the ADF, the hypotheses were set as follows:

H^0: $\beta = 1$ (Non-stationary time series)
H^1: $\beta < 1$ (Time series is stationary)

Accordingly, at levels, the null hypothesis cannot be rejected for majority of the data plots. This emphasized that the raw data is non-stationary. So, ADF was computed for the first difference, and the results reject the null hypothesis for the variables at 5% of significance level that is illustrated in table 4.3. Accordingly, LN_CCPI is stationary at I (0), while all the other variable becomes stationary at I (1).

Table 4.3 Unit root test result with 5% significances level

		ADF	
Variable	Indicator	**Level**	**1st difference**
LN_CCPI	Statistic	−2.9995	
	P-value	**0.0366**	
LN_MS	Statistic	−1.8482	−10.1131
	P-value	0.3565	**0.0000**
LN_FER	Statistic	0.9427	−23.1743
	P-value	0.5521	**0.0000**
LN_GP	Statistic	−1.8683	−12.8824
	P-value	0.3469	**0.0000**
LN_OP	Statistic	−2.5824	−11.0205
	P-value	0.0982	**0.0000**
LN_TB	Statistic	−1.7600	−11.0008
	P-value	0.3997	**0.0000**
LN_GDP	Statistic	−1.7759	−3.1989
	P-value	0.3917	**0.0215**

Table 4.4 Johansen co-integration test results

Hypothesized no. of CE(s)	Eigenvalue	Trace statistic	0.05 critical value	Prob.**
None *	0.294925	161.224	125.6154	0.0001
At most 1	0.169707	88.8874	95.75366	0.1352
At most 2	0.108095	50.3903	69.81889	0.6207
At most 3	0.064292	26.7104	47.85613	0.865
At most 4	0.026903	12.9548	29.79707	0.8936
At most 5	0.021569	7.30962	15.49471	0.5419
At most 6	0.013417	2.79609	3.841466	0.0945

Trace test indicates 1 cointegrating eqn(s) at the 0.05 level * denotes rejection of the hypothesis at the 0.05 level **MacKinnon-Haug-Michelis (1999) p-values

4.5.6 *Johansen Co-Integration Test*

This test determines the substance of long-run association between CCPI and the independent variables. The lag lengths have been determined by using Akaike information criterion (AIC) and concluded with 5 lags to conduct the test of Johansen co-integration. The co-integration has been tested for the variables using both trace test and maximum-eigenvalue test.

The hypothesis for the trace test will be developed for the test as follows:

H_0: The number of co-integration vectors is $r = r^* < k$.
H_1: $r = k$.

According to the results of the Johansen co-integration test (Table 4.4), the null hypothesis has been rejected by trace test with $P\ (0.0001) < 0.05$. Thus, it is possible to conclude that the time series data maintains a long-term equilibrium relationship.

Based on the results of Johansen co-integration test, the analysis was directed in developing error correction model (ECM) to analyze the long-run equilibrium between CCPI and independent variables.

4.5.7 *Error Correction (ECM) Model*

The series of residuals has been obtained based on the ordinary least square (OLS) regression.

$$\begin{aligned} \ln\_ccpi_t = {} & a_{01} + b_{11} \ln\_ms_{t-i} + b_{21} \ln\_fer_{t-i} + b_{31} \ln\_gp_{t-i} \\ & + b_{41} \ln\_op_{t-i} + b_{51} \ln\_tb_{t-i} + b_{61} \ln\_gdp_{t-i} + e_{1t} \end{aligned} \tag{4.1}$$

The stationarity of the residuals has been tested by using ADF test and the results concluded that the residual series is stationary at I (0) with a t-statistic of −4.7593 and $p = 0.0001 < 0.05$.

Accordingly, the ECM has been derived using both short-run and long-run effects in to consideration as follows:

$$\begin{aligned}\Delta \ln\_ccpi_t = {} & a_0 + \sum\nolimits_{i=1}^{p} a_{1i} \Delta \ln\_ccpi_{t-i} + \sum\nolimits_{i=1}^{q} a_{2i} \Delta \ln\_ms_{t-i} \\ & + \sum\nolimits_{i=1}^{q} a_{3i} \Delta \ln\_fer_{t-i} + \sum\nolimits_{i=1}^{q} a_{4i} \Delta \ln\_gp_{t-i} \\ & + \sum\nolimits_{i=1}^{q} a_{5i} \Delta \ln\_op_{t-i} + \sum\nolimits_{i=1}^{q} a_{6i} \Delta \ln\_tb_{t-i} \\ & + \sum\nolimits_{i=1}^{q} a_{2i} \Delta \ln\_gdp_{t-i} + \lambda ecm_{t-1} + e_t \end{aligned} \tag{4.2}$$

As per the results illustrated in Table 4.5, since the coefficient of the residual series (ECM (−1) in Table 4.5) is negative and it is significant $p = 0.0000 < 0.05$, we can conclude that long-run equilibrium relationship is exhibiting among LN_CCPI and the respective independent variables.

However, the short-run coefficients of the developed ECM are not significant. The coefficient of the error term has been 7.82% monthly. This emphasis that the system corrects the disequilibrium of its previous period at a speed of 7.82% monthly. Moreover, the negative sign and significance of the residual series indicate the validity of long-run equilibrium relationship between LN_CCPI and the respective independent variables.

Finally, it is possible to conclude that the ECM is not spurious since the *R*-squared (0.3542) is less than Durbin-Watson statistic (2.4420).

Table 4.5 ECM Coefficients

Variable	Coefficient	Std. error	*t*-Statistic	Prob.
C	−0.0157	0.0114	−1.3737	0.1710
D(LN_CCPI(−1))	0.5427	0.0573	9.4676	0.0000
D(LN_FER(−1))	−0.0271	0.1528	−0.1775	0.8593
D(LN_GDP(−1))	−0.1853	0.2278	−0.8132	0.4171
D(LN_GP(−1))	0.0278	0.1456	0.1912	0.8486
D(LN_MS(−1))	1.1688	0.7829	1.4930	0.1370
D(LN_OP(−1))	0.0576	0.0666	0.8652	0.3880
D(LN_TB(−1))	−0.0252	0.1156	−0.2177	0.8279
ECM (−1)	−0.0782	0.0173	−4.5170	0.0000
R-squared	0.3542	Mean dependent var		−0.0056
Adjusted *R*-squared	0.3286	S.D-dependent var		0.1001
S.E. of regression	0.0820	Akaike info criterion		−2.1228
Sum squared resid	1.3578	Schwarz criterion		−1.9798
Log likelihood	232.9548	Hannan-Quinn criter.		−2.0650
F-statistic	13.8484	Durbin-Watson stat		2.4420
Prob (*F*-statistic)	0.0000			

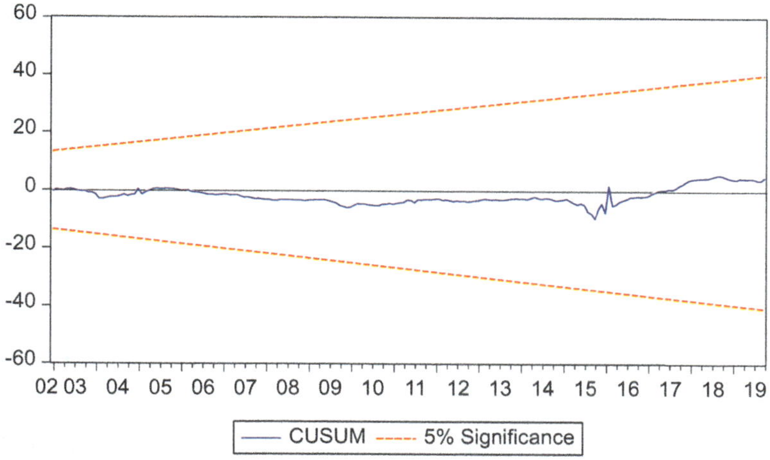

Fig. 4.2 Results of CUSUM test

4.5.8 Tests of Residuals

Residual and stability of the model have been tested to assure the efficiency of the model.

The hypothesis tested here are.

H_0 = There is no serial correlation among residuals.
H_1 = There is serial correlation among residuals.

As per the results of the Breusch–Godfrey Serial Correlation LM Test, $p = (0.0000) < 0.05$ reject null hypothesis which conclude that the residuals of the ECM is serially correlated.

The small shifts in the process mean have been monitored by using the plotted cumulative sum (CUSUM) chart and through that it has been measured the cumulative sum of deviations from the target for individual measurements and subgroup means.

The results of the CUSUM Test of recursive estimation (Fig. 4.2) shows that the model values are lying within the 5% boundary and so that we can conclude that the model is stable.

4.6 Conclusion

The success of inflation control by the Central Bank mainly depends on two factors as in (a) the degree of influence of the money supply on inflation and (b) the extent of autonomy that the Central Bank enjoys in managing the money supply (Colombage

2005). Further, the prior findings exhibit that the main source for the current inflation within Sri Lankan economy is the continuous increment in the money supply (Colombage 2005; Weerasekara 1992). When analyzing the considered macroeconomic variables along with the inflation, the ECM coefficient between money and inflation is 1.1688 which is the highest coefficient based on a sample of ($n = 212$). Thus, the findings are in line with the literature and emphasis the importance of efficient management in money supply.

After the liberalization of the economy, exchange rates and import prices added further pressure to the general price level of the country and became important factors on the general level of prices (Cooray 2008; Kulatunge 2017). As per Weerasekara (Weerasekara 1992), nominal exchange rate between rupee and US dollar is one another key factor which impacts to determine the inflation within the country. However, in contrast with the findings the current research revealed that the effect of USD to Sri Lanka rupee exchange rate is considerably lower.

Higher oil prices affect oil importing economies in two ways and could lead to an increase in firms' production costs and reduce profits (Kihangire and Mugyenyi 2005). Jayawardana and Jayasinghe (Jayawardana and Jayasinghe 2016) supports this by their findings which highlights that both in short run and in long run the oil prices are significantly affecting for the inflation within the Sri Lankan economy which disturbs the aggregate supply. The ECM coefficient reveals that there is a lower level of influence from the price of a crude oil barrel in LKR towards the inflation.

A change in interest rates is a significant factor in determining the inflation of the country (Darrat 1985). However, Kesavarajah (Kesavarajah 2009) argues against the above findings stating that the interest rates are comparatively insignificant in determining the inflation in Sri Lanka. In parallel to the above finding, the ECM coefficient shows that there is a mild influence from treasury bill rate towards the inflation.

According to Smyth (Smyth 1992), there is a negative relationship between inflation and economic growth. However, prior findings revealed that inflation does not impact to the real output in the long run, but that in the short run there exists a negative effect from inflation on output (Blanchard and Quah 1989). In parallel to the findings, the current research emphasizes that there is a low level of effect from the GDP to inflation in Sri Lanka.

The study reveals the long-run factors influencing the inflation in Sri Lanka. While interpreting the ECM results it was identified that last month CCPI has a high capacity of forecasting the CCPI of current month. Though the majority of the variables are less significant with the behavior of inflation (i.e., OP, GP, GDP, FER, TB) and MS is moderately significant with inflation the coefficient of the residual series suggested that it is possible to adjust the deviations in a speed of 7.82% monthly.

As a result of higher money supply, the currency circulation will be higher and it increases the aggregate demand in the country, which increases the domestic price level. The findings of the current research are validating the findings of the Colombage (Colombage 2005); thus, it is contrary to the findings of Kulatunge

(Kulatunge 2017). However, the research confirms the Keynesian theory of demand pull inflation. Further, the factors identified as significant are subjective to the economic performance of the country.

Since the test of residual diagnostics emphasizes an existence of auto-correlation among the residuals, the future research studies are open with an expanded sample size.

References

Alexius, A. (1997). Import prices and nominal exchange rates in Sweden. *Finnish Economic Papers, 10*(2), 99–107.

Bandara, A. (1996). *Short-run dynamics of inflation: Do monetary and exchange rate policies matter? An empirical investigation for Sri Lanka*. Staff Studies, Central Bank of Sri Lanka.

Bashir, F. (2011). Determinants of inflation in Pakistan: An econometric analysis using Johansen co-integration approach. *Australian Journal of Business and Management Research, 01*(05), 71–82.

Bhattacharya, R. (2013). *Inflation dynamics and monetary policy transmission in Vietnam and emerging Asia*. IMF Working Paper WP/13/155.

Blanchard, O. J., & Quah, D. (1989). The dynamic effects of aggregate demand and aggregate supply disturbances. *American Economic Review, 79*, 655–673.

Central Bank Annual Report (2018). Central Bank of Sri Lanka.

Central Bank of Iraq (2012). History page at the Central Bank of Iraq. Retrieved from www.cbi.iq

Chari, V. V., Christiano, L. J., & Eichenbaum, M. (1998). Expectation traps and discretion. *Journal of Economic Theory, 81*(02), 462–492.

Clarida, R., Gali, J., & Gertler, M. (2000). Monetary policy rules and macroeconomic stability: Evidence and some theory. *Quarterly Journal of Economics, 115*(01), 147–180.

Cole, J. H. (1986). Imports and domestic inflation in Latin America. *Studies in Economics and Finance, 10*(01), 72–78. https://doi.org/10.1108/eb028664.

Colombage, S. S. (2005). Determinants of inflation in Sri Lanka: An econometric analysis. *Journal of Humanities, Social Sciences & Education, 03*, 49–60.

Cooray, A. V. (2008). A model of inflation for Sri Lanka. *Review of Applied Economics, 04*(01), 35–44.

DaCosta, D., & Greenidge, K. (2002). Determinants of inflation in selected Caribbean countries. In *29th Annual Review Seminar*.

Darrat, A. F. (1985). Inflation in Saudi Arabia: An Econometric Investigation. *Journal of Economic Studies, 12*(04), 41–51. https://doi.org/10.1108/eb002605.

Goyal, A. (2011). *Inflationary pressures in South Asia*. MPDD working papers WP/11/14.

Jayawardana, D., & Jayasinghe, P. (2016). An inquiry into the causes of inflation in Sri Lanka: An eclectic approach. *NSBM Journal of Management, 02*(01), 92.

Kesavarajah, M. (2009). *Determinants of inflation in Sri Lanka after economic liberalization: An econometric analysis*. Department of Economics.

Kihangire, D., & Mugyenyi A. (2005). Is inflation always and everywhere a non-monetary phenomenon? In *Evidence from Uganda*. Bank of Uganda Working paper WP/05/05.

Kulatunge, S. (2017). Inflation dynamics in Sri Lanka: An empirical analysis. Central Bank of Sri Lanka – Staff Studies (Vol. 45).

Kumar, S., Srinivasan, N., & Ramachandran, M. (2012). A time-varying parameter model of inflation in India. *Indian Growth and Development Review, 05*(01), 25–50. https://doi.org/10.1108/17538251211224123.

Laryea, S.A., & Sumaila, U.R. (2001). Determinants of inflation Tanzania. Institute of Development Studies and Human Rights WP 2001 (p. 12).

Mallik, G., & Chowdhury, A. (2001). Inflation and economic growth-evidence from four south Asian countries. *Asia-Pacific Development Journal, 8*(01), 123–135.

Mosayeb, P., & Rahimi, M. (2009). Sources of inflation in Iran: An application of the ADRL approach. *International Journal of Applied Econometrics and Quantitative Studies, 06*(01).

Mubarik, A. (2005). Inflation and growth: An estimate of the threshold level of inflation in Pakistan. *SBP-Research Bulletin, 01*(01), 35–43.

Sahadudheen, I. (2012). A co-integration and error correction approach to the determinants of inflation in India. *International journal of Economics and Research, 03*(01), 105–112.

Shrestha, M.B., & Bhatta, G.R. (2017) Selecting appropriate methodological framework for time series data analysis. The Journal of Finance and Data Science 4 (2018):71–89. doi.org/10.1016/j.jfds.2017.11.001

Smyth, D. J. (1992). Inflation and the growth rate in the United States "natural output". *Applied Economics, 24*, 567–570.

Weerasekara, Y.M.W.B. (1992). Inflation in Sri Lanka, A Causality Analysis. The South East Asian Central Banks Staff Papers (Vol. 46).

Chapter 5
Information, Policy, and Market Disorder Under Democracy: Evidences from the United States

Purbash Nayak, Mayank Sharma, and Harshit Shandilya

5.1 Introduction

The economy functions on its own—it is organic. Though interests are highly grouped, divisions have to be stable in order to have an automatic self-regulatory economic system. This requires systematic arrangements. Some components of this system are instituted in the form of financial instruments. The investors hold portfolios which collectively forms a myopic reflection of a short- to medium-run macroeconomic performance. Anecdotally, it has been noticed that even advertisement agency sets up mind-frames in order to have a horizon long enough to get gains from the transition in the economy—their slogan: "invest in long term." Also, with opening up of the international boundaries, even the investment has increased their reach, but it must adhere to the rules of the game which principally constraints investors for maintaining profitability. This is a very strict rule. Although the rule is investor's behavior regulator, it has got nothing to do with the effectiveness within the economy provided politics is nurtured under democracy improving labor markets and the investor playing this game, under the dominance of this rule systematically, will increase the capital formation, although complex, in which the system has a balanced saddle path. Under this backdrop, this chapter observes the evolution resulting from the combinatorial behavior of the investor transiting from a politics endorsed system to a system where politics affects the system exogenously.

The methodology adopted is to first look at the literature for efficient market or use widely accepted statistical tools and then use an indicative efficient market under the macroeconomic discourse. For this purpose, this chapter has selected Wilshire

P. Nayak (✉)
Research Faculty, Gokhale Institute of Politics and Economics, Pune, India
e-mail: purbash.nayak@gipe.ac.in

M. Sharma · H. Shandilya
Postgraduate, Gokhale Institute of Politics and Economics, Pune, India

A. K. Mishra et al. (eds.), *Critical Perspectives on Emerging Economies*,
Contributions to Economics, https://doi.org/10.1007/978-3-030-59781-8_5

5000 price index and Sect. 5.1 is a short note about the same. Moving ahead, this chapter tries to formulate a three-dimensional response behavior of the investors determining their entry or exit in the market. The rate of entry though important but is expected to be deterministic by the conditions favoring market returns. Instead, this chapter also focuses on the exit part which follows the strict rule of the game, i.e., the rate of decay or the rate at which markets is not profitable. In Sect. 5.2, while exploring these three dimensions, this chapter contrasts the dimensions between the politically endorsed system and the system with political exogeneity. In order to capture the exogenous effect of politics, we have used color (Democrat or Republican) and the term of the President (first or second term) as explanatory variables. Finally, in Sect. 5.3, the chapter models state of the investors as a response of their behavior. There are three possible states in this system. The investors may belong to a state wherein their existence (i.e., maintaining profits) is possible from the functioning of the economy itself. Contrarily, the other state is where the investor's existence is independent of the macroeconomic functioning and the investors need to bear risk in order to transit (or maintain profits). The third state is the state of decay wherein the market is non-profitable for the representative investor. In this chapter, we assume that these states are independent and irrelevant to each other and at any point in time the investor is expected to be in any of these three states. This chapter uses multinomial logit framework to model the probability distribution among these three states. Analysis is followed in the same section. Section 5.4 concludes the chapter.

5.2 The Idea Behind This Chapter

The investor and the market are always in a transitory state. The idea is to study the behavior of an investor whose existence in the future is subjected to the return on the current investment. Also, the investor, in transition, follows the following rule:

Rule 1: If the assets are giving returns, the investor will continue existing in the transition.
Rule 2: There is only one rule. Either obey or perish.

This transition can also be seen through the lens in a spectrum of an N-Dimensional response of investors to their endeavors. In this chapter, we have considered three dimensions:

1. Means (Responding to a phase).
2. Monetary and Fiscal Policy (Responding to the economy).
3. Globalization (Responding to the rate of convergence).

But this system is intertwined in politics which transforms the behavior response to a 3.5[1]-dimensional space. Politics cannot affect system involving rational agents

[1]Politics as direction and not dimension—Politics directs the way the system reacts to policies.

as an independent dimension. But its presence in dynamic setup formulizes the direction, i.e., politics is an inception of another dimension. Nevertheless, civil expenditure or the fiscal resource is constraint by geopolitical and other positions in international bureaucracy, while, on the scale of resources, the fiscal expenditure is factored as civil expenditure (inside) and military expenditure (outside). An instability at the international frontiers are reflected on military resources, while instability at the economic frontiers are expected to be distributed between the fiscal and monetary resources. Pressure group demands government interventions effecting the operating system in general. This chapter also focuses on the policy of increasing the minimum wage. Also, the economy is exposed to the market failures or shocks resulting from some or the other form of information manipulation. Simultaneously, monetary policy generates several signals informing the investor about the aspects of the economy such as its growth, unemployment, demographic burden/dividend, and expected inflation. Though the monetary policy theoretically carries direct information of excess money balances, the rationally inattentive human agent intends to conceive different types of other information as well. Furthermore, the macroeconomic functioning of the era, with open borders for enterprises, have made it dependent on the economic functioning of the other parts of the world. Although including such broad measures enriches the enquiry yet one needs to be careful while selecting the arguments for such functioning. Further, we have considered two components of the globalization acting on the expected state of the investor, i.e., the growth of the world outside vis-a-vis its development. In order to proxy for the development, we have considered convergence.

This serves two purposes: firstly, it would evaluate the impact of development on the fate of investor and secondly or rather more important purpose is to test convergence as a phenomenon of economic development while interacting with electoral politics. The following sections look into each dimensions particularly (Fig. 5.1).

5.2.1 Means: Responding to a Phase

In a developed country such as the United States, the market appears to be efficient resulting from institutional arrangements. But this so-called efficiency is also associated with the elections. Furthermore, the seasonally adjusted time series of weekly differenced Wilshire 5000 price index in Fig. 5.9 of Appendix 3 suggests an increased volatility especially post Clinton's second term. Also, the nature of fluctuation is consistently more pronounced during the second term onwards. The markets also respond to different events causing spikes evident enough for the graph—a small spike in the graph is due to the Black Market crash (1987)—spikes due to dot-com bubble (also called internet bubble) and due to 2007–08 Financial Crises. Fluctuations of the similar scale have surfaced even from government's policies and have become evident in the contemporary times. As a matter of fact, US economy has seen two major crises in the contemporary times, both of which

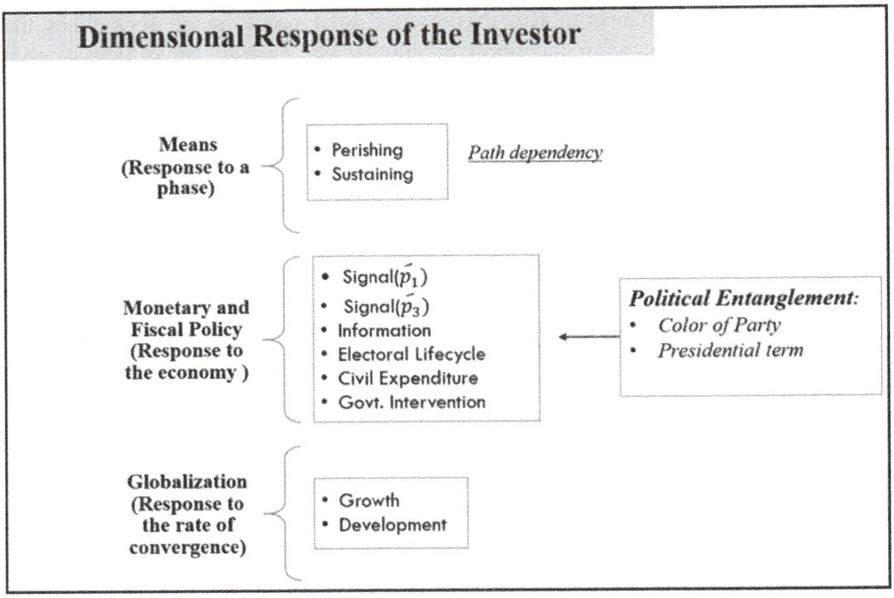

Fig. 5.1 Dimensions of the investor under which the decisions are made. Refer to Sect. 5.2.2.1 for $\widehat{p_1}$ and $\widehat{p_3}$

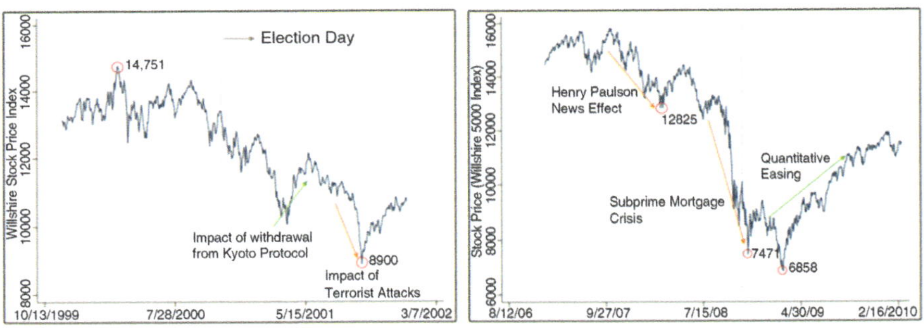

(a) *(b)*

Source Wilshire Associates.

Fig. 5.2 Stock market price by presidential terms

surfaced right before the election post the second term. In Fig. 5.2a, we closely observe the stock price index as the stock market struggles due to the intertwining of economic downturn with uncertainty related to elections particularly between George W. Bush and Al Gore in November 2000. The graph shows a sharp decline followed by withdrawal of the US Government from the Kyoto Protocol resulting in a small rise until 9/11 Terrorist Attack post which market started declining.

Table 5.1 Runs test results for testing weak form of EMH

Stock market	Developed/Emerging	Conclusion
Merval, Buenos Aires	Emerging	Inefficient
Shanghai, China	Emerging	Efficient
Sensex, India	Emerging	Inefficient
ADX, UAE	Developed	Inefficient
NYSE, USA	Developed	Efficient
HIS, Hong Kong	Developed	Efficient
TSX, Canada	Developed	Efficient
Wilshire 5000, USA	Developed	Efficient

Source: Author's calculation

The test statistic is: $Z = \left(R - \overline{R}\right)/\sigma_R$, where R = observed number of runs, $\overline{R}$ = expected number of runs, σ_R = standard deviation of the number of runs

Wald—Wolfowitz Runs test is a non-parametric statistical test that checks a randomness hypothesis for a two-valued data sequence. Refer to Table 5.5 in Appendix 1 for details

Some similar processes featured during the end of George Bush presidency as depicted by Fig. 5.2b. This figure shows the effect of U.S. Treasury Secretary of State Henry Paulson's comments on market volatility (better known as Henry Paulson News Effect) on the stock market index. Also, the graph demonstrates a sharp decline in the index due to the subprime mortgage crisis with subsequent response in the form of quantitative easing and series of bailout packages by the Government resulting in an upward trend in the index. Table 5.1 summarizes the efficiency story showing developed economies with efficient markets while emerging economies struggle (China being a case of exception) for the same. Although, detailed enquiry into the case of US economy suggests that even in developed economies market efficiency is subjected to many types of risk from the environment which is seldom independent of politics. (Refer to Table 5.6 from Appendix 2).

We applied the same test for efficiency (Runs test), but this time however disaggregating the span (Clinton's second term onwards) on the basis of the term of each Presidents for the same data of Wilshire 5000 price index. This change in experiment setup can now reveal efficiency for each period within the whole span of information. Fig. 5.3 shows cyclicity in the z-score. Also, an interesting observation from this figure is that the second term of the Presidents (irrespective of their party's affiliation) consistently appears to be inefficient.

Evidences reiterate literature (Bondt and Thaler 1985; Beaudry and Portier 2006; Shiller 2015) that the investment behavior gets affected by the policies, announcements, uncertainties, etc. But, the prime interest of any rational investor in the game is the return on portfolio subjected to the risk one has to incur in order to achieve the targeted return at any point of time. Thus, analyzing this relationship of risk and return is primary for the purpose of our enquiry. Fig. 5.4 sheds some light on this relationship using quantiles of quarterly risk and return over the timeframe of 37 years (1980–2017). Figure 5.4a shows that return curve rises with risk, but beyond the particular level this curve plateaus and one may expect loss for the

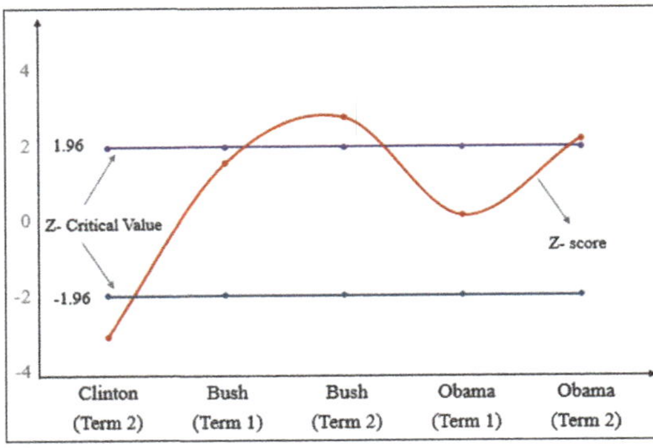

President (Term)	Year	Conclusion
Clinton (Term 2)	1997-00	Inefficient
Bush (Term 1)	2001-04	Efficient
Bush (Term 2)	2005-08	Inefficient
Obama (Term 1)	2009-12	Efficient
Obama (Term 2)	2013-16	Almost Efficient

Source: Author's calculation

Fig. 5.3 The movement of z-score (Runs test) market efficiency from Clinton to Obama's second term. Source: Author's calculation

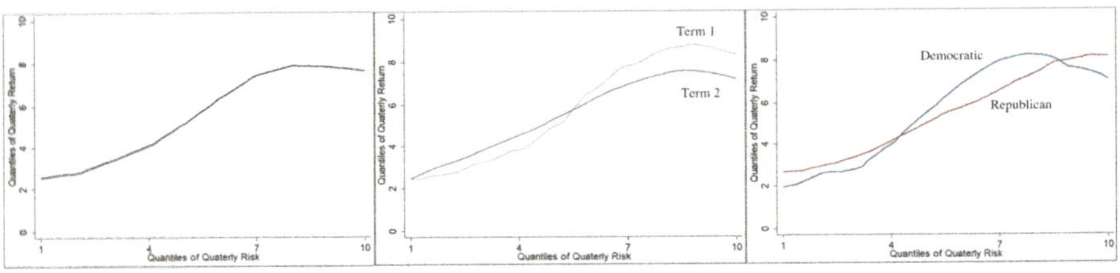

(*a*) (*b*) (*c*)

Fig. 5.4 The plot of quantiles of Quarterly Return with Quarterly Risk. (**a**) The plot of quantiles of Quarterly Return with Quarterly Risk. (**b**) The plot of Quarterly Risk with Quarterly Return under different terms of the President. (**c**) The plot of Quarterly Risk with Quarterly Return under major political parties in the United States (Democrats and Republicans)

excess (and unnecessary) risk. Figure 5.4b shows how the markets have behaved under each terms of different Presidents of the United States irrespective of their party affiliations. At lower level of risk, both *term1* and *term2* show similar result (*term2* is slightly more), but risking beyond a point generates higher return in *term1* than *term2*. Figure 5.4c shows the relation between market risk and market return under different political leadership, i.e., the Democrats and the Republicans. Here, in case of the Democratic government, after minor fluctuations at lower level of risk, the market returns start increasing at an increased rate and after a point, the curve starts bending. While in case of the Republicans, return increases with an increase in risk which eventually flattens. It is in the first term of Republicans, when the irrational exuberance among the investors may await them to expect a very high returns as they may eventually take higher risks which may be endorsed in politics unless politics is kept exogenous to the system regulating investor's behavior to ensure the same. These stylized facts suggest an existence of a political business model as suggested by Hibbs (1977) and Alesina (1987). Their literature suggests that the Democrats will stimulate the economy once elected while the Republicans, on the other hand, will contract the economy which is due to their difference in higher inflation vs higher unemployment approach.

While comparing both terms, we find that initially, that market returns and risk is lesser and relatively fluctuating in *term1* than *term2*. This trend continues for a while but somewhere in the middle of the tenure of an electoral life cycle, the returns in *term1* overtakes the return from *term2* and keeps on moving that way until the end of the *term1* before plateauing of the curve; but still the markets are giving higher returns than *term2*. The analysis of Fig. 5.4 suggests existence of a political business cycle which in its opportunistic model as proposed by Nordhaus (1975) predicts that the output and economic growth in the economy is increased in the years and a half before each elections as the incumbents implement the policies to stimulate the economic growth to improve their chances of being voted back to the government. Fig. 5.4b suggests that there is a tendency in the past US Presidents to stimulate economic growth from mid quarters of *term1* in order to improve their chances of getting re-elected from *term2*. Apart from existence of political business cycle and the rules of the game, existence of the investors in future is subjected to the returns on assets in the portfolio. And they will continue to be in the transitory state unless if, for some reasons, the portfolio's return starts decaying. It means that those returns are getting consumed by the investors who are still transiting. We intend to study this behavioral conditioning of investors from a political spectrum. We have considered two distinct systems which are two different processes, where

(a) the politics is endogenous,
(b) the politics is exogenous.

Let there be two types of investors—Investor A and Investor B. The investor A realizes its risk–return framework from its past information while assuming that the politics is already endogenized in the signaling system while investor B perceives political information independent from its framework. The latter thinks that any change in a political ecosystem might have a direct or indirect impact on the returns from their portfolio, thereby its future (or existence) in the game.

5.2.1.1 Political Endogenous System

Below is the system of equations to account for the behavior of investor A. In this system, the political information associated with the changes in political order is captured in the residual terms (ϵ_t and ϵ'_t) in the phase of risk and return, respectively, at any point in time along with other sporadic events affecting factors that can influence investor's decisions, thus his behavior.

$$\text{Risk}_t = \alpha_0 + \alpha_1.\text{Return}_{t-1} + \alpha_2.\text{Risk}_{t-1} + \epsilon_t \tag{5.1}$$

$$\text{Return}_t = \alpha'_0 + \alpha'_1.\text{Return}_{t-1} + \alpha'_2.\text{Risk}_{t-1} + \epsilon'_t \tag{5.2}$$

5.2.1.2 Political Exogenous System

Below is the system of equations to account for the behavior of investor B. In this political exogenous model, we have incorporated dummy variables for the term (*term2* = 1) and political party affiliation (Democratic = 1) of the government as the exogenous variables in the same risk–return framework. In this model, the residual terms (e_t and e'_t) capture the information in the phase of risk and return independent of changing political order.

$$\text{Risk}_t = \alpha''_0 + \alpha''_1.\text{Return}_{t-1} + \alpha''_2.\text{Risk}_{t-1} + \alpha''_3.\text{term2}_t + \alpha''_4.\text{Democratic}_t + e_t \tag{5.3}$$

$$\text{Return}_t = \alpha''_5 + \alpha''_6.\text{Return}_{t-1} + \alpha''_7.\text{Risk}_{t-1} + \alpha''_8.\text{term2}_t + \alpha''_9.\text{Democratic}_t + e'_t \tag{5.4}$$

$$\text{where Democratic} = \begin{cases} 1, \text{if the political party present during the time period is Democratic} \\ 0, \text{if the political party present during the time period is Republican} \end{cases}$$

Table 5.7 in Appendix 4 shows the results of the system of equations [Eqs. (5.1)–(5.4)]. Analyzing the result suggests that investor needs to bear risk in order to book a return for both endogenous and exogenous case. Additionally, in the exogenous model, if the investment is made in the second term of a president, then irrespective of the party's affiliation at power, the amount of risk accumulated on the portfolio, on an average, is higher than if the same investment had been made in the first term. Further, the Granger Causality test between these variables under both models show a bidirectional causality. On comparing the two results, one can conclude that irrespective of the investor's interaction with politics, one can make returns in the market only if some amount of risk is undertaken.

5.2.2 *Responding to the Economy: Monetary and Fiscal Policy*

5.2.2.1 Monetary Policy

The Central Bank or the Fed Reserve influences the money supply in the US economy based on the macroeconomic conditions. Information is published in almost all the public information platforms. And hence, both the Fed Reserve and the investors continuously evaluate the situation before making any decision. Understanding the signaling of the economy is critical as investors base their decisions on the expected action of the Central Bank. In this section, we try to model investor as a signal receiver from the economy of expected policy-move by the Central Bank, i.e., either to increase or decrease the repo rate or status quo. We assume that the investor has arrangements to decode fluctuations of macroeconomic variables (unemployment rate, GDP growth rate, expected inflation, etc.) in the form of expected possibility of increasing or decreasing repo rate using intelligence from analyzing contemporaneous events. The US economy has suffered from different economic crises/shocks. Hence, the shock and the shock recovery period has also been incorporated in the multinomial approach to study the behavior of the Fed Reserve. And, as discussed previously, as how markets like those of the United States could behave when subjected to the political business cycle being intertwining with the market, we have furthered the analysis by looking in the matter separately for *term1*, *term2* as well. We model:

$$\text{Monetary Policy} : M = \begin{cases} -1, \text{Decrease in Repo rate} \\ 0, \text{Status Quo} \\ +1, \text{Increase in Repo rate} \end{cases}$$

An investor expects the banker to make any of the policy choices and readjusts his portfolio valuations accordingly. He is also attentive towards the functioning of the macroeconomy while getting informed through continuous signals. The signal is quantified as a vector of probabilities of being in any of the state.

$$\boldsymbol{P} = \begin{pmatrix} \Pr(M = \text{Repo decrease}) \\ \Pr(M = \text{Status quo}) \\ \Pr(M = \text{Repo increase}) \end{pmatrix} = \begin{pmatrix} p1 \\ p2 \\ p3 \end{pmatrix} \text{ and } p1 = \frac{e^{X'\gamma^{-1}}}{e^{X'\gamma^{-1}} + e^{X'\gamma^{0}} + e^{X'\gamma^{+1}}},$$

$$p2 = \frac{e^{X'\gamma^{0}}}{e^{X'\gamma^{-1}} + e^{X'\gamma^{0}} + e^{X'\gamma^{+1}}},\ p3 = \frac{e^{X'\gamma^{+1}}}{e^{X'\gamma^{-1}} + e^{X'\gamma^{0}} + e^{X'\gamma^{+1}}}.$$

$$X' = \begin{pmatrix} \pi^e{}_t \\ \mu - \mu' \\ \lambda \\ r \\ \chi \\ \xi \\ 1 \end{pmatrix}, \text{ where}^{2,3,4,5}\ \lambda = \begin{cases} 1, \text{Age Dependency ratio} \geq \theta \\ 0, \text{Age Dependency ratio} < \theta \end{cases},$$

$$\chi = \begin{cases} 1, \text{shock present} \\ 0, \text{shock absent} \end{cases}, \text{ and } \xi = \begin{cases} 0, \textit{shock exists} \\ 1, 1\textit{st phase recovery} \\ 2, 2\textit{nd phase recovery} \\ 3, 3\textit{rd phase recovery} \\ 4, 4\textit{th phase recovery} \\ 5, 5\textit{th phase recovery} \end{cases}$$

$\boldsymbol{\gamma}^{-1}$, $\boldsymbol{\gamma}^{0}$, and $\boldsymbol{\gamma}^{+1}$ are MLE of parameters for an expected Central Bank policy—repo rate decrease, status quo or increase, respectively. We consider status quo as our base outcome, thus $E_{\text{S. quo}}\{M = \text{Repo decrease}\} = \frac{\Pr(M=\text{Repo decrease})}{\Pr(M=\text{Status quo})} = e^{X'\gamma^{-1}}$.

Maximum likelihood estimators (MLE) of this model using quarterly dataset since 1980 is presented in Table 5.2. Further, we divide the sample for quarters belonging first term of any president and second term, respectively, and report the MLE of the same. $\boldsymbol{\gamma}_1^{-1}$ *and* $\boldsymbol{\gamma}_2^{-1}$ would represent marginal probability of decreasing repo rate particularly for *term1* and *term2,* respectively.

Before analyzing the results, let us reiterate the rules of transition:

Rule 1: The investor can exist in the market only if there is a return on his portfolio or else the market will itself consume them, i.e., *the investors, who are transiting by following the rule, will incur profits equivalent to the valuation of the portfolios that are getting consumed by the market.*

Rule 2: There is only one rule: either obey or perish.

---

[2]Data Source: Expected Inflation—Board of Governors of the Federal Reserve System (US), Unemployment Rate—U.S. Congressional Budget Office, High Age Dependency Ratio—World Bank, Growth (US GDP)—U.S. Bureau of Economic Analysis.

[3]Where $\pi^e{}_t$ = Expected Inflation, $\mu - \mu'$ = Unemployment Rate, λ = High Age Dependency Ratio, r = GDP Growth Rate, χ = Shock, and ξ = Shock Recovery. Also, refer to Table 5.10 in Appendix 7 for the stationary test results of the variables $\pi^e{}_t$, $\mu - \mu'$ & r.

[4]Refer to Fig. 5.10 in Appendix 8 for kernel density plot of High Age Dependency.

[5]Shock recovery variable is formed to capture the post shock time periods. For instance, if a shock period sustains for 6 quarters, then the shock recovery periods will be of 6 quarters as well and are defined as first, second, third, fourth, and fifth or above shock recovery periods.

Table 5.2 Monetary policy response to information and politics using multinomial logistic approach

	Both terms	(95% Conf. int.)		Term1	(95% Conf. int.)		Term2	(95% Conf. int.)	
Decreasing repo rate	γ^{-1}	Lower	Upper	γ_1^{-1}	Lower	Upper	γ_2^{-1}	Lower	Upper
$\pi^e{}_t$	19.148****	5.72	32.57	24.511**	−0.18	49.21	41.702**	−4.45	87.85
$\mu - \mu'$	−14.036****	−24.13	−3.94	−28.529***	−51.60	−5.46	−35.701	−92.15	20.75
λ	−1.703***	−3.04	−0.37	−1.714**	−3.54	0.12	−24.883	−6216.91	6167.14
r	−22.254****	−37.73	−6.78	−41.309***	−75.05	−7.57	−47.583	−127.46	32.29
χ	1.190	−0.81	3.19	1.183	−1.00	3.37	−11.861	−32.52	8.80
ξ	−0.049	−0.49	0.39	−0.268	−0.88	0.34	−1.202	−3.90	1.50
Constant	281.793****	83.13	480.45	537.744***	98.30	977.19	640.214	−415.21	1695.64
Increasing repo rate	γ^{+1}			γ_1^{+1}			γ_2^{+1}		
$\pi^e{}_t$	−15.300*	−34.21	3.61	−20.284	−49.12	8.55	9.136	−33.72	52.00
$\mu - \mu'$	0.400	−8.69	9.49	1.233	−10.33	12.80	39.135**	−6.43	84.70
λ	−1.102**	−2.27	0.06	−1.309	−3.12	0.50	0.346	−4.07	4.76
r	0.836	−13.43	15.10	1.903	−16.11	19.92	60.134**	−7.69	127.95
χ	−13.035	−1995.80	1969.73	−14.575	−4356.42	4327.27	−0.179	−53623.73	53623.38
ξ	0.181	−0.30	0.66	0.243	−0.36	0.84	4.015*	−0.76	8.79
Constant	−10.668	−192.89	171.56	−24.571	−254.28	205.14	−793.647**	−1693.48	106.18
No. of obs	140			76			64		
Pseudo R2	0.25			0.29			0.41		
LR chi^2 (Levhari & Patinkin, 1968)	67.14			41.02			48.95		
Log likelihood	−99.15			−51.03			−35.49		

Source: Author's calculation. **** for 1%, *** for 5%, ** for 10%, * for 15% level of significance

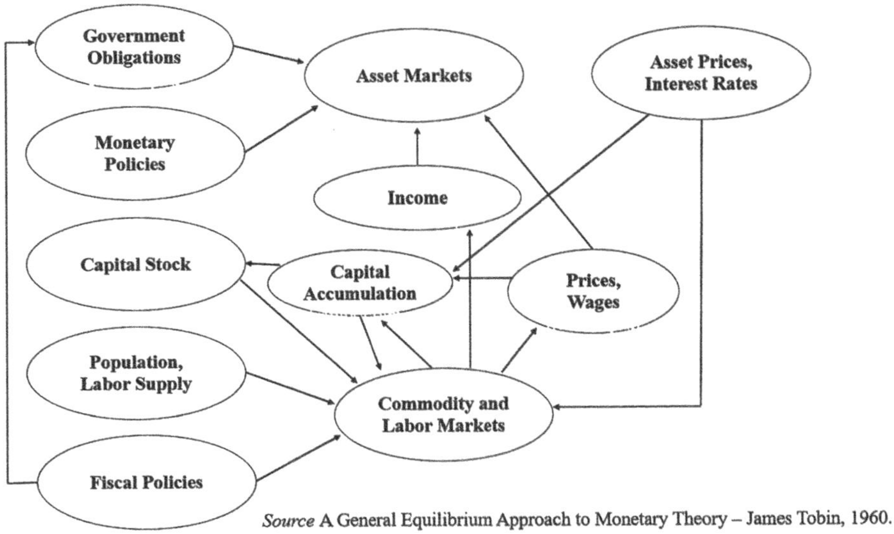

Fig. 5.5 Capital account approach (schematic). Source: a general equilibrium approach to monetary theory—Tobin (1960)

The rules of the game are a mechanism design wherein the investors participate in an environment of excessively high competition and behaving rationally is their only key to continue their existence. Furthermore, a surge in the financial market activities appeared only in the ex post institution developments as supported by the political movements since the Reagan era. It was the same time when the monetarism was discussed widely in the economic schools and the literature was filled with the mathematical models of monetarism, i.e., considering money as a commodity which is entering the utility function of a representative agent in a dynamic economy. Interestingly, the data selected for the analysis in the enquiry appears to have been generating from the aftermath of such processing in some parts of the discipline of economics. The relation of the investors with the economy is structural wherein the yield of their portfolio is resulting from the exchange activity which is happening in the core of the system, i.e., an exchange of labor and productivity with continuously evolving taste and consumption patterns. As malfunctioning of the non-viable economic activities leads to a loss in all the portfolios bearing that the investment through their capital accounts (Fig. 5.5), but who decides this rule—Tobin's Q[6] (Brainard and Tobin 1968).

While, ever since there is a shift in the discipline of economics into monetarism, the commodity price has been tampered in lieu of resonance with a representative portfolio in the economy. Thus, it was the duty of the Central Bank to dictum the investor's behavior generating the business cycle. This chapter looks at the

[6]Tobin q, shadow value.

investor's behavior in a game that is following a set of rules which generates the rationality and hence, with adaptive capacity, they will converge to a state of rational expectations where, their behavior though reactionary, but, responsive to the "information" which puts light on the expected change in order. Thus, the investors follow the Central Bank as the monetary policy itself generates a signal regarding the parameters describing the health of the economy. Table 5.2 illustrates the parameters of multinomial choice model—a probability model. Investors, at least some of them, are also observant to this game while the others participate in provisioning the demand for fluidity (liquidity). In a nutshell, response of the Central Bank in general and monetary policy in particular reveals information regarding the macroeconomy to an information seeking rational investor constrained by his capacity to arrange understanding of economic functioning. Here, we argue that investors are also seekers of information and based on event-based summary would expect the likeliest outcome. In jargon of probability-based models, investors would receive at max the signal as predicted by the above model while parameters are MLE.

Interpreting Coefficients

Standard way to interpret parameters would be to consider a utility function based on consumption and money balances under the constraints of the capital flows (Levhari. D and Patinkin. D,1967; Johnson H.G.,1967; Sidrauski. M,1967). These coefficients would then indicate the marginal probability of the policy given a macroeconomic reality. In this chapter, we would definitely like to benefit by the natural experiment that has resulted from ex post implementation of such formulations. Although, our model keeps the spirit of the ups (ξ) and downs (χ) fixated in the contemporaneous memory post Reagan. But the so-called "*players*" of this game, though rational but is suffering from a sparse sight. It would not be scientific at all to consider all types of investors being informed of the macroeconomic reality. Instead this myopic investor is continuously seeking information among a network of other co-sufferers. Experts are hired and even monetary valuations is high power for these consultancy jobs—enough evidence for demand of information. Simultaneously, there are production houses of information which empower the grid of distribution among the circuit and networks. The purpose is to forecast expected future bases on their pretense of knowledge of the economy at large. In this model, expected inflation is proxied as money supply of previous period after controlling for ups and downs in the economy, broader shift of consumption pattern through demographic change and potential threat of conflict possibly causing due to unemployment. We assume that the capacity of investor to understand the economy is subjected to attention and the parameters $\gamma^{-1}, \gamma^{+1}, \gamma_1^{+1}, \gamma_1^{-1}, \gamma_2^{-1}, \gamma_2^{+1}$ are the marginal propensity to signal a reality by a policy γ^{-1} & γ^{+1} is the vector of propensities to signal a reality vector by expansionary and contractionary monetary policy, respectively. Particularly, ${\gamma^{+1}}_{\lambda}$ would then be the marginal propensity to signal the prosperity induced due to change in demographic structure by expansionary monetary policy. Similarly, ${\gamma_2^{+1}}_{\mu-\mu'}$ is the propensity to signal increase in unemployment following the need for a contractionary monetary policy.

A decreasing repo rate would signal a very high increase in the expected inflation ${\gamma^{-1}}_{\pi^e} > 0$. In some cases, it is also a signal of recession ${\gamma^{-1}}_{r} < 0$ and sometimes even signal a demographic shift ${\gamma^{-1}}_{\lambda} < 0$—resulting in cohort-based culture propagation, while limiting the old age burden affecting consumption and henceforth everything. An increase in the repo rate by the Central Bank would signal a reduction in the expected inflation ${\gamma^{+1}}_{\pi^e} < 0$. But there is no stable signal about the GDP ${\gamma^{+1}}_{r}$ is insignificant although this may signal some version of prosperity related to diminishing old age burden ${\gamma^{+1}}_{\lambda} < 0$ in the system. But the crucial thing to note from this table would be that unemployment rate or the state of the economy (i.e., whether the economy is recovering or it is under a shock) does not reveal anything about the expected monetary policy or vice versa (at least for the ignorant one) ${\gamma^{+1}}_{\mu-\mu'}, {\gamma^{+1}}_{r}, {\gamma^{+1}}_{\chi}$, and ${\gamma^{+1}}_{\xi}$ are also insignificant. Further, while analyzing the model over both the *terms* independently, we notice that pseudo R^2 for *term2* sample has increased substantially signaling that the Central Bank's behavior is more predictive during the second term. Also, as discussed, decreasing the repo rate in *term2* does not reveal anything other than an increase in the expected inflation ${\gamma_2^{-1}}_{\pi^e} > 0$. But in *term1*, the same policy would reveal signal recession with more clarity than anything else. ${\gamma_1^{-1}}_{\lambda} < 0$, while ${\gamma_2^{-1}}_{r}$ is insignificant. While ${\gamma_1^{+1}}_{\pi^e}, {\gamma_1^{+1}}_{\mu-\mu'}, {\gamma_1^{+1}}_{\lambda}, {\gamma_1^{+1}}_{r}, {\gamma_1^{+1}}_{\chi}$, and ${\gamma_1^{+1}}_{\xi}$ are all insignificant. Surprisingly, both the policies reveal different signals about unemployment—a contractionary monetary policy increases unemployment if discreetly seen among the second terms—${\gamma_2^{+1}}_{\mu-\mu'} > 0$ while in *term1*, it is insignificant. Whereas a monetary expansionary policy signals declining unemployment ${\gamma^{-1}}_{\mu-\mu'} < 0$—in general and *term1* in particular ${\gamma_1^{-1}}_{\mu-\mu'} < 0$, while ${\gamma_2^{-1}}_{\mu-\mu'}$ is insignificant. Also, increasing the repo rate has no signal other than returns from age structure (demography) ${\gamma^{+1}}_{\lambda} < 0$ and expected decline of inflation ${\gamma^{+1}}_{\pi^e} < 0$. From the analysis of this exercise one thing is clear—*Any one signal can have many causes and all causes have possible causation behind the signal received.*

Furthermore, another important aspect in determining the behavior of an investor is his enlightenment regarding the change of order. Rationally, the investor may have arrangements designed where he receives signals as a result of his social interaction subject to the entropy (measure of disorder) constraint. Thus, three crucial measures—two of them revealing signals of monetary policy, i.e., probability of increase or decrease of repo rate predicted from the above monetary choice model and a measure to quantify information—the entropy, particularly for the purpose of this chapter, we have used the Shannon's entropy[7] (Shannon. C,1948) as our measure of

[7]In 1948, Shannon published his paper "A Mathematical Theory of Communication" in the Bell Systems Technical Journal. He showed how information could be quantified with absolute precision and demonstrated the essential unity of all information media. Telephone signals, text, radio waves, and pictures, essentially every mode of communication, could be encoded in bits. The paper provided a "blueprint for the digital age". Since the Bell Systems Technical Journal was targeted only towards communication engineers, mathematician Warren Weaver "had the feeling that this ought to reach a wider audience than (just) people in the field" recalls Betty Shannon. He met with Shannon, and together, they published "The Mathematical Theory of Communication" in 1949.

macroeconomic information intended by investor in resonance of demand for broader liquidity while some are endorsed in politics provisioning the same fluid.

The Measure

$Ip = -\widehat{p_1}\ \log\widehat{p_1} - \widehat{p_2}\ \log\widehat{p_2} - \widehat{p_3}\ \log\widehat{p_3}$, *where* $\widehat{p_1}$ *and* $\widehat{p_3}$ are the predicted probabilities of decreasing and increasing of repo rate in the system with $\widehat{p_2} = 1 - (\widehat{p_1} + \widehat{p_3})$, as the probability of the Central Bank maintaining status quo.[8]

5.2.2.2 Fiscal Policy

After making inferences from the monetary policy in the above section, this chapter focuses on understanding the transition of the investor in response to the fiscal policies which, in turn, is based on the expenditure incurred by the government as civil and military expenditures. The political party in its election campaign promises and releases manifesto explaining a series of reforms which they think might solve the problems of the country. These reforms are designed in order to meet the primary socio-economic problems associated with the beneficiaries as well as the geopolitical scenario that the government could be facing in those periods. Figure 5.6 shows the tax receipts and military expenditure of the US economy under different Presidents. The Democrats increase the government services to the people by increasing taxes. Hence, under the Democrats, increased taxation with plateauing military expenditure refers to increased civil expenditures. While, under Republican era, there is an increased military expenditure along with tax cuts. The Republicans favor the private sectors by reducing the government services by instruments of tax cuts and reducing funds. But following the 9/11 Terror Attack, the Bush administration had to increase tax to raise funds for exercising war. Hence, the Republicans show both increasing taxation and military expenditure (the cause). But, in the Global Neo-Liberal Militarism era or post Keynesian Military tailing, there is a dissonance in the direction of the instrumentation of tax. There is an ideological demand for both instruments like Tax Relief Reconciliation Act (2003) in order to stimulate the economy responding ex post economic shock and instruments responsive to exogenous impulses due to situations like war which are also instruments of increasing tax. We develop similar systems relating to the changes in the civil and military expenditures and further divide it in politically endogenous and exogenous systems.

[8]In this chapter, our measurements are based on distribution from the above monetary model wherein we have considered the whole sample consisting of information on both the terms.

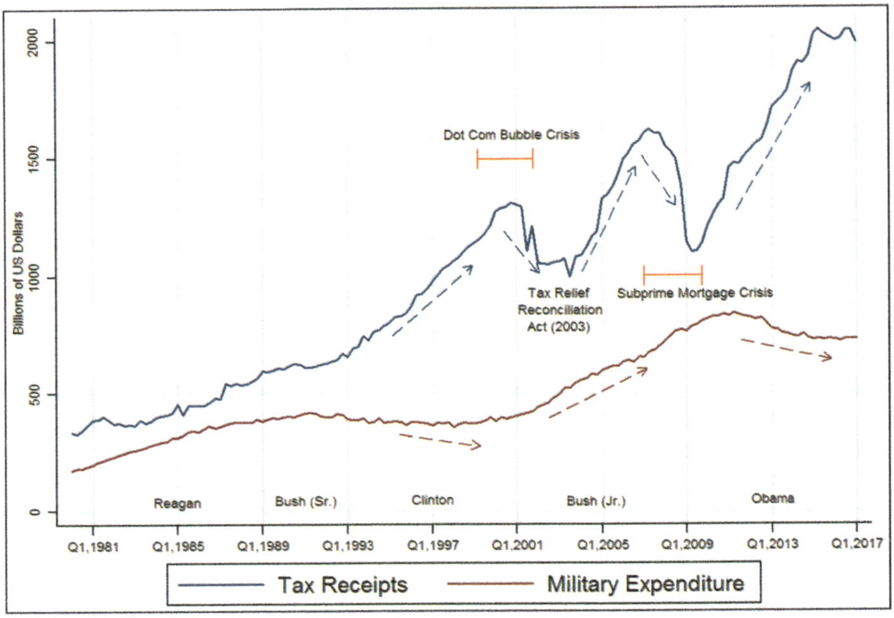

Source U.S. Bureau of Economic Analysis

Fig. 5.6 The tax receipts and the military expenditure time series plot of the United States under different Presidents. Source: U.S. Bureau of Economic Analysis

Political Endogenous System

Under this system, the policies associated with these expenditures are decided by the system of equations [Eqs. (5.5) and (5.6)]. The residual terms (ϑ_t and ϑ'_t) of the equations reflects information regarding change in civil expenditure independent of military expenditure but endogenized with political order.

$$\Delta \text{ME}_t = \beta_0 + \sum\nolimits_{i=1}^{3} \beta_i . \Delta \text{ME}_{t-1} + \sum\nolimits_{i=1}^{3} \delta_i . \Delta \text{CE}_{t-1} + \vartheta_t \tag{5.5}$$

$$\Delta \text{CE}_t = \beta'_0 + \sum\nolimits_{i=1}^{3} \beta'_i . \Delta \text{ME}_{t-1} + \sum\nolimits_{i=1}^{3} \delta'_i . \Delta \text{CE}_{t-1} + \vartheta'_t \tag{5.6}$$

where ΔME_t is the change in the military expenditure and ΔCE_t is the change in civil expenditure.[9]

[9]Total expenditure (Total tax receipts): $\text{TE}_t = \text{CE}_t + \text{ME}_t$

Political Exogenous System

While under the system of equations [Eqs. (5.7) and (5.8)], we have again included the exogenous variables similar to the approach we took for exogenous condition for risk–return framework. The residual terms (υ_t and υ_t') here refer to change in civil expenditure after controlling for both military expenditure and the political order of power.

$$\Delta \mathrm{ME}_t = \beta_0'' + \sum_{i=1}^{3} \beta_i''.\Delta \mathrm{ME}_{t-1} + \sum_{i=1}^{3} \delta_i''.\Delta \mathrm{CE}_{t-1} + \tau_1.\mathrm{term2}_t + \eta_1.\mathrm{Democratic}_t + \upsilon_t \tag{5.7}$$

$$\Delta \mathrm{CE}_t = \beta_0''' + \sum_{i=1}^{3} \beta_i'''.\Delta \mathrm{ME}_{t-1} + \sum_{i=1}^{3} \delta_i'''.\Delta \mathrm{CE}_{t-1} + \tau_2.\mathrm{term2}_t + \eta_2.\mathrm{Democratic}_t + \upsilon_t' \tag{5.8}$$

where $\Delta \mathrm{ME}_t$ is the change in the military expenditure and $\Delta \mathrm{CE}_t$ is the change in civil expenditure.

Results of the system is in Table 5.8 of Appendix 5.

Both the models show similar results as far as expenditure on military and civil needs is concerned. However, under exogenous model setup, the result shows that the expenditure in the military infrastructure, on an average, is decreased under Democrats when compared to the Republicans. Also, the Democrats invest more in the civilians by reducing military expenditure. In addition, the expenditure on the military, on an average, is increased if the president is in his second term. Also, the Granger Causality test implies a unidirectional causality with direction of causality from civil to military. Considering the trade-off between civil and military expenditure, one may conclude from these evidences that expenditure for civilian needs does restrict scope for future military expenditures but other way round is not statistically prudent at least from the contemporaneous experience of the United States. We assume that the above system of equations also ascertains the laws of motion determining contemporaneous evolution of military expenditure provisioning through tax receipts and not the other way round (i.e., provisioning public expenditure by waging war). We have seen how politics is not any dimension, but it induces direction in the functioning of dimensions, i.e., politics is not directly related to any of the investor's deed. As it is very difficult to imagine the class consisting of set of people suitable enough for investor's affiliation simultaneously demanding politicians for provisions. Instead, it is this provisioning class that also includes some investors within, as they get endorsed in politics. Interpretation of the Granger Causality table (Table 5.3) illustrates that change in civil expenditure (surplus tax after spending in military) must diminish in order to increase military spending. The Table 5.3 illustrates the test performed with the null hypothesis that the coefficients on the lags of the other endogenous variable is zero for any particular equation and we reject the same for Eq. (5.5) and (5.7) by putting $\boldsymbol{\delta}_i$ and $\boldsymbol{\delta}_i'' = 0$ followed by $\boldsymbol{\tau}_1, \boldsymbol{\tau}_2$ $\boldsymbol{\eta}_1$ and $\boldsymbol{\eta}_2$—all kept jointly zero.

Table 5.3 Granger causality tests for endogenous and exogenous system

Granger causality Wald tests		Endogenous			Exogenous		
Equation	Excluded	chi2	Df	*p*-value	chi2	Df	*p*-value
ΔME_t	ΔCE_t	8.4855	3	0.037	11.032	3	0.012
ΔME_t	All	8.4855	3	0.037	11.032	3	0.012
ΔCE_t	ΔME_t	4.8535	3	0.183	2.0898	3	0.554
ΔCE_t	All	4.8535	3	0.183	2.0898	3	0.554

Source: Author's calculation

5.2.3 *Globalization:* A Hypothesis...

In this section, we investigate the third dimension under the backdrop of theory developed. In the past few decades, there has been an increased level of cooperation and integration among the different businesses around the world. This has resulted into more connectivity and trading activities of the developed countries (the United States in particular) with the emerging economies. For example, the Chinese economy experienced high growth rates and so did India. Hence, these activities strongly direct towards the concept of convergence as a by-product of globalization which has resulted into increased economic growth and per capita income in the emerging economies. Also, the system in the United States is responsive to the global world—an average American investor is expected to gain from the world's growth and from its development. Though selfish investors have no business whatsoever from the deeds of the outside world other than his opulence, he still would want to get feuded by growth of the outside world. Our interest here is to test the hypothesis that

> *Irrational exuberance among rational but myopic investors provisions for growth friendly behavior which is often non friendly towards the concept of development but without development the endeavors of his feed from the by-product of globalization is incomplete. What solves this conflict? Our answer is Politics–in this neo-liberal era this is often practiced as instruments.*

5.3 Model Specification and Econometric Modeling

There are three possible states in this system. The investors may belong to a state wherein their existence, i.e., (maintaining profits) is possible from the functioning of the economy itself. Contrarily, the other state is where the investor's existence is independent of the macroeconomic functioning and the investor needs to bear risk in order to transit (or maintain profits). The third state is the state of decay wherein the market is non-profitable for the representative investor.

$$\text{State} : Y = \begin{cases} \text{Firm returns, dependent on the functioning of economy} \\ \text{Risky returns, independent of macroeconomic functioning} \\ \text{The Decay, this quarter no luck} \end{cases}$$

We assume the expected state of the transitory investor at any given time to be distributed between three states. Also, the probability of being in any state is assumed to be following a multinomial logistic distribution. MLE of $(\boldsymbol{\psi}, \boldsymbol{\varphi}, \boldsymbol{\phi})$ and $(\overline{\boldsymbol{\psi}}, \overline{\boldsymbol{\varphi}}, \overline{\boldsymbol{\phi}})$ are used in order to analyze this system of interactions evolving with a constant cyclicity due to elections and its effects henceforth. The idea behind this model is to be informed of the contemporaneous state of the market wherein the behavior of investor is responsible for their fate and hence we argue that the same is also deterministic wherein their responses in the dimensions as explained above puts them under a probability distribution of belonging to any of the state which is based on their relatedness with polity and is determined as:[10,11]

$$\Pr(y = \text{Risky returns}|\text{Pol.Exog}) = \frac{e^{X\,\psi}}{\left(e^{X\,\psi} + e^{X\,\varphi} + e^{X\,\phi}\right)}$$

$$\Pr(y = \text{Risky returns}|\text{Pol.Endo}) = \frac{e^{\overline{X}\,\overline{\psi}}}{\left(e^{\overline{X}\,\overline{\psi}} + e^{\overline{X}\,\overline{\varphi}} + e^{\overline{X}\,\overline{\phi}}\right)}$$

$$\Pr(y = \text{Firm returns}|\text{Pol.Exog}) = \frac{e^{X\,\varphi}}{\left(e^{X\,\psi} + e^{X\,\varphi} + e^{X\,\phi}\right)}$$

$$\Pr(y = \text{Firm returns}|\text{Pol.Endo}) = \frac{e^{\overline{X}\,\overline{\varphi}}}{\left(e^{\overline{X}\,\overline{\psi}} + e^{\overline{X}\,\overline{\varphi}} + e^{\overline{X}\,\overline{\phi}}\right)}$$

$$\Pr(y = \text{The Decay}|\text{Pol.Exog}) = \frac{e^{X\,\phi}}{\left(e^{X\,\psi} + e^{X\,\varphi} + e^{X\,\phi}\right)}$$

$$\Pr(y = \text{The Decay}|\text{Pol.Endo}) = \frac{e^{\overline{X}\,\overline{\phi}}}{\left(e^{\overline{X}\,\overline{\psi}} + e^{\overline{X}\,\overline{\varphi}} + e^{\overline{X}\,\overline{\phi}}\right)}$$

$$\textit{where } \boldsymbol{X} = \begin{pmatrix} \textbf{Response to phase} \\ \textbf{Response to economy} \\ \textbf{Response to globalization} \end{pmatrix} \text{ and}$$

$$\overline{\boldsymbol{X}} = \begin{pmatrix} \overline{\textbf{Response to phase}} \\ \textbf{Response to economy} \\ \textbf{Response to globalization} \end{pmatrix}.$$

While, **Response to phase** $= \begin{pmatrix} \text{Perishing} \\ \text{Sustainable} \end{pmatrix}$ and

Response to globalization $= \begin{pmatrix} \text{Growth} \\ \text{Development} \end{pmatrix}$ affects both the systems equally.

[10] ψ, φ, *and* ϕ are coefficients in the exogeneous system.

[11] $\overline{\psi}, \overline{\varphi}$, *and* $\overline{\phi}$ are coefficients in the endogenous system.

$$\textbf{Response to economy} = \begin{pmatrix} \text{Signal}(\widehat{p_1}) \\ \text{Signal } (\widehat{p_3}) \\ \text{Information } (\widehat{I_p}) \\ \text{Democratic} \\ \text{Term2} \\ \text{Civil.Exp}(\Delta CE_t) \\ \text{Govt.Intervention} \\ \text{Elec.Lifecycle} \\ 1 \text{ (apolitical)} \end{pmatrix},$$

while

$$\overline{\textbf{Response to economy}} = \begin{pmatrix} \text{Signal } (\widehat{p_1}) \\ \text{Signal } (\widehat{p_3}) \\ \text{Information } (\widehat{I_p}) \\ \text{Civil.Exp}(\Delta CE_t) \\ \text{Govt.Intervention} \\ \text{Elec.Lifecycle} \\ 1\ \overline{\text{(political)}} \end{pmatrix}.$$

$\boldsymbol{\psi}, \boldsymbol{\varphi}, \textit{and}\ \boldsymbol{\phi}$ are coefficients of the expected state of the investor—risky returns, firm returns, and decay, respectively. $\widehat{p_1}, \widehat{p_3}, and\ \widehat{I_p}$ are predicted probabilities from the monetary model described in Sect. 5.2.2.1. Also, growth here is the first difference of log of world GDP net of the United States and development here is referred as convergence which is measured as first difference of the ratio of GDP of emerging to developed economies.[12,13,14]

Further,

$$\text{Democratic} = \begin{cases} 1, \text{if the ruling party is Democratic} \\ 0, \text{if the ruling party is Republican} \end{cases},$$

$$\text{Term 2} = \begin{cases} 1, \text{if } 2^{\text{nd}} \text{ presidential term of the ruling party} \\ 0, \text{if } 1^{\text{st}} \text{ presidential term of the ruling party} \end{cases},$$

[12]This refers to *path dependency*. These are dummy variables indicating the type of shift in the existed state of the previous period. If in the previous period, risk has increased, i.e., the difference in quarterly variance of the daily series—we call it risky quarter. Similarly, if the difference in quarterly income (the difference in price over a month) is negative, we call these quarters—*Perishing phase*. Non-risky and non-perishing quarters are in *Sustainable phase*.

[13]Sources *Democratic& Term* 2—The Miller Center, *Govt. Intervention*—U.S. Department of Labor.

[14]Refer to Table 5.10 in Appendix 7 for stationary test results.

$$\text{Govt.Intervention} = \begin{cases} 1, \text{if government increases the min wage} \\ 0, \text{if government keeps status quo} \end{cases},$$

$$\text{and Elec.Life cycle} = \begin{cases} 0, \text{if Election year} \\ 1, \text{if first year after election} \\ 2, \text{if second year after election} \\ 3, \text{if one year left for election} \end{cases}$$

The model, however, is unidentified in the sense that there is more than one solution to $\psi, \varphi, and\ \phi$ that leads to the same probabilities for Pr(y = Firm returns), Pr (y = Risky returns), and Pr(y = The Decay). To identify the model, we set $\phi = 0$, the remaining coefficients $\psi\ and\ \varphi$ will measure the change relative to y = The Decay. The relative Pr(y = Risky returns) to the base outcome is $\frac{\Pr(y=\text{Risky returns})}{\Pr(y=\text{The Decay})} = e^{X\psi}$. $\psi\ and\ \overline{\psi}$ are listed in Table 5.4, while $\varphi\ and\ \overline{\varphi}$ are listed in Table 5.9 of Appendix 6.

Table 5.4 The investor's position using multinomial logistic approach[5]

	Endogenous Model			Exogenous Model		
	Coefficient	[95% Conf. Interval]		Coefficient	[95% Conf. Interval]	
Risky returns	$\overline{\psi}$	Lower	Upper	ψ	Lower	Upper
Perishing	1.777****	0.56	2.99	1.632****	0.40	2.87
Sustainable	−0.630	−2.04	0.78	−0.869	−2.32	0.58
Signal ($\widehat{p_3}$)	2.562***	0.08	5.05	3.983***	0.86	7.10
Signal ($\widehat{p_1}$)	5.637****	1.56	9.71	7.527****	1.86	13.19
Information ($\widehat{I_p}$)	−2.151**	−4.62	0.32	−2.480**	−5.20	0.24
Democratic	–	–	–	1.223*	−0.29	2.74
Term2	–	–	–	−0.207	−1.43	1.01
Δ civil Exp (ΔCE_t)	0.013**	0.00	0.03	0.011*	0.00	0.03
Govt. intervention	−0.209	−1.45	1.03	−0.466	−1.77	0.83
World GDP	8.264**	−1.26	17.79	13.866***	1.83	25.91
Δ convergence	0.894	−0.77	2.56	1.316	−0.62	3.25
Elec. Life cycle						
First	2.354****	0.77	3.94	2.715****	1.04	4.39
Second	1.145*	−0.25	2.54	1.135*	−0.28	2.55
Third	1.437***	0.03	2.85	1.365**	−0.08	2.81
Constant	−3.411****	−5.69	−1.13	−4.497****	−7.25	−1.75
No. of obs	140			140		
Pseudo R2	0.21			0.23		
LR $\text{chi}^2(24)\vert(28)$	61.23			65.88		
Log likelihood	−112.55			−110.23		

Source: Author's calculation (**** for 1% level of significance, *** for 5% level of significance, ** for 10% level of significance, * for 15% level of significance)

5.3.1 Interpretation of Coefficients

Considering $\boldsymbol{\phi} \& \overline{\boldsymbol{\phi}} = \mathbf{0}$ would mean that $\psi \& \overline{\psi}$ can be interpreted as marginal opulence of the concerned factor in politically exogenous and endogenous system, respectively. While $\varphi \& \overline{\varphi}$ would represent marginal utility of the factor for an informed and rational investor with its respective relation to politics.

The responses to the life cycle of politics is color (politics) invariant. Further, a politically cohesive investor makes the financial market an instrument of politics, i.e., provisioning. Such politically endorsed portfolios are very structural. In autarky, such a system is more likely to end up as higher return portfolio. $\psi_o(y = \text{Risky means}|\text{Pol.Exog}) < \overline{\psi}_0(y = \text{Risky means}|\text{Pol.Endo}\ ) > 0$, where $\overline{\boldsymbol{\psi}}_{\mathbf{0}}$ is the constant term of the politically endorsed model. But the deviance is very costly as revising in such a system leads to uncertainty spirals. Though, it ensures yield over the firm means, extent of bias is huge, wherein politically endorsed investors have natural avenues for risk diversification.

Among the coefficients of Table 5.4, the constant term refers to the election year of the first term for Republicans where the investors can ensure very high return by taking equivalently higher risk. But it is the election year requiring huge investments for the political entrepreneurs and not so much for economic agents who are destined to face uncertainty spiral. The politically endorsed behavior often results in an increased animal spirit type of entrepreneurship. Their collective gain rivalry often overpowers the loss of cooperation; thus, dynamic stability allows a knife edge panache. These types of systems are very closed. But even business cycle has to be responsive to the election cycle.[15] This is not a confounding result as it is the election which decides most of the game. This episteme around this citizenship's duty is invariant of the type of investor. As can be seen confirmed in Table 5.4. Juxtaposing, this politically endorsed investor to a rational investor will shed more light in our endeavor to understand the investment behavior under political information. In this case, this rational investor is more certain to gain from both the monetary contraction and expansion. Of course, there is an uncertainty of losing from monetary mis-balances, but a responsible institution can fix this volatility provided adequate trust is present. $\boldsymbol{\psi}_{\boldsymbol{p}_1} > \bar{\boldsymbol{\psi}}_{\boldsymbol{p}_1} > 0, \boldsymbol{\psi}_{\boldsymbol{p}_3} > \bar{\boldsymbol{\psi}}_{\boldsymbol{p}_3} > 0, \textit{and}\ \boldsymbol{\psi}_{\boldsymbol{Ip}} < \bar{\boldsymbol{\psi}}_{\boldsymbol{Ip}} < 0$ where $\overline{\boldsymbol{\psi}}_{\boldsymbol{p}_1}$ *and* $\overline{\boldsymbol{\psi}}_{\boldsymbol{p}_3}$ are the coefficients of the signal of monetary policy and $\overline{\boldsymbol{\psi}}_{\boldsymbol{Ip}}$ is the coefficient of information regarding change of macroeconomic order. We found that investors are more likely to transit during Democratic governments ($\overline{\boldsymbol{\psi}}_{\mathbf{Democratic}} > 0$) although term of the presidency has no significant impact. Civil expenditure is also a cost that these rationalist investors have to bear, still, given a Democratic functioning and with restoration of freedom of civilians and necessary interventions, the investor is highly likely to be better off. Also, here the system is assumed to be responsive to functioning of the global world—contemporaneously an average American investor has gained more from the world's growth but not from its development. Particularly,

[15]Refer Figs. 5.7 and 5.8.

$\psi_{W.GDP} > \overline{\psi}_{W.GDP} > 0$. Although, this rational investor's behavior had no effect whatsoever from the deeds of the outside world other than his opulence. The coefficient of convergence is not statistically significant for any of the model while expecting risky return states— $\psi_{con}, \overline{\psi}_{con}, and$ even φ_{con} are insignificant. Also, $\psi_S > \overline{\psi}_S > 0$, *where* $\overline{\psi}_S$ is the coefficient of structure in politically endorsed model. This result refers to the return of the investors as market faces high rate of decay, again such risky form of returns is more favorable devoid of politics, i.e., in the politically exogenous type model reiterating the rules of market:

Rule 1: If the assets are giving returns, the investor will continue existing in the transition.
Rule 2: There is only one rule. Either obey or perish.

Corollary *If assets are not giving any returns, then these returns are getting consumed by those who are transiting in this continuously evolving financial markets.*

Perversely, allowing politics in the system, devoid of institution, devalues the market ethics—without institutions, the financial markets decay, given that the investors cannot be independent of politics. Further, the concept—development seems of no use for the rational investor independent of politics as the famous claim—"convergence is development" seems to fade away in giving any virtue to the investor (animal) as (ψ_{con} *and* $\overline{\psi}_{con}$) are insignificant. Evaluation suggests that development has no impact on the fate of investor bearing risk, though such generalizations need to test convergence as a phenomenon of economic development while interacting with electoral politics.

In lieu of assurance of feeding oneself with opulence, investors desire to free themselves from the development of outside world but this is not in their hands. In fact, it depends on the ability of functioning independently from politics although the purpose of the chapter is not to test whether convergence brings development. That is theoretically impossible for an organized system involving human, their doing and being. This chapter sheds light on the question of how and not whether, convergence can possibly impact the investor. The answer is a significant $\overline{\varphi}_{\text{con}} > 0$. Also, all coefficients of φ_1 ***and*** $\overline{\varphi}$ are insignificant except φ_1 *and* $\overline{\varphi}_{\text{con}}$. This itself is a bias in the set of information, i.e., p-value [ψ] is in acceptable limits but not p-value [φ]. Literature suggests that if markets were efficient, predicting returns is non-deterministic (Fama 1970). But our findings suggest that while prices may or may not reflect information, the behavior of the investor is very predictable. Under this natural experiment wherein the players follow the rules strictly, hence, are behaviorally constrained. The huge bias in the scale of predictability is reserved in the interaction of risk as action and risk as state present in the surrounding environment created within the game. This predictability allows broader institutes in the society to use market as an instrument. This deterministic behavior due to super rational attire is a distinct feature of the market and investors. This explains pretty much the story of an investor from a state of transition (accumulating returns but at the cost of others). But even then the only possible deterministic factor responsible for maintaining the transitory state without risking but through functioning, featured as $\boldsymbol{\varphi}$ ***and*** $\overline{\boldsymbol{\varphi}}$ parameters in our model, is like a time bracket borrowed from election and its demand of politics—referring to our model, only $\overline{\boldsymbol{\varphi}_1} > \boldsymbol{\varphi}_1 > 0$ and significant. Thus, it can be inferred that the lens required to cure myopia of investors seem to be working only by the virtue of limited allocation of time and resource between civilians and its ruler trading with each other over provisioning of factors into the production system. All other variables are insignificant except for convergence, which is again but conditioned on politics, i.e., $\overline{\boldsymbol{\varphi}}_{\mathbf{con}} > 0$ and significant. Although convergence has no effect on opulence, i.e., $\overline{\boldsymbol{\psi}}_{\mathbf{con}}$ is insignificant, as investor's fetish for opulence itself makes the time a riskier affair. While investors were busy feeding on all that once perished, convergence as a process is still significant and effects the economic cores particularly that of the developed countries, but again requires sufficient political endorsement before it seems to be beneficial to investors. Nevertheless, the politically endorsed investor is at least spared of assurance, while, being rational and keeping the politics exogeneity allows gain in the first year after election when compared to the politically endorsed one, but post second year, the economy revised its political spending towards the next election making it unprofitable for politically exogenous investor when compared to its politically endorsed counterpart. In reality, both these types and system of investors are co-existing and the complexity weigh more than the scope of this chapter. But we do attempt to decompose this decaying of investors perplexed in both the behavior forms in a spectrum of time, i.e., time in reference to the elections (citizen duty). Figs. 5.7 and 5.8 shows that the decaying rate converges during the election year post which building the institution along with required belief-system reduces the rate of decay. But, the force of a citizen duty cushions mostly those endorsed by the politics, while those who are independent perish with nearing of the election dates. The rate of decay increases further for an institutional apolitical investor resulting in the increase in their trust-deficit.

5.4 Conclusion

It seems incorrect that market is unbiased and fair. But it is easy to instrument market since the market makes the behavior predictable (the behavior of players playing the game) though market might not be modellable—reactions of investors are. These reactions are often used by "big-shots" to control the masses in their game. Information for the market is in three dimensions, but underneath all these, there runs an undercurrent of election cycle. Investors in sync with the cycle or playing the game of this cycle transit easily consuming the losses made by others. Is transiting possible in this system just by being in sync with the election cycle and playing the game of election? Does this imply that financial markets are just a hog wash and a mask for politically engrained investors to make money and perhaps indulge in exuberance? The answer is beyond the scope of the chapter though here, we try to put light on a

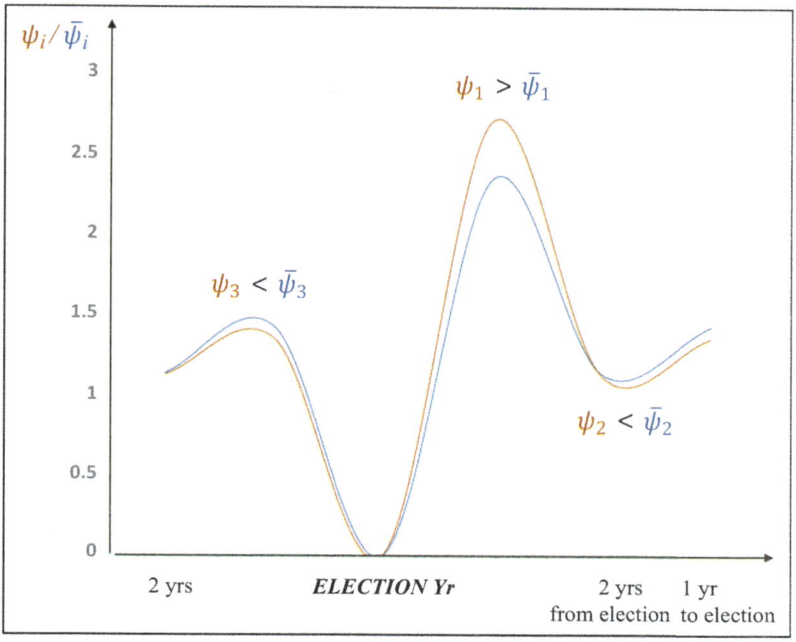

ψ_i *and* $\bar{\psi}_i$ are opulence rate in a political cycle for politically exogeneous and endogeneous investors respectively. *Source* Author's calculation.

Fig. 5.7 Political cycle (short memory). ψ_i*and* $\overline{\psi}_i$ are opulence rate in a political cycle for politically exogenous and endogenous investors, respectively. *Source* Author's calculation

way to look at these problems, i.e., through the kaleidoscope of attention and information.

Attention is a scarce resource. The entrepreneurs seek investor's attention for financing. They respond through the financial market. Similarly, there are political entrepreneurs. Also, the cyclicity of political investments are symmetrically fixed designed by democracy through the modes of citizen's duty. There is a fixed time for election, i.e., after every 4 years for the United States. The initial election year's demand for the political investment increases regardless of their performance or "effective" demand. Over the years, the financial market has evolved responding to the complexity and through the lens of observing the decaying rate in a spectrum of politics. Though *Reaganisation*[16] in American politics was responsible for the advent of the modern financial markets but soon, they went through an impulse of shock (Black Monday, 19th October, 1987). These players in those days were also ensnared with information sets related to the positions of Republican politics. The civilians exogenous to this game were also affected and did not allow Bush Sr. his

[16]We refer this term to describe—Amalgamation of terms like *"Reagan Revolution" and "Reaganomics"* among popular media parlance.

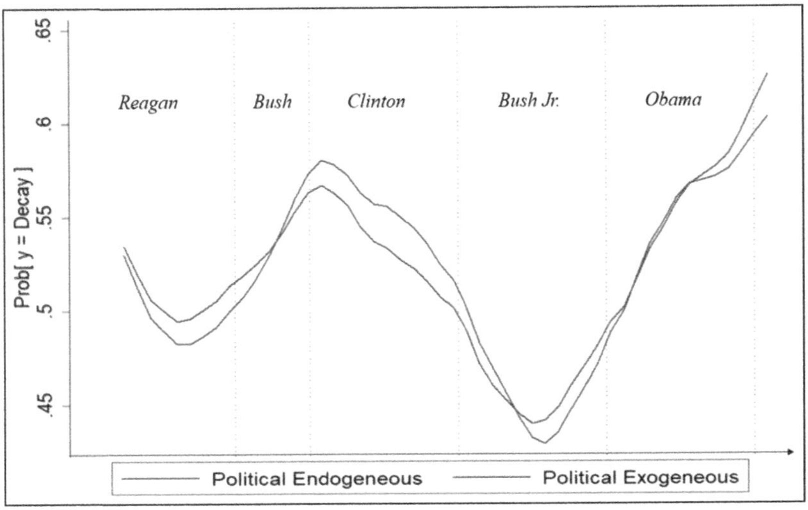

Source Author's calculation.

Fig. 5.8 Political business cycle (long memory)

second term while Clinton, being a Democrat brought down military spending thereby increasing civil expenditures. Analysis of our model suggests that myopic players in the market do not like to rhyme with development of the masses. In some sense, with enough significant statistical information, this chapter argues that the exuberance created around the dot-com generation is reflected by the parameters ψ and as described in Fig. 5.7 and 5.8, particularly from the short memory of political cycle that the civilians activities around the election times created a state of conflict. The bubble which was present as latent (evolving in long memory) surfaced out during this period when $\overline{\psi}_2, \overline{\psi}_3 > \psi_2, \psi_3$. Similarly, the second period of Bush or 2008 crisis can be described as a phenomenon wherein the higher politically endogenous returns on risks during the election pressures resulted in surfacing of system-breakdown from what was then the latent exuberance among the players.

The advent of financial markets during Reagan era was a system where decay rate $(\phi_t^{Reagan} > \bar{\phi}_t^{Reagan})$ was more for politically exogenous systems and continued to have the same until the last phase of Bush senior. Clinton era is characterized by increased civil expenditure which reverses the systems' relations $(\phi_t^{Clinton} < \bar{\phi}_t^{Clinton})$. This is the time when decay rate is lesser for investors with politics as exogeneity in their system—financial market activities actually spurred since this arrangement—as can be confirmed from Fig 5.9 in Appendix 3 but ended with a shock as the economy and the market in particular responded to the impulse from dot-com bubble crash—comes the Bush Junior era wherein instruments of tax cuts were made popularized to woo the animals from their human spirits. Markets responded partially until the terrorist attack on the World Trade Center which changed the arrangements reshifting the gears to high tax period but devoid of civil expenditures. Our model illustrates in its long memory phase that this Bush period anomaly over the directional cause of the instrumentation tax makes the game shift in the favor of politically ensnared class of investors (ex post rising spending on war). This is a structural change and figure confirms the same. When the economy is or is not always booming, the investor should be bullish only when the investments are made more through risk free or firm means. The trend $\phi_t^{Bush\ Jr.} < \bar{\phi}_t^{Bush\ Jr.}$ before the "*Iraq War, 2003*" and $\phi_t^{Bush\ Jr.} > \bar{\phi}_t^{Bush\ Jr.}$ after its response, i.e., *tax cut reversal*. This pattern is very similar (the change is vice versa in Bush Snr. and Bush Jnr.) to the single term era of Bush Snr. where $\phi_t^{Bush\ Sr.} > \bar{\phi}_t^{Bush\ Sr.}$ before "*The Persian-Gulf-War tensions, 1990*" post which the state of relations $\phi_t^{Bush\ Sr.} < \bar{\phi}_t^{Bush\ Sr.}$. The trend continues and then both the system converges, but since Obama's second term politically endogenous systems were favored, $\phi_t^{Obama.} \geq \bar{\phi}_t^{Obama}$. Also, Table 5.4 suggest that the excess return ($\overline{\psi}_{\mathbf{Democratic}} > 0$) in the stock market is higher under Democratic than Republican presidencies.[17]. The answer to this *Presidential puzzle* has contextual as well as structural components. Contextually, it is still ambiguous but one possible structural candidate appearing from our analysis is the schizophrenic instrumentation of tax. On one end, the Republicans use tax cuts as stimulants whereas their entanglement with war is often at the cost of civil expenditure which according to our model reduces yield over value at stake, $\overline{\psi}_{\mathbf{\Delta CE}} > \psi_{\mathbf{\Delta CE}} > 0$. Further involvement in war requires persistent funding which is inconsistent with the Republican's tax cut policy and brings a dilemma i.e *tax cut reversal*.

Evidences are sufficient to nullify the *Efficient Market theory*. The so-called efficiency is subjective to the information set accessible to any agent. Under information theory, an agent maximizes utility subject to an entropy constraint.[18] Market always adjusts with a lag and such lag varies when the information seeker looks at it in modules. Under this framework, the market efficiency is not binary but is a continuum which is also contextual. What is structural is the fate of the investor. And, in the presence of politics, the financial markets decay irrespective of the investor's behavioral system. It appears that development does not matter to rational investor but our evidences suggest that instead it is development in terms of political commitment of the government that keeps them independent from the market. If market is in the utility function of the planner, then politics will be instrumented to grab that cash and it will be them who will be making the stash. If investors want returns, they would need the nurturing from economic functioning and hence, can seldom transit.

$\overline{\varphi}_{\mathbf{con}}, > 0, \overline{\psi}_{\mathbf{\Delta CE}} > \psi_{\mathbf{\Delta CE}} > 0$, and $\overline{\psi}_{\mathbf{Democratic}} > 0$ —Civil expenditure favors opulence but gains are more for the politically endorsed system. Similarly,

---

[17] 9% for the value-weighted and 16% for the equal-weighted portfolio. The difference that comes from higher real stock returns and lower real interest rates is statistically significant and is robust in subsamples as stated by Pedro Santa-Clara and Rossen Valkanov, in their famous: "The Presidential Puzzle: Political Cycles and the Stock Market."

[18] A new class of literature has emerged since Christopher A. Sims coined the term "Rational Inattention" in his seminal work "Implications of rational inattention," published in Journal *of monetary Economics* 50, no. 3 (2003): 665–690.

convergence favors functioning but only to politics. In order to reach a favorable state, one needs to first identify broader aspects of developmental processes (Tables 5.5, 5.6, 5.7, 5.8, 5.9, and 5.10).

Appendix 1

Table 5.5 shows that the stock prices (adjusted close price) of ADX, NYSE, Merval & SENSEX exhibit weak form of market efficiency. As null hypothesis is not rejected, the market is weakly efficient in most of the cases. In 6 out 10 stock exchange markets, Z test value is between Z critical value, i.e., −1.96 & 1.96 (5% sig.). Also, at universal level, the evidences do not reject the null hypothesis and therefore favor the random walk theory.

On the basis of empirical results given by runs tests, we conclude that New York Stock Exchange (NYSE), Sensex, Buenos Aires Stock Exchange and Abu Dhabi Securities Exchange (A.D.X.) did not accept the null hypothesis and hence were not efficient. One the other hand, NASDAQ, Moscow Stock Exchange (MSE) Shanghai Stock Exchange (SSE), Hong Kong Stock Exchange (SEHK), Frankfurt Stock Exchange (DAX), National Stock Exchange (NSE) and Toronto Stock Exchange (TSX) accepted the null hypothesis and hence, are weakly form of efficient market.

Table 5.5 Runs test results of stock markets. Source*:* Author's calculation

Company	Positive (n_1)	Negative (n_2)	Mean (μ)	std dev (σ)	Upper limit	Lower limit	Runs (r)	Z-value	$Z_{critical}$	$Z_{critical}$	Hypothesis testing at level of sig. 5%
ADX	1283	1208	1245.37	24.93	1294.23	1196.51	1137	-4.35	1.96	-1.96	H_0 rejected
NYSE	1339	1172	1250.95	24.94	1299.83	1202.07	1304	2.13	1.96	-1.96	H_0 rejected
HSI	1260	1198	1229.22	24.77	1277.76	1180.67	1226	-0.13	1.96	-1.96	H_0 not rejected
NSEI	1259	1156	1206.30	24.52	1254.37	1158.24	1161	-1.85	1.96	-1.96	H_0 not rejected
MSE	1236	1219	1228.44	24.77	1276.99	1179.90	1245	0.67	1.96	-1.96	H_0 not rejected
Merval	1316	1115	1208.19	24.48	1256.17	1160.21	1082	-5.16	1.96	-1.96	H_0 rejected
TSX	1323	1125	1216.99	24.57	1265.15	1168.83	1222	0.20	1.96	-1.96	H_0 not rejected
Shanghai	1324	1076	1188.19	24.23	1235.67	1140.70	1141	-1.95	1.96	-1.96	H_0 not rejected
Sensex	1290	1183	1235.19	24.81	1283.82	1186.55	1171	-2.59	1.96	-1.96	H_0 rejected
NASDAQ	1384	1122	1240.30	24.75	1288.82	1191.79	1259.00	0.76	1.96	-1.96	H_0 not rejected

Appendix 2

Table 5.6 List of important events since Clinton's second term

Bill Clinton's second term	
Date	Event
9/3/1996	President Clinton orders missile strikes on Iraq.
8/7/1998	U.S embassies bombed in Kenya, Tanzania.
12/16/1998	President Clinton orders 3-day retaliatory attacks on Iraq.
3/8/2000	Bill introduced in Congress asking for permanent trade relations with China.
11/7/2000	A close election with no winner between vice-president Gore and Governor Bush.
George W. Bush's first term	
Date	Event
3/29/2001	Kyoto protocol rejected by the Bush administration.
6/7/2001	President Bush signs $1.35 trillion dollar tax cut into law.
9/11/2001	September 11 terrorist attack on the World Trade Centre, the Pentagon and Pennsylvania countryside.
10/7/2001	President Bush announces Operation "Enduring Freedom".
10/17/2001	The Capital shuts down amidst Anthrax scare.
9/4/2002	President seek support for action against Iraq.
10/10/2002	Congress authorizes the Bush administration to use force against Iraq.
3/19/2003	President Bush addresses the American people that U.S is at war with Iraq.
3/25/2003	The Senate approves the reduction of President Bush's tax cut plan to $350 billion.
5/22/2003	The UN Security Council votes to lift sanctions on Iraq.
5/28/2003	President Bush signs third largest tax cut in history.
11/03/2004	President Bush re-elected for second term.
George W. Bush's second term	
Date	Event
10/9/2007	The Dow Jones industrial average at its all-time high.
1/18/2008	President Bush proposes $145 billion stimulus package in response to housing crises & oil price.
2/7/2008	The Senate passes $170-billion stimulus package.
9/7/2008	U.S. Treasury takes over of Fannie Mae, Freddie Mac.
10/3/2008	President Bush signs largest bailout in history.
11/4/2008	Barack Obama elected as the next president of the United States.
12/16/2008	Federal Reserve cuts the interest rates to an all- time low (set at 0%).
12/19/2008	President Bush issues a $17.4 billion auto bailout to General Motors and Chrysler.
Barack Obama's first term	
Date	Event
2/4/2009	President Obama forces companies to a cap on top executive pay at $500,000.
2/17/2009	American Recovery and Reinvestment Act of 2009 signed into law by President Obama.

(continued)

Table 5.6 (continued)

Barack Obama's first term	
Date	Event
1/14/2010	President Obama pledges $100million to assist Haiti to recover from the earthquake.
7/21/2010	The Dodd-Frank Wall Street Reform and Consumer Protection Act signed by President Obama.
11/29/2010	The President freezes two-year pay on federal employees to get the deficit under control.
12/17/2010	The Tax Relief, Unemployment Insurance Reauthorization and Job Creation Act of 2010 becomes law.
8/2/2011	The Budget Control Act becomes law.
9/8/2011	President Obama present American Jobs Act to the joint session of Congress.
11/6/2012	President Obama re-elected.
Barack Obama's second term	
Date	Event
01/02/2013	President Obama signs the American Taxpayer Relief Act.
10/01/2013	Government shutdown
02/07/2014	The Federal Agriculture Reform and Risk Management Act of 2014 is signed into law
02/12/2014	An executive order to increase the minimum wage is signed by President Obama
11/10/2016	Presidential election: Trump wins

Source: The Miller Center
The Miller Center is a nonpartisan affiliate of the University of Virginia that specializes in presidential scholarship, public policy, and political history.

Appendix 3

Figure 5.9 displays the market returns, i.e., weekly difference in price of Wilshire 5000 Price Index, by presidential term served starting from President Reagan (1981–1988) till Obama (2009–2016).

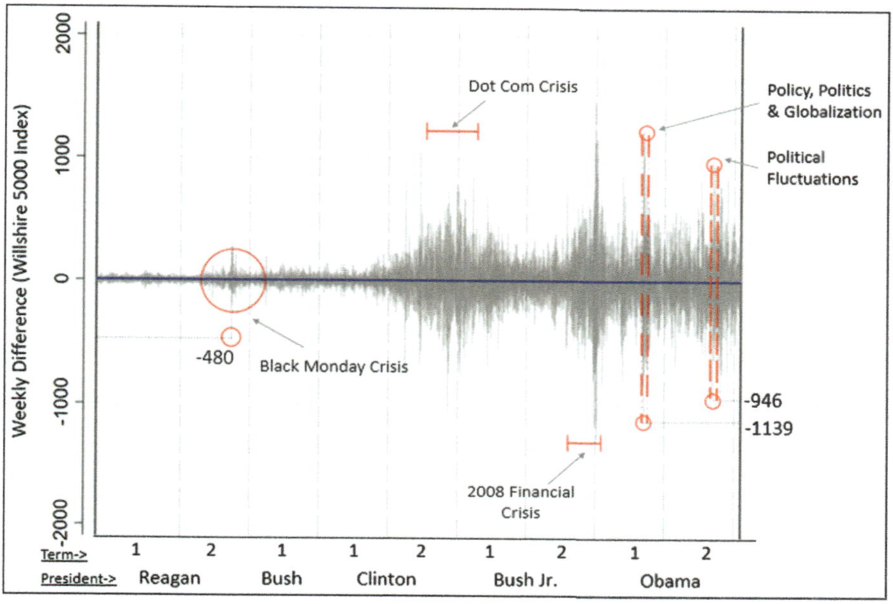

Fig. 5.9 Market Returns by presidential term, 1981 to 2016

Appendix 4

Political Endogenous System

$$\text{Risk}_t = \alpha_0 + \alpha_1.\text{Return}_{t-1} + \alpha_2.\text{Risk}_{t-1} + \epsilon_t \tag{5.9}$$

$$\text{Return}_t = \alpha'_0 + \alpha'_1.\text{Return}_{t-1} + \alpha'_2.\text{Risk}_{t-1} + \epsilon'_t \tag{5.10}$$

Political Exogenous System

$$\text{Risk}_t = \alpha''_0 + \alpha''_1.\text{Return}_{t-1} + \alpha''_2.\text{Risk}_{t-1} + \alpha''_3.\text{term2}_t + \alpha''_4.\text{Democratic}_t + e_t \tag{5.11}$$

$$\text{Return}_t = \alpha''_5 + \alpha''_6.\text{Return}_{t-1} + \alpha''_7.\text{Risk}_{t-1} + \alpha''_8.\text{term2}_t + \alpha''_9.\text{Democratic}_t + e'_t \tag{5.12}$$

Table 5.7 The risk and return framework under Politics Endogenous and Exogenous model

	Politics endogenous model			Politics exogenous model		
		[95% Conf. Interval]			[95% Conf. Interval]	
	Coefficient	Lower	Upper	Coefficient	Lower	Upper
Returns (Qtr.)						
Returns (Qtr.)						
Δ(lag 1)	−0.407****	−0.542	−0.273	−0.411****	−0.546	−0.275
Risk(Qtr.)						
Δ(lag 1)	0.013****	0.008	0.018	0.013****	0.008	0.018
Democratic	–	–	–	−1.198	−166.910	164.515
term2	–	–	–	3.882	−162.143	169.907
Constant	7.384	−73.120	87.888	1.870	−126.354	130.095
Risk (Qtr.)						
Returns (Qtr.)						
Δ(lag 1)	−5.044***	−9.132	−0.956	−5.140***	−9.175	−1.104
Risk(Qtr.)						
Δ(lag 1)	−0.270****	−0.424	−0.115	−0.288****	−0.441	−0.135
Democratic	–	–	–	−3557.463	−8505.304	1390.378
term2	–	–	–	6113.457***	1156.273	11070.640
Constant	133.833	−2319.537	2587.203	−974.224	−4802.762	2854.314
No. of obs	147.0			144.0		
AIC	37.4			37.5		
HQIC	37.5			37.5		
SBIC	37.5			37.7		
Log likelihood	−2744.4			−2687.2		

Source: Author's calculation (**** for 1%, *** for 5%, ** for 10%, * for 15% level of significance.)

Granger causality Wald tests		Endogenous			Exogenous		
Equation	Excluded	chi2	Df	*p*-value	chi2	Df	*p*-value
Returns (Qtr.)	Risk (Qtr.)	26.54	1	0.000	26.16	1	0.000
Returns (Qtr.)	All	26.54	1	0.000	26.16	1	0.000
Risk (Qtr.)	Returns (Qtr.)	5.8482	1	0.016	6.2319	1	0.013
Risk (Qtr.)	All	5.8482	1	0.016	6.2319	1	0.013

Source: Author's calculation (**** for 1%, *** for 5%, ** for 10%, * for 15% level of significance)
Refer to Table 5.10 in Appendix 7 for the stationary test results of the variables used in this table.

Appendix 5

Politics Endogenous Model

$$\Delta ME_t = \beta_0 + \sum\nolimits_{i=1}^{3} \beta_i.\Delta ME_{t-1} + \sum\nolimits_{i=1}^{3} \delta_i.\Delta CE_{t-1} + \vartheta_t \quad (5.13)$$

$$\Delta CE_t = \beta'_0 + \sum\nolimits_{i=1}^{3} \beta'_i.\Delta ME_{t-1} + \sum\nolimits_{i=1}^{3} \delta'_i.\Delta CE_{t-1} + \vartheta'_t \quad (5.14)$$

Politics Exogenous Model

$$\Delta ME_t = \beta''_0 + \sum\nolimits_{i=1}^{3} \beta''_i.\Delta ME_{t-1} + \sum\nolimits_{i=1}^{3} \delta''_i.\Delta CE_{t-1} + \tau_1.\text{term2}_t + \eta_1.\text{Democratic}_t + \upsilon_t \quad (5.15)$$

$$\Delta CE_t = \beta'''_0 + \sum\nolimits_{i=1}^{3} \beta'''_i.\Delta ME_{t-1} + \sum\nolimits_{i=1}^{3} \delta'''_i.\Delta CE_{t-1} + \tau_2.\text{term2}_t + \eta_2.\text{Democratic}_t + \upsilon'_t \quad (5.16)$$

Table 5.8 The civil and the military expenditure framework under Political Endogenous and Exogenous model

	Politics endogenous model			Politics exogenous model		
		(95% Conf. interval)			(95% Conf. interval)	
	Coefficient	Lower	Upper	Coefficient	Lower	Upper
Military exp						
Military exp						
Δ(lag 1)	−0.032	−0.187	0.124	−0.123*	−0.281	0.035
Δ(lag 2)	0.238****	0.088	0.388	0.155***	0.003	0.307
Δ(lag 3)	0.268****	0.113	0.424	0.205****	0.051	0.359
Civil exp						
Δ(lag 1)	0.013	−0.022	0.048	0.012	−0.021	0.046
Δ(lag 2)	−0.031**	−0.064	0.002	−0.033***	−0.065	−0.001
Δ(lag 3)	−0.037***	−0.072	−0.002	−0.043***	−0.077	−0.009
Democratic	–	–	–	−5.746****	−9.023	−2.469
term2	–	–	–	2.112*	−0.726	4.949
Constant	2.359***	0.560	4.158	4.960****	2.141	7.778
Civil exp						
Military exp						
Δ(lag 1)	−0.405	−1.149	0.339	−0.277	−1.055	0.500
Δ(lag 2)	−0.412	−1.130	0.307	−0.249	−0.999	0.500
Δ(lag 3)	−0.448	−1.191	0.295	−0.396	−1.155	0.363

(continued)

Table 5.8 (continued)

	Politics endogenous model			Politics exogenous model		
		(95% Conf. interval)			(95% Conf. interval)	
	Coefficient	Lower	Upper	Coefficient	Lower	Upper
Civil exp						
Δ(lag 1)	0.044	−0.121	0.210	0.038	−0.127	0.203
Δ(lag 2)	0.308****	0.150	0.466	0.312****	0.154	0.470
Δ(lag 3)	0.072	−0.095	0.238	0.073	−0.094	0.240
Democratic	–	–	–	8.824	−7.326	24.974
term2	–	–	–	0.042	−13.941	14.026
Constant	8.861***	0.268	17.454	4.109	−9.781	18.000
No. of obs	145.0			144.0		
AIC	17.6			17.5		
HQIC	17.7			17.7		
SBIC	17.9			17.9		
Log likelihood	−1259.6			−1243.7		

Source: Author's calculation (**** for 1% level of significance, *** for 5% level of significance, ** for 10% level of significance, * for 15% level of significance)
Refer to Table 5.10 in Appendix 7 for the stationary test results of the variables used in this table

Appendix 6

Table 5.9 The investor's position under political endogenous and exogenous model using multinomial logistic approach

	Endogenous Model			Exogenous Model		
		[95% Conf. Interval]			[95% Conf. Interval]	
	Coefficient	Lower	Upper	Coefficient	Lower	Upper
Firm returns	$\overline{\varphi}$			φ		
Perishing	16.681	−1345.31	1378.67	17.169	−1675.89	1710.23
Sustainable	14.714	−1347.27	1376.70	15.265	−1677.79	1708.32
Signal ($\widehat{p_3}$)	0.861	−1.84	3.56	0.362	−2.98	3.71
Signal ($\widehat{p_1}$)	2.375	−2.16	6.91	2.071	−3.89	8.03
Information $\widehat{(I_p)}$	−0.291	−2.86	2.27	−0.397	−3.18	2.38
Democratic	–	–	–	−0.505	−2.05	1.04
Term2	–	–	–	−0.099	−1.35	1.15
Civil Exp (ΔCE_t)	0.000	−0.01	0.01	0.001	−0.01	0.01
Govt intervention	−0.202	−1.46	1.05	−0.081	−1.39	1.23
World GDP	5.062	−4.93	15.05	3.2	−8.67	15.07
Δ convergence	1.321*	−0.33	2.98	1.172	−0.63	2.98
Elec lifecycle						
First	1.562**	−0.01	3.13	1.487**	−0.15	3.12
Second	0.780	−0.53	2.09	0.819	−0.50	2.13
Third	0.524	−0.85	1.90	0.51	−0.87	1.89

(continued)

Table 5.9 (continued)

	Endogenous Model			Exogenous Model		
		[95% Conf. Interval]			[95% Conf. Interval]	
	Coefficient	Lower	Upper	Coefficient	Lower	Upper
Constant	−17.687	−1379.67	1344.30	−17.615	−1710.68	1675.45
Risky returns	$\overline{\psi}$			ψ		
Perishing	1.777****	0.56	2.99	1.632****	0.40	2.87
Sustainable	−0.630	−2.04	0.78	−0.869	−2.32	0.58
Signal ($\widehat{p_3}$)	2.562***	0.08	5.05	3.983***	0.86	7.10
Signal ($\widehat{p_1}$)	5.637****	1.56	9.71	7.527****	1.86	13.19
Information $\left(\widehat{I_p}\right)$	−2.151**	−4.62	0.32	−2.480**	−5.20	0.24
Democratic	–	–	–	1.223*	−0.29	2.74
Term2	–	–	–	−0.207	−1.43	1.01
Civil Exp (ΔCE_t)	0.013**	0.00	0.03	0.011*	0.00	0.03
Govt intervention	−0.209	−1.45	1.03	−0.466	−1.77	0.83
World GDP	8.264**	−1.26	17.79	13.866***	1.83	25.91
Δ convergence	0.894	−0.77	2.56	1.316	−0.62	3.25
Elec lifecycle						
First	2.354****	0.77	3.94	2.715****	1.04	4.39
Second	1.145*	−0.25	2.54	1.135*	−0.28	2.55
Third	1.437***	0.03	2.85	1.365**	−0.08	2.81
Constant	−3.411****	−5.69	−1.13	−4.497****	−7.25	−1.75
No. of obs	140			140		
Pseudo R2	0.21			0.23		
LR $chi^2(24)\|(28)$	61.23			65.88		
Log likelihood	−112.55			−110.23		

**** for 1% level of significance, *** for 5% level of significance, ** for 10% level of significance, * for 15% level of significance

Source: Author's calculation

Refer to Table 5.10 in Appendix 7 for the stationary test results of the variables

Appendix 7

The stationary test results for the variables used in Tables 5.2, 5.3, and 5.4 and Appendices 4, 5, and 6. It was done to make these variables time-invariant.

Table 5.10 Stationary test results

Dickey-Fuller test for unit root	Test statistic ($Z(t)$)	Interpolated Dickey-Fuller 1% critical value	5% critical value	10% critical value	p-value for $Z(t)$
Expected Inflation[a]	−3.597	−3.497	−2.887	−2.577	*0.0058*
Δ unemployment rate[a]	−3.251	−3.494	−2.887	−2.577	*0.0172*
Δ growth (US GDP)[a]	−8.579	−3.494	−2.887	−2.577	*0.0000*
Δ civil Exp[b]	−10.312	−3.494	−2.887	−2.577	*0.0000*
Δ military Exp[b]	−10.458	−3.494	−2.887	−2.577	*0.0000*
Δ growth (world GDP)[c]	−3.58	−3.494	−2.887	−2.577	*0.0062*
Δ Convergence[c]	−4.166	−3.494	−2.887	−2.577	*0.0008*
Quarterly Returns[d]	−7.094	−3.494	−2.887	−2.577	*0.0000*
Quarterly Risk[d]	−2.783	−3.494	−2.887	−2.577	*0.0607*

Source: Author's calculations
[a]Represents variables used in Table 5.2, Sect. 5.2.2.1
[b]Represents variables used in Table 5.3 and Table 5.8, Appendix 5
[c]Represents variables used in Table 5.4, and Table 5.9, Appendix 6
[d]Represents variables used in Table 5.7, Appendix 4

Appendix 8

Figure 5.10 shows the kernel density estimate of variable, age dependency ratio; from whicha binary variable, High ADR is created referring to the period when age dependency was comparatively higher than the rest of the period.

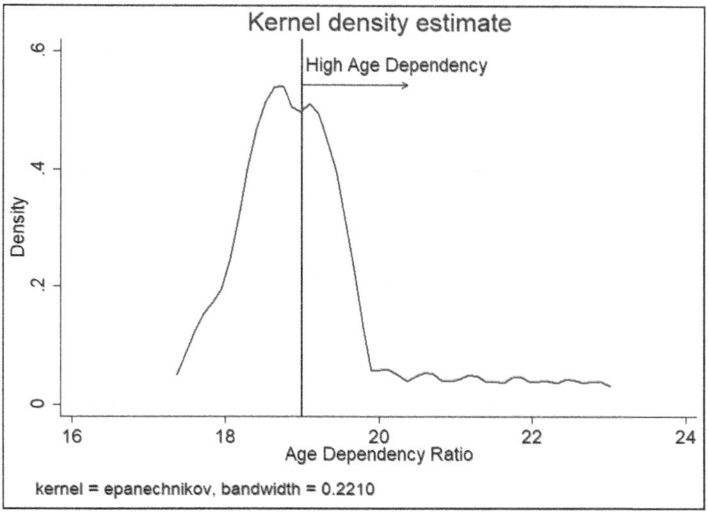

Fig. 5.10 Kernel density estimate of Age Dependency Ratio

References

Alesina, A. (1987). Macroeconomic policy in a two-party system as a repeated game. *Quarterly Journal of Economics, 102*(3), 651–678.

Beaudry, P., & Portier, F. (2006). Stock prices, news, and economic fluctuations. *The American Economic Review, 96*(4), 1293–1307.

Bondt, W. F., & Thaler, R. (1985). Does the stock market overreact? *The Journal of Finance, 40*(3), 793–805.

Brainard, W. C., & Tobin, J. (1968). Econometric models: Their problems and usefulness pitfalls in financiai, model building. *American Economic Review, 58*(2), 99–122.

Cameron, C., & Trivedi, P. K. (2009). *Microeconometrics Using Stata*. College Station, TX: Stata Press.

Fama, E. F. (1970). Efficient capital markets: A review of theory and empirical work. *Journal of Finance, 25*, 383–420.

Greene, W. H. (2008). *Econometric analysis* (6th ed.). Upper Saddle River, NJ: Prentice Hall.

Hamilton, L. C. (1993). *sqv8: Interpreting multinomial logistic regression. Stata Technical Bulletin 13: 24–28. Reprinted in Stata Technical Bulletin Reprints, vol. 3, pp. 176–181. College Station, TX: Stata Press, 2013. Statistics with Stata: Updated for version 12* (8th ed.). Boston: Brooks/Cole.

Hibbs, D. A. (1977) Political Parties and Macroeconomic Policy. American Political Science Review 71 (04):1467-1487

Johnson, H. G. (1967). The possibility of income losses from increased efficiency or factor accumulation in the presence of tariffs. *The Economic Journal, 77*(305), 151–154.

Kaldor, N. (1966). Marginal productivity and the macro-economic theories of distribution: Comment on Samuelson and Modigliani. *Review of Economic Studies, 33*(4), 309–319.

Levhari, D., & Patinkin, D. (1968). The role of money in a simple growth model. *The American Economic Review, 58*(4), 713–753. Retrieved June 20, 2020 from www.jstor.org/stable/1815530.

Lutkepohl, H. (1993). *Introduction to multiple time series analysis* (2nd ed.). New York: Springer.

Nordhaus, W. D. (1975, April). The political business cycle. *The Review of Economic Studies, 42* (2), 169–190.

Persson, T., & Svensson, L. E. O. (1989, May). Why a stubborn conservative would run a deficit: Policy with time- inconsistent preferences. *The Quarterly Journal of Economics, 104*(2), 325–345.

Rogoff, K., & Sibert, A. (1988, January). Elections and macroeconomic policy cycles. *The Review of Economic Studies, 55*(1), 1–16.

Santa-Clara, P., & Valkanov, R. (2003, October). The presidential puzzle: Political cycles and the stock market. *The Journal of Finance, 58*(5), 1841–1872.

Shannon, C. E., & Weaver, W. (1949). *The mathematical theory of communication*. Urbana, IL: University of Illinois Press.

Shiller, R. J. (2015). *Irrational exuberance*. Princeton: Princeton University Press.

Sidrauski, M. (1967). Rational choice and patterns of growth in a monetary economy. *The American Economic Review, 57*(2), 534–544.

Sims, C. A. (2003). Implications of rational inattention. *Journal of Monetary Economics, 50*(3), 665–690.

Sims, C. A. (2006). Rational inattention: Beyond the linear-quadratic case. *American Economic Review Papers and Proceedings, 96*(2), 158–163.

Tobin, J. (1969). A general equilibrium approach to monetary theory. *Journal of Money, Credit and Banking, 1*(1), 15–29.

Watson, M. W. (1994). Vector autoregressions and cointegration. In R. F. Engle & D. L. McFadden (Eds.), *Handbook of econometrics* (Vol. 4). Amsterdam: Elsevier.

Chapter 6
Eliciting Time, Risk, and Social Preferences: Experimental Evidence from India

Aswini Kumar Mishra, Pratyush Pradhan, and Divya Satish Revankar

6.1 Introduction

Psychologists say that a human's behaviour is a reflection of his surroundings. Behaviour is an integral part of the human life which becomes a reflection of what one sees in the society. People's behaviour changes with time, age, experience, and situations. These changes may also be economical, political, environmental, and cultural. The Indian society is seeing a gradual shift from conservatism to liberalism. People are welcoming and imbibing new attitudes, beliefs, and culture in the new society. As the societal make-up plays an important role in determining behaviours; thus, it is important to study each country in isolation and then see how the behaviours change between countries.

We hear many stories regarding the risk-seeking attitude among people and investing in business and then this business flourishing. Greater the risks, greater the rewards, is saying based on which people are willing to take the risk and invest in the financial market. Apart from using trading strategies, a large number of traders use their "Gut Feeling". This gut feeling is an indication of the appetite for risk they are willing to bear. Another example seen of high-risk preferences is seen in entrepreneurship. Leaving a steady paying job, for undertaking a journey with no fixed or definite reward in the end, is highly risky. Entrepreneurship is on trust in one's ability and patience. For it may take many years for a company to become successful.

This brings us to our next behaviour, time preference. As an investor in the financial market, time plays a crucial role. Every second, there are changes taking place in the market considering the price, economic conditions, political conditions, demand and supply, cost, etc. Government policies are the perfect example to

A. K. Mishra (✉) · P. Pradhan · D. S. Revankar
Department of Economics and Finance, BITS Pilani, K K Birla Goa Campus, Sancoale, Goa, India
e-mail: aswini@goa.bits-pilani.ac.in

A. K. Mishra et al. (eds.), *Critical Perspectives on Emerging Economies*,
Contributions to Economics, https://doi.org/10.1007/978-3-030-59781-8_6

understand patience levels of a country. A government's developmental project is usually planned keeping in mind the level of demand at least 10–15 years from now. Thus, how the population reacts to them gives us an indication of the time preferences exhibited. Moreover, with time, risk preferences change becoming higher or lower.

With these psychological changes taking place in the society at individual level. Economists aim to develop models of human behaviour and interactions in markets and other economic settings. Human mind behaves differently in every different situation. Although we try to make rational decisions, we have limited cognitive abilities and limited willpower. While our decisions are often guided by self-interest, we also care about fairness and equity. Moreover cognitive abilities, self-control, and motivation can vary significantly across different individuals (Thaler 2017).

Many theories of human behaviour, in economics and neighbouring disciplines, assume that a set of preferences drives individual decision-making. This includes preferences about risk, the timing of rewards, and in the social domain, reciprocity, altruism, and trust (Falk et al. 2018).

This chapter aims at exploring six facets of human behaviour in the context of India:

1. **Risk Preference:** It refers to the attitude people hold towards risks, which is a key factor in studies on investors' decision-making behaviour. (Wen et al. 2014).
2. **Time Preference:** The definition of time preference we have used states that a person with a lower time preference favours having a good sooner rather than later.
3. **Positive Reciprocity:** Positive reciprocity occurs when an action committed by one individual that has a positive effect on someone else is returned with an action that has an approximately equal positive effect.
4. **Negative Reciprocity:** Negative reciprocity occurs when an action committed by one individual that has a negative effect on someone else is returned with an action that has an approximately equal negative effect.
5. **Altruism:** Willingness to do things that bring advantages to others, even if it results in disadvantage for yourself.
6. **Trust:** Firm belief in the reliability, truth, or ability of someone or something.

This study focuses on these factors and tries to capture these subjects accurately. For this, we adapted a survey by Falk et al. (2016). The values of the monetary benefits offered were converted on the basis of PPP. Although our work is heavily influenced by the same work, we take a departure from the work by creating our own dataset with 614 university students and parents. We have then used regional, gender, and age-based analysis to get a broader look of the divisions in the sample. This is not performed in Falk et al. (2018). We use age as a discontinuous variable in the form of age groups as compared to a continuous variable which is used in Falk et al. (2018). Another important departure that we make is the use of principal component analysis. This helped us determine the variables to be chosen for the regressions which explain the highest variance in time, risk, and social preferences. The objectives of the study are as follows:

- Exploring the correlation among the six attributes and seeing if it is in line with the GPS report.
- Primary analysis of components of all factors and analysing which are the best independent variables for the regression.
- Regression and comparison of coefficients for under 25 years, over 40 years, and the total sample.

Then, analysis of the study begins with describing the sample, its various variables, heterogeneity among it. PCA is used to determine the factors under all five attributes. These attributes are tested among themselves for any correlation. Further regression is run among the attributes and age-based cohorts to check their significance levels.

In the cultural and economic point of view, this study related to research measured in variations in preference across society selecting smaller groups. The study has focused on students as their subjects wherein we capture their attitude towards risk—averse or seeking.

The IEPS has the potential for further research with respect to other variable/ variations. Such as the role of demography, fertility, women participation, lifestyle, economic situations in the country could be considered for further study.

6.2 Literature Review

In this chapter, we look at three behavioural traits of a person and what factors play a part in determining them and how they vary across India. These three behavioural traits are time preference or patience, risk preference, and social preference. These traits have been studied extensively in various methodologies internationally and contexts of specific countries. Falk et al. (2018) lays down the basis for our work. We shall analyse the literature on each trait.

6.2.1 Time Preferences

Time preferences are a major area of study in the behavioural economics world. Many papers have been written trying to analyse the nature of time preferences and how they can be estimated. Andreoni and Sprenger (2012) looks at how time preferences can be estimated using convex budget curves while Rubinstein (1985) tries to explain it by using a bargaining model. Wang et al. (2016)'s study was the first large-scale international survey on time preferences in 52 countries and how they differ based on hyperbolic discounting patterns. They performed this study in over 53 countries. They found that cultural dimensions play a significant role in time discounting. Hofstede (2009) proposed the Hofstede cultural dimensions which were used here. They also found that waiting tendency is correlated with innovation, environmental protection, credit rating, and BMI. Meier and Sprenger (2015) looked at temporal stability of time preference and found they remain relatively stable over the two-year period studied.

Time preferences also help understanding how the country will react to different types of disasters, financial, and geographical. This is explored in Cassar et al. (2017). They show that natural disasters make people more patient. Sawada and Kuroishi (2015) explores this in Philippines using convex budget curves.

Variation of time preferences are found to vary across gender (Dittrich and Leipold 2014), age (Fung et al. 2001), education (Perez-Arce 2017), energy efficiency (Newell and Siikamäki 2015), and culture (Breuer et al. 2011). This leads us to believe that time preferences are not entirely explored and that each individual country will have different factors contributing the time preferences of the local population. Country-wise studies of time preferences have been performed in the form of survey. Yesuf and Bluffstone (2008) and Tanaka et al. (2010) explored Ethiopia and Vietnam, respectively, and calculated discounting factors for them. Yesuf and Bluffstone (2008) explored the linkages with the mortgage markets too. Poulos and Whittington (2000) explored time preferences in six developing countries.

India-specific studies for time preferences have been very few. Kurosaki (2001) looked at only rural India while Mehar et al. (2017) looks at the role it plays in agricultural selection. No study that we came across has explored the role of gender, age, education, and cognitive ability with a special focus on India before.

6.2.2 Risk Preferences

Risk preferences are also a major topic study in behavioural economics. It has real-world effects in the world of finance, entrepreneurship, and simple life choices. Andreoni and Sprenger (2012) explains the main differences between time and risk preferences. The main stumbling block in calculating risk preferences is eliciting them in the first place. Harrison et al. (2005) came with a theoretical backing to show the methods being used had certain flaws. Charness et al. (2013) and Dave et al. (2010) explore the various methods that can be followed to elicit the right kind of responses. Freeman et al. (2019) uses choice lists using pairwise lotteries to elicit risk preferences. Coppola (2014) explores the use of socioeconomic surveys and debates if the short form of DOSPERT scale (Weber et al. 2002) is the right method. Rieger et al. (2014) takes ahead the work of Wang et al. (2012) and explore the effect of culture.

Risk preferences are also known to be different on and individual level and a country level; the causes of risk preferences to change are being studied extensively. Apicella et al. (2008) explores the role testosterone plays. Genetics are also considered ion economics risk preferences (Zyphur et al. 2009). Freese (2004) uses the WVS data to explore the effect of gender and religion on risk preferences. Miller and Hoffmann (1995) serves as the precursor to the study. Charness and Gneezy (2012) shows that men are more risk taking that woman. Cardenas and Carpenter (2008) looks at Sweden and Columbia and explores how different the role of gender is a developing economy vis-vis a developed economy.

An important study by Fehr and Hoff (2011) showed that society plays a major impact in determining on the preference of the individual. Miller (2000) explores the Asian societies and the relationship they have with risks. The Indian society is unique: with the multitude of languages and internal migration, poverty levels, education level, and inter-regional differences. Country-level risk preferences have been studied beforehand. To illustrate, while Kachelmeier and Shehata (1992) examines the case of China, Kahsay and Osberghaus (2018) analyses the same in the context of Germany, but to the best of our knowledge, we have not come across with any study that focuses on India.

6.2.3 *Social Preferences*

Social preferences are broken down into four main qualities—positive reciprocity, negative reciprocity, altruism, and trust (Falk et al. 2016). Social preferences help us understand the make-up of the society. Social preferences have a strong impact of the entrepreneurial sprits of the society (Caliendo et al. 2014). They also have impacts in the labour market (Pereira et al. 2006; Charness 2004). Charness et al. (2007) performed an experiment where he explored the effect of distance on the type of behaviour shown by a person.

Reciprocity is a crucial social preference, be it positive or negative. Games are commonly used for determining reciprocity. Cox (2004) lays down the theoretical backing for this. McCabe et al. (2003) uses trust games, while Yamagishi et al. (2012) states that ultimatum game methods are not accurate.

Dohmen et al. (2008) talked about the determinants and the prevalence of trust. Dunning et al. (2012) explores the noneconomic considerations that need to be taken while considering trust behaviour. Trust games are popular study mediums. Croson and Buchan (1999) uses trust games to explore the differences caused by gender and culture. Social inclusion induced trust game were the based on a study by Hillebrandt et al. (2011). Trust is known to have a close relationship with education. Hooghe et al. (2012), Hakhverdian and Mayne (2012), and Borgonovi (2012) all explore this. Developing countries are often studied for trust levels. Johansson-Stenman et al. (2009)'s study examines trust experiment among religious groups in Bangladesh. Castilla (2015) only focuses on the relationship between husbands and wives and not how people react in the society.

Altruism is a concept where someone does something good for another without expecting anything in return. Altruism and its effect on economics were explored in Simon (1993) and Zamagni (1995) since then it has become an important element of human behaviour. Carter and Castillo (2002) provided an experimental approach to determine the economics effects of altruism. Bekkers (2007) uses dictator games to measure altruistic behaviour. Zizzo (2011) explores whether this is actually the right method. Fehr and Schmidt (2006) provides some interesting theories on how effect the economy, but it is Schwarze and Winkelmann (2005) paper that provides us with models to calculate the effect of altruism.

Falk et al. (2016, 2018) is a unique set of papers, which first devises a unique survey which can help estimate all the risk, time, and social preferences in a single survey. They also provide interesting results on how countries behave on an aggregate level. We have used the survey designed by Falk et al. (2016) and focus only Indian population and look how factors unique to India play a role in determining the behaviours of the Indian population.

6.3 Data Sample

The data was collected during the start of the academic year of 2019 using a web survey it primarily focused on college students along with their parents. The survey was live from august 2019 to September 2019. The sample collected is limited to students, alumni, and their relatives over the age group of 18 years and above. The study uses stratified sampling technique based on the age cohorts among the students enrolled in the educational institutes along with their parents. The entire student population list was available from the administration office in the campus. The invitation to take part in the survey was sent via e-mails. This link introduced them to the topic of the survey; its objective, further taking them into the survey, where they had to affirm their assent to the informed consent statement.

The survey was conducted in one phase, where 1-month time was given to the students along with their parents for participation. They were given 1-month time to fill in the survey. The subjects were reminded twice for filling up the questionnaire—first, in the last 15 days and 10 days before we closed the collection of data via the link.

Apart from asking questions regarding the behavioural factors, many questions which helped us determine the socioeconomic and demographic profiles of the user were present in the survey. Average monthly expenditure, state of origin, marital status, highest education, social group, industry, type of employment of head of household, age group, mother tongue, and whether the subject is a student or not.

In a month's time, 3000 students received the e-mails with about 614 completing the survey. The overall response rate was about 20% which is seemingly low for survey research, but is consistent with the lower response seen in the online surveys. The lower response rate might have occurred due to the e-mail address being incorrect, invalid, or users using anti-spam programmes. The length and complexity of the survey could also have been the factor (Fig. 6.1).

Most of the response captures from the subjects belong to the age groups of 15–20 and 21–25 years. Age-wise distribution of the sample was lopsided towards the younger population as the survey was predominantly distributed among college students. Table 6.1 shows the age distribution. The subjects where 480 were male subjects and 134 were female subjects. The sample is similar to the demographic profile of the college students, where the campus has majority of male student

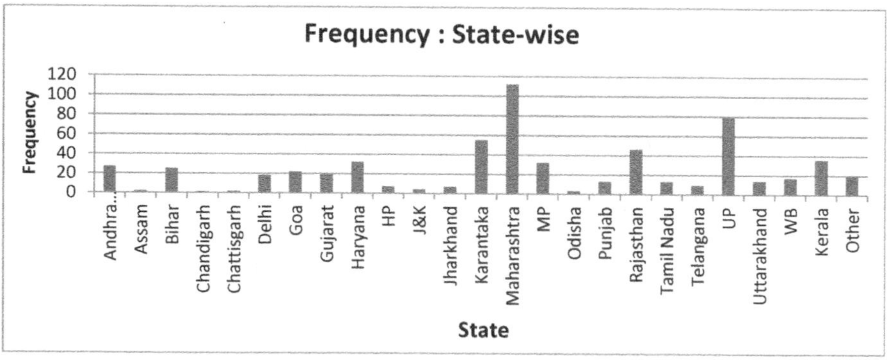

Fig. 6.1 State-wise distribution of sample. Source: All data from the conducted survey

Table 6.1 Age-wise distribution of the subjects

Age	Freq.	Percent	Cum.
18–20	289	47.0684	47.0684
21–25	195	31.75896	78.82736
26–30	28	4.560261	83.38762
31–40	33	5.374593	88.76221
41–50	39	6.351792	95.11401
Above 50	30	4.885993	100
Total	614	100	

Source: All data from the conducted survey

enrolment more than that of the females. The sample consisted of data of people from more than 26 states of India speaking more than 25 languages.

6.4 Methodology

The design of the survey is based of Falk et al. (2016). Questions are designed to capture the preferences of the subject. For each behavioural preference, at least three questions are asked and a weighted average is taken to create an index between 0 and 1.

For time preference the questions asked includes a step-wise ladder question of choice between a collecting a payment of X amount today and a payment of Y amount 1 year from now. X was kept constant and Y was increased or decreased based on the answers of the subject. The subject who chose the option of payment today was assigned level 1 while the subject who always chose the payment at a later date was assigned L32. Intermediate levels were also assigned based on answers. The second part of the time preferences was determined by the question "How willing are you to give up something that is beneficial for you today in order to benefit more from that in the future?" The subject was asked to answer this on a 1–10 scale.

For risk preference, a similar step-wise ladder question was used. Here, the subjects had an option between accepting a sure payment of X amount or take a 50/50 chance of receiving amount Y. X was kept constant and Y was changed depending on the answers. The subject who chose the sure payment in all questions was assigned the lowest risk level (L1) while the subject who chose the 50/50 chance in all questions was assigned the highest risk level (L32). Intermediate levels were assigned based on answers. The second part of the risk preferences was determined from 1 to 10 scale answer of the question "I tend to postpone tasks even if I know it would be better to do them right away".

For positive reciprocity, the subject was described a situation where a stranger helps the subject in time of need. The willingness to gift the stranger a reward and the value of the gift was recorded. On the 1–10 scale, the subject was then asked to rate how willing he/she was to return a favour. For negative reciprocity, three main questions were asked. The first two questions dealt with how willing the subject was to punish someone when unjust had been done to someone else or self. While the third question asked the subject to estimate his willingness to take revenge. All answers were recorded on a 1–10 scale.

For altruism, the subject's willingness to give to good causes was recorded. The subject was also presented with a situation where he/she receives an unexpected reward and is asked how much of it will he be willing to donate. Trust and cognitive ability were determined by single question like "I assume that people have only the best intentions" and "I am good at math". Both these questions are known to have sufficient explanatory power over these factors (Falk et al. 2016) and hence were the only questions required.

Once all responses were recorded a correlation matrix was created using the indexes made using the weights mentioned in Table 6.2.

The next part involved performing a principal component analysis (PCA). Principal component analysis is a statistical technique by which possibly correlated variables are decomposed into a set of linearly uncorrelated variables. Orthogonal transformations are used to create Eigen vectors which have zero correlations between each other. The main use of PCA is to help explain the variance in the independent variable. By limiting the number of components to be created, we reduce the percentage of variance described. We find that by limiting to five components we find satisfactory explanatory power in all properties.

The last set part of the paper involves performing OLS regressions of the preferences using the variables which have the maximum explanatory power as per the results of the PCA analysis. This is done three times once for the entire sample, then for all under the age of 25 and lastly for all above the age of 40. The results for sample and the subsamples are then compared. Further OLS regressions are carried out to find the effect of risk preferences and time preferences on self-employment and higher education.

Table 6.2 Preference-wise assignments of weights

Property	Questions	Weights
Time preference	How willing are you to give up something that is beneficial for you today in order to benefit more from that in the future?	0.29
	Situation: Choice between receiving payment today and 12 months from now	0.71
Risk preference	I tend to postpone tasks even if I know it would be better to do them right away	0.53
	Situation: Choice between accepting sure payment and 50/50 chance	0.47
Positive reciprocity	Situation: Value of gift for help	0.515
	When someone does me a favour, I am willing to return it	0.485
Negative reciprocity	How willing are YOU to punish someone who treats YOU unfairly, even if there may be costs for you?	0.313
	How willing are you to punish someone who treats OTHERS unfairly, even if there may be costs for you?	0.313
	If I am treated very unjustly, I will take revenge at the first occasion, even if there is a cost to do so	0.373
Altruism	How willing are you to give to good causes without expecting anything in return?	0.365
	Situation: Donation from unexpected reward	0.635
Trust	I assume that people have only the best intentions	1
Cognitive ability	I am good at math	1

Source: Adapted from Falk et al. (2018)

6.5 Results

6.5.1 Correlations and Averages

The correlations are an interesting method to see how two traits are related and how they are related to each other and the nature of the effect they have on each other. Table 6.3 shows that time preference and positive reciprocity display significant positive correlation. This is not expected as Falk et al. (2018) suggests that there is no major relationship between these two factors. Prosociality factors (positive reciprocity, altruism, and trust) are found to be significantly correlated. This is in line with our expectations. An interesting result is that negative reciprocity and higher risk preferences are positively correlated significantly which shows that highly risky are willing to hurt others for their own gains. This shows a possibility of selfishness being displayed. Cognitive ability and trust are also found to have a significant relationship which indicates that people with higher cognitive ability trust others more as compared to ones with lower cognitive ability.

Next, we look at how the time, risk, and social preferences between genders, age groups, and region are based. Table 6.4 clearly shows that females are more prosocial as they have higher average values of Positive reciprocity, altruism, and trust which is as per expectation. Male respondents were found to be more willing to

Table 6.3 Pairwise correlation table across different preference groups

	Time preference	Risk preference	Positive reciprocity	Negative reciprocity	Altruism	Trust	Cognitive ability
Time preference	1						
Risk preference	0.0267	1					
Positive reciprocity	0.1442*	−0.0644	1				
Negative reciprocity	0.0268	0.1708*	0.0299	1			
Altruism	−0.0398	−0.0414	0.1899*	0.0252	1		
Trust	−0.0262	0.0336	0.0914*	0.0332	0.01661*	1	
Cognitive ability	0.0582	0.0016	0.0243	0.0709**	0.0375	0.1432*	1

Significance level: *$p < 0.05$, **$p < 0.1$
Source: Same as Table 6.1

Table 6.4 Gender-based means

Gender		Time preference	Risk preference	Positive reciprocity	Negative reciprocity	Altruism	Trust
Male	Mean	0.552354	0.542139	0.713225	0.476006	0.399994	0.500212
		(0.254878)	(0.182672)	(0.179239)	(0.21099)	(0.196134)	(0.2797703)
Female	Mean	0.535637	0.516581	0.739416	0.459776	0.458861	0.515152
		(0.234939)	(0.21347)	(0.162767)	(0.211842)	(0.19007)	(0.262543)
Total	Mean	0.548783	0.537038	0.719081	0.472409	0.412862	0.503483
		(0.250629)	(0.189276)	(0.175893)	(0.211107)	(0.196188)	(0.275894)

Standard error in parenthesis.
Source: Same as Table 6.1

take risk and also were slightly more inclined to show negative reciprocity. Males were found to be more patient that the females. Age group wise the results are in line with many previous researches. Table 6.5 shows clear patterns with a steady decrease in time preferences and risk preferences as age increases. Decreasing time preferences suggest that the youth are more willing to wait as compared to older people as they have longer lives ahead of them. Decreasing risk preferences with an increase in age is a common theory used in the world of finance and is clearly displayed here. The trusting behaviour of people is also shown to increase with an increase in age.

Table 6.6 shows the averages for time, risk, and social preferences based on regions—North (N), South (S), East (E), West (W), Central (C) India, and Others (O). Others is used to refer to all those respondents that did not now choose to respond to the question. East Indians were found to be very patient as compared to rest. They were also the most trusting and showed the high positive reciprocity. North Indians showed the low altruism as they also displayed high negative reciprocity. Although we found negative reciprocity and risk preferences to be correlated on an individual level this is not observed on regional level. The respondents that chose not to disclose their location were unsurprisingly found to have the lowest trust and patience levels.

6.5.2 Principal Component Analysis

Principal component analysis is a technique used to determine the components of any dependent variable. It uses Eigen vectors to calculate the percentage of variance in the dependent variable explained by the variance in the independent variables. Here, we have used a PCA analysis to see which variables contribute and how much of the variance of our time, risk, and social preferences are being explained by them. The Rho values in all the PCA models are found to be greater than 0.7 (refer Appendix). This shows that we are able to explain more 70% variance is all our dependent variables can be explained by the use of five components. These five components are gender, age group, dummy for age squared, highest education, and cognitive ability. Thus, these five variables are chosen to be used for our regression-based analysis.

6.5.3 Regressions of Time, Risk, and Social Preferences

The result was used in the regressions shown in Table 6.7. Due to constraints in data, we find that not all the variables are found to significant and the R^2 values are low. This is expected in primary data studies.

In the regression for positive reciprocity, we find that age group and dummy for square of age are both significant at a 95% confidence level. We find that age group

Table 6.5 Age groups-based means

Age group		Time preference	Risk preference	Positive reciprocity	Negative reciprocity	Altruism	Trust
18–20	Mean	0.557112 (0.243232)	0.55798 (0.169159)	0.722015 (0.166529)	0.481871 (0.204929)	0.406313 (0.195064)	0.485512 (0.276443)
21–25	Mean	0.546373 (0.251539)	0.546661 (0.173969)	0.698967 (0.18034)	0.490212 (0.194169)	0.392025 (0.190234)	0.472021 (0.274895)
26–30	Mean	0.540508 (0.264535)	0.503194 (0.218909)	0.742512 (0.199957)	0.357656 (0.23699)	0.463574 (0.196567)	0.562963 (0.243608)
31–40	Mean	0.501968 (0.272557)	0.526401 (0.230227)	0.6848 (0.203064)	0.477819 (0.271745)	0.47836 (0.227732)	0.554546 (0.281837)
41–50	Mean	0.616875 (0.256295)	0.421302 (0.295885)	0.756162 (0.167905)	0.40139 (0.231815)	0.426858 (0.175576)	0.591892 (0.259678)
Above 50	Mean	0.465617 (0.255415)	0.434732 (0.186585)	0.777844 (0.1795)	0.452255 (0.217225)	0.475515 (0.21233)	0.656667 (0.248698)
Total	Mean	0.548783 (0.250629)	0.537038 (0.189276)	0.719081 (0.175893)	0.472409 (0.211107)	0.412862 (0.196188)	0.503483 (0.275894)

Standard error in parenthesis.
Source: Same as Table 6.1

Table 6.6 Region-based means

Zone		Time preference	Risk preference	Positive reciprocity	Negative reciprocity	Altruism	Trust
Central	Mean	0.573051 (0.232789)	0.514046 (0.185054)	0.745403 (0.151515)	0.447091 (0.246185)	0.433588 (0.175624)	0.55625 (0.261432)
East	Mean	0.763462 (0.179821)	0.550479 (0.125265)	0.71231 (0.156987)	0.409055 (0.271537)	0.416475 (0.188527)	0.5 (0.255841)
North	Mean	0.531355 (0.246037)	0.522272 (0.193407)	0.714853 (0.180565)	0.484567 (0.201678)	0.384793 (0.184292)	0.509917 (0.267121)
South	Mean	0.52529 (0.261964)	0.538828 (0.190813)	0.726284 (0.182662)	0.460046 (0.211786)	0.434303 (0.192603)	0.483688 (0.306274)
West	Mean	0.571856 (0.247181)	0.561332 (0.189134)	0.72107 (0.170089)	0.475146 (0.204687)	0.433526 (0.217143)	0.507285 (0.261559)
Other	Mean	0.469075 (0.254023)	0.571412 (0.19316)	0.632591 (0.17101)	0.513039 (0.249895)	0.408538 (0.225822)	0.435714 (0.33422)
Total	Mean	0.548783 (0.250629)	0.537038 (0.189276)	0.719081 (0.175893)	0.472409 (0.211107)	0.412862 (0.196188)	0.503483 (0.275894)

Standard error in parenthesis.
Source: Same as Table 6.1
Note: *Central*: Chhattisgarh; Madhya Pradesh. *East*: Assam; Odisha; West Bengal. *North*: Bihar, Chandigarh, New Delhi; Haryana; Himachal Pradesh; Jammu and Kashmir; Jharkhand; Punjab; Rajasthan; Uttar Pradesh; Uttarakhand. *South*: Andhra Pradesh; Karnataka; Tamil Nadu; Kerala; Karnataka. *West*: Goa, Gujarat; Maharashtra. *Other*: Other states

Table 6.7 Regression results of entire population

	Time preference	Risk preference	Positive reciprocity	Negative reciprocity	Altruism	Trust
Gender	−0.0125 (0.0271)	−0.0279 (0.0206)	0.0307 (0.0179)	−0.0019 (0.0212)	0.0592** (0.0194)	0.0218 (0.0270)
Age group	0.0314 (0.0398)	−0.006 (0.0301)	−0.0531* (0.2069)	0.0007 (0.0319)	−0.226 (0.0289)	−0.0278 (0.0404)
Age2	−0.00442 (0.0058)	−0.00355 (0.00443)	0.00936* (0.00394)	−0.00076 (0.0047)	0.00495 (0.00425)	0.00932 (0.00594)
Highest education	−0.0211 (0.012)	0.00196 (0.00897)	0.0038 (0.0081)	−0.0132 (0.0095)	0.00935 (0.00866)	0.00406 (0.0121)
Cognitive ability	0.0664 (0.052)	−0.0188 (0.0397)	0.0328 (0.0348)	0.06833 (0.413)	0.0524 (0.0373)	0.204*** (0.0520)
_Cons	0.517*** (0.0565)	0.585*** (0.0429)	0.729*** (0.0377)	0.459*** (0.045)	0.353*** (0.0409)	0.335*** (0.0572)
N	524	514	572	586	608	599
R-squared	0.011	0.047	0.02	0.013	0.03	0.54

Standard errors in parenthesis, $*p < 0.05$, $**p < 0.01$, $***p < 0.0001$
Source: Same as Table 6.1

has a coefficient with a negative sign and the coefficient for the dummy for square of age is positive this is completely different as compared to global level results of Falk et al. (2018). The signs of both these independent variables are flipped. This suggests that Indians show changes in positive reciprocity with age is a different manner as compared to the general populace of the world. Gender plays an important role is determine in altruism. Females are generally known to show greater altruism. The results here are consistent with the literature. The coefficient of cognitive ability is found to highly significant for trust; this is in line with the fact that we found significant correlation between these two variables. Causality may be one-way or two-way, this can be tested in future research.

Since a large section of our sample under the age of 25, we decided to see how the results of the regressions would change if only this subsample was used. In Table 6.8, we find that the dummy for age squared loses its significance in the regression of positive reciprocity. Gender becomes even more significant is the altruism. An interesting result shows that gender becomes significant in Trust suggesting that younger women are usually trusting but with an increase in age they become less trusting in nature. This is against the increase in average trust level with age that we observed earlier. For subjects over the age of 40, we found that although our sample was small, certain results were significant. Table 6.9 shows that Gender has a significant effect on positive reciprocity. This shows that older females are more likely to show positive reciprocity as compared to males. This result is similar to Falk et al. (2018). Another interesting result is the effect of square of age on time preference. The coefficient is found to be negative and significant. This shows that time preferences reduce at as Indians grow older which is can be because they may be scared of death and want to create as many experiences as possible.

Table 6.8 Regression of Sample with Age under 25

	Time preference	Risk preference	Positive reciprocity	Negative reciprocity	Altruism	Trust
Gender	−0.00278 (0.0315)	−0.00991 (0.0219)	0.0099 (0.0205)	0.02 (0.0234)	0.0749*** (0.0221)	0.0619* (0.0314)
Age2	0.0038 (0.00952)	−0.00409 (0.00659)	−0.011 (0.0064)	0.00471 (0.00724)	−0.00973 (0.00679)	−0.00864 (0.00974)
Highest education	−0.0217 (0.00127)	0.00191 (0.00886)	0.00673 (0.00854)	−0.00821 (0.00967)	0.0112 (0.00908)	0.00423 (0.0130)
Cognitive ability	0.0344 (0.0605)	0.0044 (0.0421)	−0.00167 (0.04030)	0.0556 (0.0450)	0.0265 (0.0429)	0.0234*** (0.0611)
_Cons	0.566*** (0.0526)	0.557*** (0.0374)	0.721*** (0.0352)	0.446*** (0.0402)	0.363*** (0.0378)	0.3*** (0.0539)
N	408	415	450	465	482	474
R-squared	0.008	0.002	0.007	0.006	0.028	0.036

Standard errors in parenthesis, $*p < 0.05$,$**p < 0.01$,$***p < 0.0001$
Source: Same as Table 6.1

Table 6.9 Regression for sample over 40 years

	Time preference	Risk preference	Positive reciprocity	Negative reciprocity	Altruism	Trust
Gender	−0.0497 (−0.66)	−0.0827 (−1.00)	0.110* −2.36	−0.0394 (−0.61)	−0.0108 (−0.20)	−0.1 (−1.39)
Age2	−0.0127* (−2.09)	0.00239 (−0.37)	0.0042 (−1.1)	0.00388 (−0.73)	0.00543 (−1.24)	0.00548 (−0.92)
Highest education	−0.00184 (−0.04)	0.00669 −0.14	−0.0173 (−0.61)	−0.00707 (−0.18)	0.0318 (−0.98)	0.0153 (−0.35)
Cognitive ability	0.0736 (−0.5)	−0.0403 (−0.27)	−0.0783 (−0.85)	−0.0359 (−0.28)	0.205 (−1.94)	0.121 −0.84
_Cons	0.895** (−3.14)	0.37 (−1.16)	0.730*** (−4.04)	0.38 (−1.53)	0.0294 (−0.14)	0.344 (−1.22)
N	64	52	66	65	67	66
R-squared	0.08	0.027	0.11	0.022	0.084	0.062

Standard errors in parenthesis, $*p < 0.05$, $**p < 0.01$, $***p < 0.0001$.
Source: Same as Table 6.1

6.6 Conclusion

Given that our sample is restricted, our results may not be accurate estimates for the entire population of India but our results are some of the first for an India-specific study. More scope exists for exploring the way the culture and languages affect the behaviours of Indians. The correlation between cognitive ability and trust is also an interesting result which deserves to be explored further. The positive correlation between time preferences and positive reciprocity may suggest that Indians are more likely to spend time doing activities which need not have a direct benefit to them.

The analysis of regional diversity shows that the make-up of the society plays an important part in how the time, risk, and social preferences of a person are shaped. The analysis based on genders shows that females show greater prosociality as compared to men. This is expected as previous studies have also shown that females are prosocial than males. An important result is the reducing risk preferences with age which show the potential for investments. The younger population are more risk friendly and thus will make more risky investment and career decisions. This can work in favour of a country like India which wants to grow at a fast rate.

We have shown that positive reciprocity changes differently with age as compared to the rest of the world. We find that it deceases at a decreasing rate while it increases at a decreasing rate as per Falk et al. (2018). The younger population sample shows that females are much more likely to show altruism, and trust as compared to males. These results are based on a small sample and show considerable need for exploration. India is a goldmine for behavioural economics experiments and this is just a slight peek into the mind of this interesting society.

References

Andreoni, J., & Sprenger, C. (2012). Estimating time preferences from convex budgets. *American Economic Review, 102*(7), 3333–3356.

Apicella, C. L., Dreber, A., Campbell, B., Gray, P. B., Hoffman, M., & Little, A. C. (2008). Testosterone and financial risk preferences. *Evolution and Human Behavior, 29*(6), 384–390.

Bekkers, R. H. (2007). Measuring altruistic behavior in surveys: The all-or-nothing dictator game. *SurveyResearch Methods, 1*(3), 1–11.

Borgonovi, F. (2012). The relationship between education and levels of trust and tolerance in Europe 1. *The British Journal of Sociology, 63*(1), 146–167.

Breuer, W., Hens, T., Salzmann, A. J., & Wang, M. (2011). Time preferences, culture, and household debt maturity choice. In *National Centre of Competence in Research Financial Valuation and Risk Management,* Working paper.

Caliendo, M., Fossen, F. M., Kritikos, A., & Wetter, M. (2014). The gender gap in entrepreneurship: Not just a matter of personality. *CESifo Economic Studies, 61*(1), 202–238.

Cardenas, J. C., & Carpenter, J. (2008). Behavioural development economics: Lessons from field labs in the developing world. *The Journal of Development Studies, 44*(3), 311–338.

Carter, M. R., & Castillo, M. (2002). *The economic impacts of altruism, trust and reciprocity: An experimental approach to social capital* (No. 1800-2016-142366).

Cassar, A., Healy, A., & Von Kessler, C. (2017). Trust, risk, and time preferences after a natural disaster: Experimental evidence from Thailand. *World Development, 94*, 90–105.

Castilla, C. (2015). Trust and reciprocity between spouses in India. *American Economic Review, 105*(5), 621–624.

Charness, G. (2004). Attribution and reciprocity in an experimental labor market. *Journal of Labor Economics, 22*(3), 665–688.

Charness, G., & Gneezy, U. (2012). Strong evidence for gender differences in risk taking. *Journal of Economic Behavior & Organization, 83*(1), 50–58.

Charness, G., Haruvy, E., & Sonsino, D. (2007). Social distance and reciprocity: An internet experiment. *Journal of Economic Behavior & Organization, 63*(1), 88–103.

Charness, G., Gneezy, U., & Imas, A. (2013). Experimental methods: Eliciting risk preferences. *Journal of Economic Behavior & Organization, 87*, 43–51.

Coppola, M. (2014). Eliciting risk-preferences in socio-economic surveys: How do different measures perform? *The Journal of Socio-Economics, 48*, 1–10.
Cox, J. C. (2004). How to identify trust and reciprocity. *Games and Economic Behavior, 46*(2), 260–281.
Croson, R., & Buchan, N. (1999). Gender and culture: International experimental evidence from trust games. *American Economic Review, 89*(2), 386–391.
Dave, C., Eckel, C. C., Johnson, C. A., & Rojas, C. (2010). Eliciting risk preferences: When is simple better? *Journal of Risk and Uncertainty, 41*(3), 219–243.
Dittrich, M., & Leipold, K. (2014). Gender differences in time preferences. *Economics Letters, 122* (3), 413–415.
Dohmen, T., Falk, A., Huffman, D., & Sunde, U. (2008). Representative trust and reciprocity: Prevalence and determinants. *Economic Inquiry, 46*(1), 84–90.
Dunning, D., Fetchenhauer, D., & Schlösser, T. M. (2012). Trust as a social and emotional act: Noneconomic considerations in trust behavior. *Journal of Economic Psychology, 33*(3), 686–694.
Falk, A., Becker, A., Dohmen, T. J., Huffman, D., & Sunde, U. (2016). The preference survey module: A validated instrument for measuring risk, time, and social preferences. IZA Discussion Paper No. 9674
Falk, A., Becker, A., Dohmen, T., Enke, B., Huffman, D., & Sunde, U. (2018). Global evidence on economic preferences. *The Quarterly Journal of Economics, 133*(4), 1645–1692.
Fehr, E., & Hoff, K. (2011). *Tastes, castes, and culture: The influence of society on preferences*. Washington, DC: The World Bank.
Fehr, E., & Schmidt, K. M. (2006). The economics of fairness, reciprocity and altruism–experimental evidence and new theories. *Handbook of the economics of giving, altruism and reciprocity, 1*, 615–691.
Freeman, D. J., Halevy, Y., & Kneeland, T. (2019). Eliciting risk preferences using choice lists. *Quantitative Economics, 10*(1), 217–237.
Freese, J. (2004). Risk preferences and gender differences in religiousness: Evidence from the world values survey. *Review of Religious Research, 46*, 88–91.
Fung, H. H., Lai, P., & Ng, R. (2001). Age differences in social preferences among Taiwanese and mainland Chinese: The role of perceived time. *Psychology and Aging, 16*(2), 351.
Hakhverdian, A., & Mayne, Q. (2012). Institutional trust, education, and corruption: A micro-macro interactive approach. *The Journal of Politics, 74*(3), 739–750.
Harrison, G. W., Igel Lau, M., Rutström, E. E., & Sullivan, M. B. (2005). Eliciting risk and time preferences using field experiments: Some methodological issues. In *Field experiments in economics* (pp. 125–218). Greenwich, CT: Emerald Group Publishing Limited.
Hillebrandt, H., Sebastian, C., & Blakemore, S. J. (2011). Experimentally induced social inclusion influences behavior on trust games. *Cognitive Neuroscience, 2*(1), 27–33.
Hofstede, G. (2009). Dimensionalizing cultures: The hofstede model in context. Online readings in pychology and culture (Unit 17, Chapter 14). ©International Association for Cross-Cultural Psychology.
Hooghe, M., Marien, S., & de Vroome, T. (2012). The cognitive basis of trust. The relation between education, cognitive ability, and generalized and political trust. *Intelligence, 40*(6), 604–613.
Johansson-Stenman, O. L. O. F., Mahmud, M., & Martinsson, P. (2009). Trust and religion: Experimental evidence from rural Bangladesh. *Economica, 76*(303), 462–485.
Kachelmeier, S. J., & Shehata, M. (1992). Examining risk preferences under high monetary incentives: Experimental evidence from the People's Republic of China. *The American Economic Review, 82*, 1120–1141.
Kahsay, G. A., & Osberghaus, D. (2018). Storm damage and risk preferences: Panel evidence from Germany. *Environmental and Resource Economics, 71*(1), 301–318.
Kurosaki, T. (2001). Consumption smoothing and the structure of risk and time preferences: Theory and evidence from village India. *Hitotsubashi Journal of Economics, 42*, 103–117.
McCabe, K. A., Rigdon, M. L., & Smith, V. L. (2003). Positive reciprocity and intentions in trust games. *Journal of Economic Behavior & Organization, 52*(2), 267–275.

Mehar, M., Yamano, T., & Panda, A. (2017). The role of gender, risk, and time preferences in Farmers' Rice variety selection in eastern India. *Asian Journal of Agriculture and Development, 14*(1), 17–36.
Meier, S., & Sprenger, C. D. (2015). Temporal stability of time preferences. *Review of Economics and Statistics, 97*(2), 273–286.
Miller, A. S. (2000). Going to hell in Asia: The relationship between risk and religion in a cross cultural setting. *Review of Religious Research, 42*, 5–18.
Miller, A. S., & Hoffmann, J. P. (1995). Risk and religion: An explanation of gender differences in religiosity. *Journal for the Scientific Study of Religion, 34*, 63–75.
Newell, R. G., & Siikamäki, J. (2015). Individual time preferences and energy efficiency. *American Economic Review, 105*(5), 196–200.
Pereira, P. T., Silva, N., & eSilva, J. A. (2006). Positive and negative reciprocity in the labor market. *Journal of Economic Behavior & Organization, 59*(3), 406–422.
Perez-Arce, F. (2017). The effect of education on time preferences. *Economics of Education Review, 56*, 52–64.
Poulos, C., & Whittington, D. (2000). Time preferences for life-saving programs: Evidence from six less developed countries. *Environmental Science and Technology, 34*, 14.
Rieger, M. O., Wang, M., & Hens, T. (2014). Risk preferences around the world. *Management Science, 61*(3), 637–648.
Rubinstein, A. (1985). Choice of conjectures in a bargaining game with incomplete information. In *Game-theoretic models of bargaining* (pp. 99–114). Cambridge: Cambridge University Press.
Sawada, Y., & Kuroishi, Y. (2015). How does a natural disaster affect people's preference? The case of a large scale flood in the Philippines using the convex time budget experiments. In *Disaster risks, social preferences, and policy effects: Field experiments in selected ASEAN and East Asian Coutries* (pp.57–84).
Schwarze, J., & Winkelmann, R. (2005). What can happiness research tell us about altruism? Evidence from the German Socio-Economic Panel.
Simon, H. A. (1993). Altruism and economics. *The American Economic Review, 83*(2), 156–161.
Tanaka, T., Camerer, C. F., & Nguyen, Q. (2010). Risk and time preferences: Linking experimental and household survey data from Vietnam. *American Economic Review, 100*(1), 557–571.
Thaler, R. H. (2017). Behavioral economics. *Journal of Political Economy, 125*(6), 1799–1805.
Wang, C. X., Webster, S., & Zhang, S. (2012). Newsvendor models with alternative risk preferences within expected utility theory and prospect theory frameworks. In *Handbook of newsvendor problems* (pp. 177–196). New York, NY: Springer.
Wang, M., Rieger, M. O., & Hens, T. (2016). How time preferences differ: Evidence from 53 countries. *Journal of Economic Psychology, 52*, 115–135.
Weber, E. U., Blais, A. R., & Betz, N. E. (2002). A domain-specific risk-attitude scale: Measuring risk perceptions and risk behaviors. *Journal of Behavioral Decision Making, 15*(4), 263–290.
Wen, F., He, Z., Gong, X., & Liu, A. (2014). Investors' risk preference characteristics based on different reference point. *Discrete dynamics in nature and society, 2014*, 1–9.
Yamagishi, T., Horita, Y., Mifune, N., Hashimoto, H., Li, Y., Shinada, M., et al. (2012). Rejection of unfair offers in the ultimatum game is no evidence of strong reciprocity. *Proceedings of the National Academy of Sciences, 109*(50), 20364–20368.
Yesuf, M., & Bluffstone, R. (2008). *Wealth and time preference in rural Ethiopia* (No. dp-08-16-efd).
Zamagni, S. (1995). *The economics of altruism*. Cheltenham: Edward Elgar Publishing.
Zizzo, D. J. (2011). Do dictator games measure altruism? In L. Bruni & S. Zamagni (Eds.), *Handbook on the economics of philanthropy, reciprocity and social enterprise*. Cheltenham: Edward Elgar.
Zyphur, M. J., Narayanan, J., Arvey, R. D., & Alexander, G. J. (2009). The genetics of economic risk preferences. *Journal of Behavioral Decision Making, 22*(4), 367–377.

Chapter 7
Inflation Targeting and Exchange Rate Pass-Through in India: An Empirical Investigation

Arshid Hussain Peer and Mirza Allim Baig

7.1 Introduction

One of the economic phenomena that affects every citizen, almost every day, is inflation (Reddy 1999). Monetary policy is considered to be an essential policy response for the control of inflation. One of the key elements of the Washington Consensus is that low and stable inflation is critical for market-driven growth and monetary policy is the most direct determinant of inflation (Bernanke et al. 1999). Monetary policy being the most flexible tool for achieving stabilization in the short run, has led central banks around the world to strive for developing strategies to control inflation and contribute to the stability and growth of the respective economies. Inflation targeting is one of those strategies which New Zealand pioneered, followed by Canada, the United Kingdom, and others. Currently, 41 countries (both developing and developed countries) following different exchange rate regimes have adopted the inflation targeting framework. The list of countries following inflation targeting regimes are presented in Appendix, Table 7.1).

Inflation targeting is defined loosely as a monetary policy strategy characterized by public announcement of quantitative targets of inflation rate for a particular period, and by the explicit acknowledgment that price stability is the primary goal of monetary policy in the long run. The other features of the monetary policy framework are an instrument and operational independence, transparency in policymaking, and accountability of the monetary authority. These features are the critical components of the inflation targeting framework (Kamber et al. 2015; Walsh 2015). According to Bernanke et al. (1999), the inflation targeting framework serves two essential functions in an economy, i.e., (1) improving communication between policymakers and the public, and (2) the accountability and discipline in monetary

A. H. Peer · M. A. Baig (✉)
Department of Economics, Jamia Millia Islamia (Central University), New Delhi, India
e-mail: mabaig@jmi.ac.in

A. K. Mishra et al. (eds.), *Critical Perspectives on Emerging Economies*,
Contributions to Economics, https://doi.org/10.1007/978-3-030-59781-8_7

policymaking. These functions help in reducing uncertainty, and thereby reducing volatility in the economy.

In the emerging markets, the exchange rate was at the heart of the macroeconomic debate for decades as it was either used to bring inflation down or tax the export sector (Edwards 2006). Historically, the appropriateness of exchange rate regime particularly for the emerging economies are always being debated and discussed. However, inflation targeting is being adopted irrespective of exchange rate regimes. After the Asian and Russian financial crises, several countries adopted the combination of the flexible exchange rate and inflation targeting. Though this move made exchange rate less central in policy debates of most emerging markets, however, with the adoption of inflation targeting, several relevant exchange rate-related questions, many of them being new, brought exchange rate back into policy debates implying no sign of cooling down of the relationship between the exchange rate and monetary policy.

Eichengreen (2002) argues that inflation targeting in open and emerging economies is complicated than the closed economy as the additional channel of the exchange rate is activated. The exchange rate channel makes emerging economies open and vulnerable to foreign shocks. The shock can be in the commodity market or financial market. This change in the exchange rate implies the monetary policy as an external factor impact the domestic goal of price stability. Further, Blanchard (2004) argues that in an open economy, an increase in interest rate will make the domestic debt more attractive and hence, appreciation of the currency. However, if the probability of debt is high (due to adverse fiscal conditions), the depreciation of currency takes place increasing the initial level of debt. Similarly, Taylor (2000) found a positive relationship between the level of inflation and exchange rate pass-through.

In the case of inflation targeting, the monetary authority commits to control inflation at a low and stable level. In other words, when a country adopts inflation targeting as a monetary policy rule then the exchange rate pass-through should decline. The exchange rate pass-through to domestic prices can be defined as two-stage process. In the first stage, there is change in import prices due to unit change in exchange rate; and in second stage, there is change in consumer prices due to change in import prices. In an open economy, the exchange rate pass-through relates the inflation and exchange rate. It is of particular importance to monetary policymakers as the size and speed of transmission of the exchange rate pass-through are important for proper forecasting of inflation, management, and assessment of monetary policy.

During the period 2006–2013, the Indian economy experienced a very high inflationary pressure. The average inflation during the period remained higher than 9% (Ghate and Kletzer 2016). The RBI and central government tried various measures to control the inflation, and finally, in 2013, a committee was constituted for review and strengthening of the monetary policy. The committee emphasized on price stability as the principal objective of monetary policy. The price is to be controlled within the range of 4%, with a standard deviation of 2% in the medium term. The central government, in consultation with RBI, will determine the "target" in terms of consumer price index (CPI) once in 5 years.

India is one of the emerging economies which has adopted inflation targeting in 2015. In Indian context, it is essential to understand the dynamics of exchange rate pass-through, as the RBI has the commitment of price stability under the inflation targeting regime. The magnitude of pass-through enlightens the policymakers about the influence of external factors on domestic inflation, which is the policy objective. The analysis of pass-through on the newly available CPI-combined provides the country-specific shreds of evidence under changing monetary policy regime and subsequent low-inflation environment, which is entirely different from the pre-IT bouts of food and fuel inflation. Further, India also provides the near laboratory conditions to understand the relationship between exchange rate pass-through and inflation targeting for other open and emerging economies.

The main objective of this chapter is to examine empirically the impact of exchange rate pass-through on consumer prices in India. The rest of the chapter is organized as follows. The literature review is presented in Sect. 7.2. The Sect. 7.3 deals with methodology of the study. The empirical result is discussed in Sect. 7.4. Finally, the Sect. 7.5 presents the conclusion of the study.

7.2 Literature Review

Researchers in the field of economics have traditionally made many simplifying assumptions concerning inflation and exchange rate. According to the Law of One Price (LOOP), the price of a tradeable good should be the same in every country when expressed in the same currency unit. The purchasing power parity (PPP) theory was developed on the back of the LOOP. The PPP provides an explanation of the equalization of general price level in different countries when expressed in the same currency. The empirical literature has found little support for the complete pass-through of costs, or in other words, PPP does not hold in general. Many studies on the modeling of exchange rate determination starts with the assumption that PPP does not hold perfectly (e.g., Baig et al. 2003).

There are many explanations that have been put forward for the incomplete pass-through of exchange rate fluctuation to domestic prices. Krugman (1987) and Dornbusch (1987) put forward the microeconomic aspects of imperfect competition and pricing to market as reasons for incomplete pass-through. Under new open-economy macroeconomic models, the pass-through is expounded through local currency pricing and producer currency pricing models. The former maintains that foreign exporters price the good in terms of the domestic market, thus resulting in zero pass-through. In the latter case, the pricing of the product is done in the currency of the country of origin, thereby giving rise to pass-through and hence, a divergence of prices, which are more than transportation costs.

Taylor (2000) related the exchange rate pass-through with the level of inflation. The pass-through was found to be low in countries having a credible monetary policy. McCarthy (2007) uses the VAR model with quarterly data from 1976Q1-1994Q4 to estimate the pass-through effect of the exchange rate and import prices to domestic inflation for nine industrialized countries. The impact of external factors was found to be modest, implying central banks have been successful in managing inflationary expectations. This indirectly highlights the role that domestic policies have in stabilizing and controlling inflation in the integrated world. Ca' Zorzi et al. (2007) examined the exchange rate pass-through in 12 emerging economies using the VAR method and found the evidence in favor of the Taylor hypothesis when the two outliers Turkey and Argentina are excluded. The study found high pass-through in the United Kingdom and the USA challenging the conventional wisdom that pass-through is high in emerging countries than developed countries. The study also found an insignificant relation between pass-through and openness of the economy.

On the relationship between inflation targeting and exchange rate, there is no clear answer to the question of whether the former has any impact on the later or not. Eichengreen (2002) highlighted the complicated nature of inflation targeting in open and emerging economies. The exposure to external shocks makes the control and forecasting of inflation difficult. Further, most of these economies have liabilities in foreign currencies, which makes the monetary authorities to intervene in foreign exchange management, thereby sacrificing the flexibility which inflation targeting framework provides to stabilize the economy in the short run. The credibility of central banks of emerging economies are below par when compared with the advanced economies. To gain credibility for monetary policy, these central banks will be forced to adopt a strict version of inflation targeting when flexible target perhaps may be the most valuable option for them. In the same vein, Olivier Blanchard (2004) argues that fiscal policy is an excellent tool to control inflation in a country having a high level of initial debt and a high proportion of foreign debt or if the probability to default on the debt is high. The author first develops a model containing interaction between exchange rate, interest rate, and the likelihood of default on debt. The data from the Brazilian economy is used to test the claim. The policy followed by Brazil during the 2002 crisis to control inflation is found in line with the predictions of the model.

Gagnon and Ihrig (2004) developed a theoretical model which hypothesize that credible monetary policy leads to low exchange rate pass-through. The model is then put to the test on quarterly data of 20 industrialized countries for the period 1971–2003. The authors split the country-specific sample from the date of adoption of official inflation targets or inflation targeting. Though the estimated rate of pass-through varied from country to country, it declined in the second period. The long-run pass-through was found to be around 0.23 for the full sample period. The pass-through for the first period was found to be higher than the second period. The decline was found significant in countries where authorities adopted inflation targets. The authors also regressed the pass-through on mean and standard deviation of inflation individually, and again the pass-through was found lower in the second period. The coefficient of inflation suggested that one-third of the decline in pass-through is due to a low-inflation environment in the second period as a result of credible monetary policy. The import share of GDP was found insignificant in the exchange rate pass-through model. The study attributed that the change in monetary policy objective to price stability is the primary determinant factor in explaining the decline of pass-through to domestic prices.

Edwards (2006) explores the relationship between inflation targeting and exchange rate using the least square method on quarterly data from 1985 to 2005. The study considers a mixed bag of the seven economies, where two are advanced and five are emerging economies. The results obtained by the study point that the exchange rate pass-through has declined in post-inflation targeting period. The decline has been more in the case of non-tradable goods prices than tradable goods prices. Regarding the exchange rate volatility, the study found no evidence of its rise under inflation targeting regime. On the question of the exchange rate as the variable in the model, it was found that countries that had a history of high inflation have put actual weight on exchange rate during the inflation targeting period.

Similarly, Daboussi and Thameur (2014) conducted the cross-country comparative study of the exchange rate pass-through in six emerging inflation targeting economies and found a decline in the pass-through after the adoption of inflation targeting. Taguchi and Bolortuya (2019) provide empirical evidence for the loss of exchange rate pass-through in Mongolia in the inflation targeting regime. The authors argue that the forward-looking nature of the targeting framework results in the anchoring of expectations. The anchoring of expectations occurs in less focus of domestic agents on exchange rate movements and a resultant loss of pass-through.

In the Indian context, there are few studies available in the literature on exchange rate pass-through. The brief reviews of selected studies are presented here. Ghosh and Rajan (2007) explored the relation of CPI and exchange rate in India using bivariate error correction mechanisms, assuming home demand conditions and foreign prices exogenous to the system. They found that a 100% change in exchange leads to around 40–50% change in CPI. Using the split sample technique, they did not find any significant change in the exchange rate pass-through between pre- and post-reform periods. Khundrakpam (2007) estimated the exchange rate pass-through into the wholesale price index (WPI) in India using monthly data for the period 1991:08–2005:03. The study found that the degree of pass-through in India is low. A 10% change in the exchange rate increases final prices by 0.6–0.9% only. By incorporating dummies, the study found the pass-through coefficients are higher during appreciation of exchange rate than depreciation of the exchange rate. Finally, the rolling regression technique revealed no declining trend of exchange rate pass-through. An increase in import penetration, lowering import tariff associated with liberalization, and increased inflation persistence are conjectured as plausible reasons for non-declining exchange rate pass-through in India. The study drew the monetary policy lesson that the more excellent monitoring of the impact of the exchange rate may be assumed to lowering the pass-through which entails underrating future inflation.

Bhattacharya et al. (2008) examined the relationship between inflation and the exchange rate in India by estimating the impact of a change in the nominal exchange rate on both WPI and CPI using monthly data for the period 1997–2007. The study used the frameworks of VAR and VECM with variables of CPI, WPI, nominal exchange rate, world commodity prices, and crude oil prices. The study found a moderate exchange rate pass-through in India. In the long run, the elasticity for CPI varies between 3.1 and 17% and that of WPI is 28.6%. The world food prices and crude oil prices also show a moderate level of impact on Inflation in India. The crude oil shows an insignificant effect on CPI, which may be supported by the fact that fuel prices in India were administrated.

Mendali and Das (2017) examined the exchange rate pass-through to wholesale price index using five-variable VAR model for the period April 1992–November 2013. The results from the study revealed the insignificant impact of exchange movements on WPI. The authors attribute the oil prices and persistence of inflation as the primary determinants of inflation. The WPI is found to be explaining 70–90% variation in inflation while oil prices and exchange rate are explaining the same, respectively, around 9–15% and 5.7% over 1 month. Patra et al. (2018) conducted a study on exchange rate pass-through from April-2005 to March 2016 using the VAR framework. The study found time-varying and nonlinear pass-through of the exchange rate to domestic prices. The exchange rate pass-through effects are also found asymmetric with the strongest pass-through when there is a small depreciation. This has consequences for monetary policy in terms of policy effectiveness and transmission mechanism. The study found a significant decline in exchange rate pass-through during post-2014. The study reveals that before 2013–2014, pass-through is found to be around 15% over 5 years, which is declining continuously since then.

The brief literature survey, both in the international and Indian context revealed the broad scenario of exchange rate pass-through on prices. The different methods and methodologies are adopted to study the relationship between exchange rate pass-through and prices during pre-inflation targeting regime and inflation targeting regime. A number of researchers found that after the adoption of inflation targeting as a goal of monetary policy exchange rate pass-through declines (e.g., Gagnon and Ihrig 2004, Edwards 2006, Lamia and Djelassi 2017, and, López-Villavicencio and Pourroy 2019). In nutshell, we can say that there is exchange rate pass-through to the prices, albeit, the degree of the pass-through varies from one study to the other.

7.3 Data and Methodology

In an open-economy model, exchange rate not only influences the price but is also influenced by many domestic factors—price level being one of the important factors. The vector auto-regression (VAR) model is commonly used in the literature to understand the dynamics of monetary policy (e.g., Ramachandran and Baig 2004). The VAR is preferred over a single equation model due to its properties of being simple while at the same time helping to study the reinforcing mechanisms among different variables (Ito and Sato 2008). In the present study, we examine the exchange rate pass-through to the consumer prices using the monthly data on the Indian economy for the period January 2011–October 2019. The sample period is subdivided under two scenarios, pre-inflation targeting period (January 2011–October 2015) and post-inflation targeting period (November 2015–October 2019).

The study uses the variables, monthly trade-based NEER-36 for exchange rate, and combined-CPI for prices. It is to be noted that the trade-based NEER-36 may be considered as the better proxy for the studies on exchange rate pass-through. To understand the importance of the exchange rate on headline inflation, we use combined-CPI in the study. The combined-CPI provides the broader measure available for inflation at the consumer level, and it is also the measure that RBI targets under inflation targeting framework of the monetary policy. The Index of Industrial Production (IIP) is used as a proxy for output as the monthly GDP data is not available in India. The crude oil data is the monthly price of one-barrel oil in rupee terms. The oil price is indexed with the base year 2010–11. The interest rate used in the study is the weighted average of Call Money Rate (CMR) as such rate is a good indicator of monetary policy actions in the short run.

The study used VAR model for the empirical estimation. Mathematically, the VAR model can be expressed as:

$$Y_t = \mathrm{C} + \sum_{i=1}^{p} \phi_i Y_{t-1} + \epsilon_t \tag{7.1}$$

where Y_t represents the vector of endogenous variables, C is a vector of constants, ϕ_i denotes the matrices of auto-regressive coefficients, and ϵ_t is a vector of white noise processes. The model is used in the study is similar to McCarthy (2007), with the exception that we are only concerned with its impact on domestic inflation measured in terms of CPI.

7.4 Empirical Results

In order to examine the impact of exchange rate pass-through on consumer prices in India, we have estimated VAR model using monthly data for the period January 2011–October 2019. The sample period is further subdivided under two scenarios, pre-inflation targeting period (January 2011–October 2015) and post-inflation targeting period (November 2015–October 2019). It is to be noted that even though RBI signed the inflation targeting monetary policy framework agreement in February 2015, we use November 2015 as a starting point to account for monetary policy lag up to two quarters. We also decided the break point on the basis of empirical estimation of the model.

All the variables are seasonally adjusted before using in the estimation of the model. Since all the explanatory lag variables are predetermined, and there is no dependency among the explanatory variables within the system, thus there is no problem of simultaneity and identification; hence, we can estimate the system of equations by ordinary least square (OLS) method. The identification of the structural shock is achieved by appropriately ordering the variables of interest and applying a Cholesky decomposition to the variance-covariance matrix of the reduced form residuals ϵ_t.

As a first step, we check the condition of stationarity of all the variables using ADF and PP tests with constant and trend levels. The variables were found to be

Table 7.2 Results of variance decomposition of variables for the sub-period January 2011–October 2015

Period	S.E.	D_OIL	D_IIP	D_CMR	D_NEER	D_CPI
1	0.385917	2.901952	0.286940	1.163281	4.914239	90.73359
2	0.407631	10.19271	0.407698	9.699185	8.499161	71.20125
3	0.447049	10.20770	0.801001	11.05772	8.460011	69.47357
4	0.457923	9.934865	1.010146	15.13860	8.049852	65.86654
5	0.469585	9.786411	2.390428	15.07989	7.957262	64.78601
6	0.475502	9.358785	3.279356	16.53724	8.828301	61.99632
7	0.476700	9.314652	3.267933	16.95795	8.806839	61.65263
8	0.47707	9.455660	3.499376	16.75562	9.308048	60.98129
9	0.478822	9.439714	3.692826	16.69858	9.337522	60.83135
10	0.478928	9.443211	3.687559	16.79696	9.340250	60.73202

Source: Authors' estimation based on data from data base on Indian Economy, RBI

non-stationary at the level form but stationary at first difference. The co-integration test shows no-integration among the variables. This helps us to use standard VAR model for estimating the relation between exchange rate and domestic inflation.

We estimate the VAR model as specified in Eq. (7.1) with five variables on consumer inflation, index for industrial production, exchange rate, short-term interest rate, and oil prices. The optimum lag length in the model is decided on the basis Akaike Information Criteria (AIC). The impulse response and variance decomposition are used to assess the pass-through from exchange rate movements to consumer prices. The impulse response to exchange rate shock is computed over the time horizon of 10 months. The variance decomposition shows the percentage of forecast variance in domestic prices attributed to the exchange rate and hence providing an idea of its importance for domestic inflation. The important results are discussed below.

7.4.1 Variance Decomposition of Inflation

The results of variance decomposition for the sub-periods January 2011–October 2015 and November 2015–October 2019 are presented, respectively, in Tables 7.2 and 7.3. The result shows how vital the shocks of exchange rate have been to consumer prices. For consumer price, the one standard deviation exchange rate shocks show different impacts before- and after-inflation targeting. The exchange rate explains around 9.34% variation in domestic inflation during pre-inflation targeting period (Table 7.2), which declines to only 5.87% in inflation targeting period (Table 7.3) over 10 months. Also, the variations over the periods are very low during pre-inflation targeting period as compared to the inflation targeting period except period 1 to period 2 (See Tables 7.2 and 7.3).

The persistence of inflation explains around 68–81% under inflation targeting period (Table 7.3) whereas, before IT framework, it varies around 60–91%

Table 7.3 Results of variance decomposition of variables for the sub-period November 2015–Ocotber 2019

Period	S.E.	D_OIL	D_IIP	D_CMR	D_NEER	D_CPI
1	0.116262	1.961060	2.086048	13.39717	1.329862	81.22586
2	0.123838	2.540222	6.516856	16.12616	4.972049	69.84471
3	0.124535	2.518825	7.508328	15.84858	5.696300	68.42796
4	0.124606	2.518375	7.540746	15.81259	5.865038	68.26325
5	0.124614	2.519164	7.542734	15.81135	5.875781	68.25097
6	0.124614	2.519554	7.542636	15.81132	5.876655	68.24984
7	0.124614	2.519574	7.542640	15.81139	5.876652	68.24974
8	0.124614	2.519576	7.542650	15.81139	5.876650	68.24973
9	0.124614	2.519576	7.542651	15.81139	5.876651	68.24973
10	0.124614	2.519576	7.542651	15.81139	5.876651	68.24973

Source: Authors' estimation based on data from Data Base on Indian Economy, RBI

(Table 7.2) over 10 months. The monetary policy impact also remains almost same, which highlights the predictable monetary policy under inflation targeting period during the sub-period November 2015-Ocotber 2019 as compared to the multiple indicator approach being adopted during the sub-period January 2011–October 2015.

7.4.2 *Impulse Response of Inflation to Exchange Rate Shock*

The results of impulse response of inflation to exchange rate shock for the sub-periods January 2011–October 2015 and November 2015–October 2019 are presented, respectively, in Figs. 7.1 and 7.2. The result of impulse response function shows the muted impact of the exchange rate on CPI during inflation targeting regime (Fig. 7.2), while before inflation targeting regime, the exchange rate causes fluctuations in domestic inflation (Fig. 7.1). It seems, over the period, the response of inflation is broadly converging to zero for both the sub-sample periods under study. However, the main feature that needs special attention is that under inflation targeting regime, the impact of different shocks remains almost constant and, hence, predictable. This is important from the perspective of economic agents as it removes the uncertain implications of different shocks on domestic prices resulting in optimal decision-making.

7.5 Conclusion

The empirical investigation of the study to understand the impact of exchange rate pass-through on consumer prices before- and during-inflation targeting regimes is carried out using variance decomposition and impulse response functions under

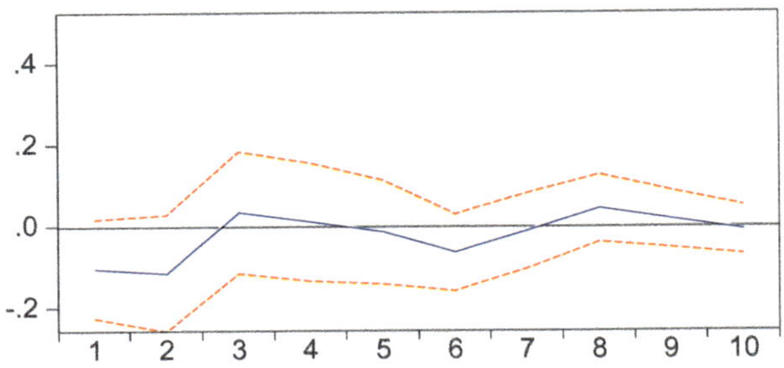

Fig. 7.1 Impulse response of CPI to NEER for the sub-period January 2011–October 2015. Source: Authors' estimation based on data from data base on Indian Economy, RBI. Note: The solid lines indicate the accumulated impulse response to shocks and the dotted lines indicate ±2 standard errors confidence bands around the estimates

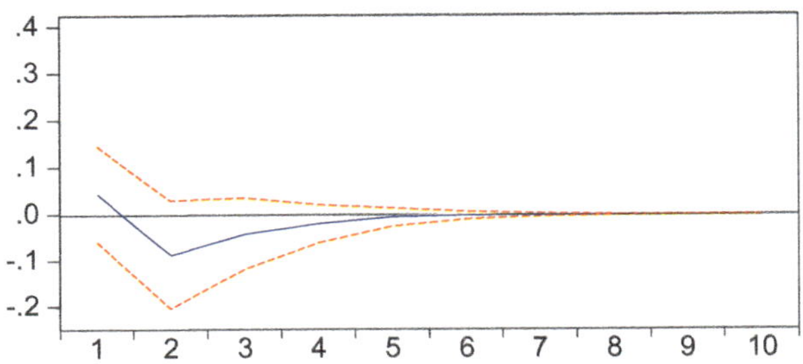

Fig. 7.2 Impulse response of CPI to NEER for the sub-period November 2015–Ocotber 2019. Source: Authors' estimation based on data from data base on Indian Economy, RBI. Note: The solid lines indicate the accumulated impulse response to shocks and the dotted lines indicate ±2 standard errors confidence bands around the estimates

VAR framework. The study finds that there is a significant decline of exchange rate pass-through under inflation targeting regime as compared to its previous regime, i.e., the multiple indicator approach regime. This finding is in line with the important study by Patra et al. (2018). The study also supports the Gagnon and Ihrig (2004) theory which maintains a decline in exchange rate pass-through under inflation targeting framework. The chapter suggests that the decline in exchange rate pass-through via imported inflation may be helpful for monetary policy to achieve the target of inflation in India.

Acknowledgments This is the part of PhD work of the first author carried out under the supervision of the second author in the Department of Economics, Jamia Millia Islamia, New Delhi.

The earlier version of this chapter was presented in the second International Conference on Economics and Finance (ICEF-2020), Organized jointly by D/o Economics, BITS Pilani & Trulaske College of Business, University of Missouri, USA BITS, at Pilani K K Birla Goa Campus, Goa during 23-25 January 2020. The authors duly acknowledge the suggestions given in the conference for the improvement of this chapter. However, the authors owe the responsibility of errors and omissions in the chapter, if any.

Appendix

Table 7.1 List of countries following inflation targeting regimes

Country	Exchange rate regime	Year	Target	Country	Exchange rate regime	Year	Target
Albania	Floating	2009	(3+/−1)	Thailand	Floating	2000	(0.5–3)
Armenia	Floating	2006	(4.5+/−1.5)	Turkey	Floating	2006	(5.5+/−2)
Brazil	Floating	1999	(4.5+/−2)	Uganda	Floating	2011	5
Colombia	Floating	1999	(2–4)	Ukraine	Floating	2016	(6+/−2)
Czech Republic	Floating	1997	(3+/−1)	Uruguay	Floating	2007	(3–7)
Georgia	Floating	2009	3	Australia	Free floating	1993	(2–3)
Ghana	Floating	2007	(8.5+/−2)	Canada	Free floating	1991	(2+/−1)
Hungary	Floating	2001	(3+/−1)	Chile	Free floating	1999	(3+/−1)
Iceland	Floating	2001	(2.5+/−1.5)	Japan	Free floating	2013	2
India	Floating	2015	(2–6)	Mexico	Free floating	2001	(3+/−1)
Israel	Floating	1997	(2+/−1)	Norway	Free floating	2001	(2.5+/−1)
Jamaica	Floating	2017	(4–6)	Poland	Free floating	1998	(2.5+/−1)
Kazakhstan	Floating	2015	4	Russia	Free floating	2015	4
Korea	Floating	2001	(3+/−10)	Sweden	Free floating	1993	2
Moldova	Floating	2013	(3.5–6.5)	United Kingdom	Free floating	1992	2
New Zealand	Floating	1990	(1–3)	Guatemala	Stabilized arrangement	2005	(5+/−1)
Paraguay	Floating	2011	4.5	Indonesia	Stabilized arrangement	2005	(5+/−1)
Peru	Floating	2002	(2+/−1)	Costa Rica	Crawl-like arrangement	2018	(2–4)
Philippines	Floating	2002	(4+/−1)	Dominican Republic	Crawl-like arrangement	2012	(3–5)
Romania	Floating	2005	(3+/−1)	Serbia	Crawl-like arrangement	2006	(4–8)
South Africa	Floating	2000	(3–6)				

Source: Authors' own compilation from annual report on exchange arrangements and exchange restrictions, IMF, 2018

References

Baig, M. A., Narasiman, V., & Ramachandran, M. (2003). Exchange market pressure and the Reserve Bank of India's intervention activity. *Journal of Policy Modeling, 25*, 727–748.

Bernanke, B. S., Laubach, T., Mishkin, F. S., & Posen, A. S. (1999). *Inflation targeting: Lessons from the international experience*. Princeton, NJ: Princeton University Press.

Bhattacharya, R., Patnaik, I., & Shah, A. (2008). *Exchange rate pass-through in India*. New Delhi: National Institute of Public Finance and Policy. Retrieved from: http://macrofinance.nipfp.org.in/PDF/BPS2008_erpt.pdf.

Blanchard, J. O. (2004). Fiscal dominance and inflation targeting: lessons from Brazil. In *National Bureau of Economic Research*, Working paper series (10389), Cambridge.

Ca' Zorzi, M., Hahn, E., & Sánchez, M. (2007). Exchange rate pass-through in emerging markets. In *The European Central Bank*, Working Paper (739), 2–33.

Daboussi, O. M., & Thameur, N. (2014). (2014). Inflation targeting and exchange rate pass-through: A comparative study in emerging markets. *International Journal of Innovation and Applied Studies, 9*(1), 317–324.

Dornbusch, R. (1987). Exchange rates and prices. *American Economic Review, 77*, 93–106.

Edwards, S. (2006). The relationship between exchange rates and inflation targeting revisited. In *National Bureau of Economic Research*, Working paper series (12163), Cambridge.

Eichengreen, B. (2002). Can emerging markets float? Should they inflation target? In *Central Bank of Brazil*, Working paper series (36), Brasilia.

Gagnon, J. E., & Ihrig, J. (2004). Monetary policy and exchange rate pass-through. *International Journal of Finance and Economics, 9*(4), 315–338.

Ghate, C., & Kletzer, M. K. (Eds.). (2016). *Monetary policy in India: A modern macroeconomic perspective*. New Delhi: Springer.

Ghosh, A., & Rajan, S. R. (2007). How high is exchange rate pass-through in India? Has it changed over time? *The Journal of International Trade & Economic Development, 16*(3), 373–382.

Ito, T., & Sato, K. (2008). Exchange rate changes and inflation in post?crisis Asian economies: Vector autoregression analysis of the exchange rate pass?through. *Journal of Money, Credit and Banking, 40*(7), 1407–1438.

Kamber, G., Karagedikli, I., & Smith, C. (2015). Applying an inflation-targeting lens to macroprudential policy 'institutions. *Journal of Central Banking, 11*(4), 395–429.

Khundrakpam, J. (2007). Economic reforms and exchange rate pass-through to domestic prices in India. In *Bank for International Settlements*, Working paper no. 225.

Krugman, P. (1987). Pricing to market when the exchange rate changes. In *National Bureau of Economic Research*, Working paper no. 1926.

Lamia, B., & Djelassi, M. (2017). The relationship between exchange rate and inflation targeting in emerging countries. *Asian Economic and Financial Review, 7*(11), 1028–1038.

López-Villavicencio, A., & Pourroy, M. (2019). Does inflation targeting always matter for the ERPT? A robust approach. *Journal of Macroeconomics, 60*, 360–377.

McCarthy, J. (2007). Pass-through of exchange rates and import prices to domestic inflation in some industrialized economies. *Eastern Economic Journal, 33*(4), 511–537.

Mendali, G., & Das, S. (2017). Exchange rate pass-through to domestic prices: The Indian experience. *Foreign Trade Review, 52*(3), 135–156.

Patra, Michael D., Khundrakpam, J., & John, J. (2018). Non-linear, asymmetric and time-varying exchange rate pass-through: Recent evidence from India. In *Reserve Bank of India*, Working paper (02/2018), Mumbai.

Ramachandran, M., & Baig, M. A. (2004). Exchange market pressure and monetary policy. In R. Correa & L. G. Burange (Eds.), *Reforms, Institutions and Policies: Challenges Confronting the Indian Economy* (pp. 299–312). Mumbai: Himalaya Publishing House.

Reddy, Y. V. (1999). Inflation in India: status and issues. Retrieved 27 September 2019, from https://rbidocs.rbi.org.in/rdocs/Speeches/PDFs/8431.pdf

Taguchi, H., & Bolortuya, J. (2019). Inflation targeting and the pass-through effect in Mongolia. *Business and Economic Research, 9*(2), 57.

Taylor, B. J. (2000). Low inflation, pass-through and the pricing power of firms. *European Economic Review, 44*(7), 1389–1408.

Walsh, C. (2015). Goals and rules in central bank design. In *CESifo*, Working paper series 5293. Munich: CESifo Group.

Chapter 8
Indoor Fuel Choice and Women Empowerment: A Demand-Side Analysis

Sabitri Dutta

8.1 Introduction

There is a close link between the gender and the type of fuel used inside the household. Usually, women are the main cook and suffer the maximum exposure arises due to the pollution content of the fuel used for cooking and heating. This exposure is a cause of various diseases like chronic obstructive pulmonary disease, acute lower respiratory track infection, bronchial asthma, tuberculosis, hypertension and heart diseases, cataract, etc. Literatures show strong to moderate evidences of these illnesses due to indoor air pollution. Women's health is disproportionately affected in comparison to men because of their higher exposure. In addition, collection of biomass fuel in poor households to meet the energy needs is burden of women and girls. Several hours are spent on this. It reduces the time available for women to participate in other livelihood strategies. Girls miss schools to assist their mothers.

The exposure mainly depends on the type of fuel used by the household. However, the ventilation of the cooking area, the location of the kitchen, the type of cooking hearth and the time spent by the victim in cooking activities also play an important role. The fuel choice of the household again is a function of the income, awareness, access and availability of the fuel. As fuel is a normal good, rise in income should bring a shift towards a cleaner fuel with less pollution content. In other words, household moves higher in the energy ladder. The chance of improved cooking stove with chimney to be chosen in place of traditional cooking stove (chulha) also increases with better affordability. Income to afford cleaner fuel is necessary to get rid of energy poverty. However, it is not enough. The decision on the choice of fuel depends more on awareness than on affordability. The awareness of the head of the household matters as he is generally the main decision taker on the

S. Dutta (✉)
DumDum Motijheel Rabindra Mahavidyalaya, Kolkata, India

A. K. Mishra et al. (eds.), *Critical Perspectives on Emerging Economies*, Contributions to Economics, https://doi.org/10.1007/978-3-030-59781-8_8

purchase of household needs. The intra-household power relation also matters when the household head decides about the fuel. This decision can be influenced by the other members as well. This again depends on the awareness of those members. If the woman who cooks and hence gets most exposure is sufficiently aware and has the empowerment to influence the decision regarding fuel choice, then choice can be efficient enough to reduce the exposure of the cook.

This chapter attempts to measure the empowerment of the woman and its impact on the cooking arrangement in the households of rural India. It is general belief that indoor air pollution is an outcome of poverty and therefore solution is sought generally in the subsidized supply of cleaner fuel, improved cook stoves, etc. It is true that these have important role to play in reducing the indoor air pollution. But use of cleaner fuel is sometimes restricted due to lack of awareness on the part of the user as well as of the main decision taker in the family. Even if, the awareness is there, it happens that women, the primary user of fuel in the household is not empowered enough to take the decision driving towards purchase of cleaner fuel. This chapter has a policy implication that it finds the importance of women empowerment in choosing the fuel and in turn, can perhaps explain the limited use of the cleaner fuels even after subsidized supply of the same. Policies that enhance the awareness of the women and the thereby empower them to have better voice in choosing the fuel, cooking mode, kitchen structure may put an end to the menace in the longer run.

8.2 Literature Review

There are literatures that show evidences that intra-household relationship matters in case of fuel choice. Fuel is needed for performing household chores like cooking, heating, lighting, etc. Much of this use is done by the women. Sustainable energy development puts increasing prominence on the gender issues over last few decades (Cecelski 2003). The relation between energy and poverty has a gender dimension. Within households, the division of labour is gender based. The household responsibilities are borne by the women who are the main collectors, producers and users of household energy. Reddy and Nathan (2012) pointed out that reduced drudgery for women and increased access to cleaner fuels for household use have dramatic impacts on women's health and education. Women's limited access to the decision-making process limits their ability to influence the resource allocation on many issues including energy (Clancy et al. 2003). Women have different energy needs than men due to their different roles and responsibilities, but policies seldom offer due consideration to their needs and concern (Human Development Report, UNDP 2011). The effectiveness of energy policies in promoting gender empowerment is discussed in Skutch (2005). She argues for increasing the political and decision-making power for women. Access to range of energy services can enhance the growth and sustainability of the women and create environment for empowerment (Groot et al. 2017). Muchiri (2008) emphasizes that investment in the energy should target increased access to energy and reduced drudgery for women who are the main users of firewood for cooking and lighting. The study found that in response to fuel scarcity in some parts of rural Kenya women use potentially toxic options like cow dung, agricultural wastes, old plastic containers, which are injurious to their health and could accentuate respiratory illnesses due to persistent exposure to smoke. It has been noted by Reddy (2000) that use of energy is linked with the position of women in the household. Wealthier households enjoy higher choices in their energy carrier and use cleaner and more efficient fuel including kerosene, LPG and electricity. ESMAP report (2004) indicated that a large portion of women's time in rural India is spent on collecting fuel for cooking and heating. It also concluded that rural women in India benefit substantially from improved energy services.

8.3 Objective of the Study

8.3.1 The main objective of the study is to measure the empowerment of the woman by constructing a Woman Empowerment Index (WEI).

8.3.2 To analyse the contribution of women empowerment in the household fuel choice.

8.4 Data Description and Methodology

8.4.1 Data Description

The study uses India Human Development Survey-II data (IHDS-II) (Desai et al. 2011). The survey was conducted through the time period 2011–2012. It is a multitopic survey carried out at the national level. It covers all states and union territories of India except Andaman/Nicobar and Lakshadweep. It represents 42, 152 households from 1, 503 villages and 971 urban neighbourhoods across India. It covers topic like health, education, employment, economic status, marriage, fertility, gender relations and social capital. The Primary Sampling Units (PSU) are the districts and urban blocks. The number of urban blocks is determined from the list of urban areas in a state following probability proportional to size sampling methodology. The blocks are selected for enumeration with the help of Registrar General of India. For selecting rural households, the methodology of the survey titled Human Development Profile of India (HDPI) conducted by NCAER in 1993–1994 is followed. About half of the households selected in IHDS-II were interviewed initially by NCAER in 1993–1994. Other half of the samples were drawn from the districts surveyed in HDPI as well as those which were not covered by HDPI.

Table 8.1 Education attainment by woman and spouse

Education level	Woman (%)	Spouse (%)
No education	49.33	25.22
Up to primary level	7.90	9.46
Up to secondary level	35.36	44.12
Up to higher secondary level	4.60	7.90
More than higher secondary	2.81	13.30
Total	100	100

Source: Author's calculation

The present study uses the data for rural women of India. The study is carried out on 25, 663 individuals. Among them, 20.51% are poor as per Tendulkar's poverty line definition, 2012. Using weights provided in IHDS data the percentage of poor among the entire population is 21.83%. Mean age of the sampled women is around 36 years with a minimum age 15 and maximum age 78 years. Population mean comes to be the same. 89.59% women are of the age group 15–49 which is considered as the reproductive age group. All women studied here are married. Among the population of married women, around 85% are currently married, spouse of 8.5% are absent, 5.6% are widowed and near about 1% are separated or divorced. Median monthly income per capita for the population is INR 12147. The income distribution is highly skewed with a skewness measure 32.4. The education of women as well as spouse's education are divided into five groups. Those having zero years of education are termed as having no education, those with 1–4 years of education are considered to be having up to primary level education, up to secondary level with 5–10 years of education, up to higher secondary level with 11–12 years of education and those with more than 12 completed years of education are taken as educated above higher secondary level. 49.33% of rural women have no education or less than 1 year of education and 35.36% have more than primary and up to secondary level education. Most spouses have the education level of more than primary level and up to secondary level. Around 25.22% spouses have no education and 13% have education more than higher secondary level. These are projected population figures obtained using the sample weights. The detailed picture of educational attainment is shown in Table 8.1.

29% of the population of rural women in the age group 15 to 78 use clean fuel which constitute kerosene and liquid petroleum gas (LPG). 71.08% use fuels with high pollution content like firewood, dung cake, crop residue and coal. These fuels are termed as dirty fuels in this study. 54% of women belong to households that use traditional chulha without chimney, 21.4% cook in open fire (three stone) chulha. Only 8.49% use improved chulha and 15.92% cook with stoves other than those mentioned. 51.23% reside in houses that do not have separate kitchen out of which in 26.14% and 25% stay in houses where cooking is done in living areas and outdoors, respectively. 52.47% of rural women cook without any ventilation in the cooking area. Average number of meals cooked is 3. Stoves or chulhas burn for 3 h a day on average for cooking, heating, making tea, etc. More than 83% women have access to the electricity in their home. As large as 68.77% women collect firewood, 83.19%

collect dung cake, 93% collect crop residue, either from their own land or from village or other places and around 12% collect coal. For those who use LPG, the mean expenditure on it in the preceding month of survey was INR 307. On average people spend INR 58 for kerosene, INR 184 for crop residue, INR 193 for dung cake, INR 334 for firewood, INR 343 for coal and INR 312 for LPG. The figures suggest that there are households who use multiple fuel for domestic use instead of using a single type. So, a portfolio of fuels is maintained by the rural households in the country.

8.4.2 Methodology

The objective of this work is to find the influence of women empowerment on the use of fuel in the household after controlling for related factors. It starts with some descriptive study and cross tabulation of the variables included in order to understand the possibility of any causal relationship. The study attempts to quantify women's empowerment by constructing a Women Empowerment Index (WEI) and uses that as one of the determinants of fuel choice in the household. Women empowerment is known to be a multidimensional study. Empowerment, by definition, cannot be directly measured as it is not observed. So, it can be treated as a latent unobservable variable. The empowerment can be expressed in terms of indicators which represent the decision-taking power of woman about the household matters, freedom that she enjoys, representation she makes in different associations, her possessions and decision regarding her employment. These factors are interdependent and interact with each other building up a sense within the person that enhances confidence and hence empowers her. Empowerment signifies freedom of choice and hence action that leads to enhanced ability to influence their course of life and decisions that affect them. The interdependence of the underlying latent dimensions defines empowerment. The achievements in each dimension can be measured at the individual level. The achievements reflect the performance in the associated dimension. The indicators used here for each dimension are available in the dataset and are described in the following paragraph. They may be qualitative or quantitative in nature. The model used here for the construction of WEI and the subsequent analysis of causal relation between the expenditure on clean fuel and WEI is the structural equation analysis (path analysis). The analysis consists of two models—(1) measurement model (2) structural model. Maximum likelihood estimation is used here, and the missing data is addressed by the model. The indicators/variables used for the construction of WEI are as follows:

(a) *Women's freedom to take decisions in financial matters (WEIF):* Women can enjoy freedom in taking decisions unconditionally in the financial matters in the households. Five sub-indicators are considered here. They are—whether the woman decides about purchasing expensive items (yes/no), whether she decides about buying land/property (yes/no), whether she decides about wedding expenses (yes/no), whether she does food shopping (yes/no), and whether she possess cash in hand for household expenditure (yes/no). In each case, 1 is assigned if the response is "yes" and 0 for a "no". WEIF is constructed by summing up the values for these five indicators, and hence WEIF has a range of values from 0 to 5.

(b) *Women's freedom to go outside home (WEIO):* Going outside alone is an indicator of enjoying freedom and hence empowerment. It consists of three sub-indicators. They are—whether the woman can visit health centre alone (yes/no), whether she can visit relative/friend's house alone (yes/no), and whether she can go short distance by train/bus alone (yes/no). WEIO is the sum of these three and hence can vary between 0 and 3.

(c) *Women's participation in associations as members (WEIM):* Being a member of different groups or associations enhance the information and knowledge base of the woman and empowers her by enhancing the self-confidence. Here membership of four such associations is considered, namely Mahila Mandal, self-help group, credit/saving society and political organization. All are dichotomous (yes/no) in nature. WEIM is the sum of all these four types of membership and takes value between 0 and 4.

(d) *Women's possession (WEIP):* The physical asset of the women raises her status within the household and empowers her. Two indicators are considered—whether she has her name in the bank account and whether her name is there on the home ownership or rental paper. Both are binary variables. WEIP is the sum of these two and have three possible values 0, 1 and 2.

(e) *Women's participation in work (WEIW):* Participation in work or freedom to take decision regarding the participation makes the woman confident. This is taken to be one of the most important indicators of empowerment. Three possible indicators have been chosen here, namely whether the woman is currently working for pay or wages, whether she has the most say about work and whether she is allowed to work if suitable job is found. WEIW can take values between 0 and 3.

The measurement model uses above-mentioned five variables for the construction of WEI which has a latent structure. Another latent variable about arrangement of cooking in the household is constructed on the basis of the three observed exogenous variables. They are as follows:

1. *Separate kitchen (SK):* This is a binary variable with 1 assigned for the household (where the individual woman belongs to) has a separate kitchen. 0 is given if there is no separate kitchen.
2. *Ventilation in the cooking area (V):* This is again dichotomous by nature. Presence of ventilation gets value 1, 0 otherwise.
3. *Chulha type (CH):* Improved chulha with chimney and chulhas that are suitable for LPG, kerosene, etc. combinedly form clean chulha and is put a value 1. All other kind including traditional chulha gets a value 0.

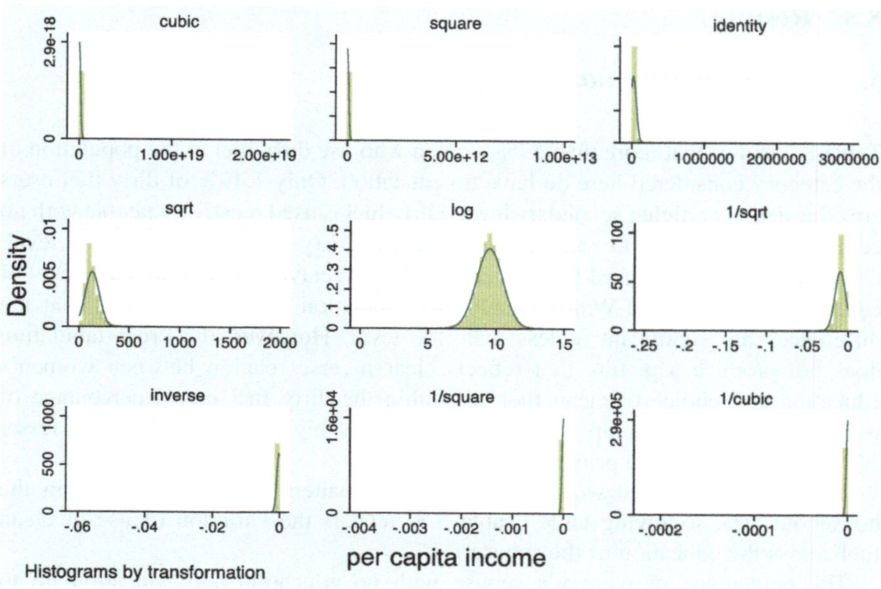

Fig. 8.1 Possible transformations (GLADDER): variable—per capita income

These three variables constitute the variable 'cooking' and weights are determined by the measurement model. The interdependence between the latent variables, i.e. WEI and 'cooking' is also taken care of by the model.

The structural model depicts the causal relation between the choice of fuel in the household and the WEI. The dependent variable is expenditure on the clean fuel spent by the household (EXCF) and hence continuous in this case. The expenditure is measured by taking a sum of the money spent on two clean fuels, kerosene and LPG, in the last 30 days preceding the survey by the household to which the woman belongs. The sum is expressed in terms of Indian Rupee (INR). The other determinants of fuel choice the study uses, apart from WEI, are the per capita income of the individual (LNPCI, taken in logarithmic form), years of education completed by the woman member (EW) and also by her spouse (ES), the number of meals cooked per day (MC) and the number of hours the stove/chulha burns per day (SB). The variables are denoted by the terms mentioned in the parentheses. Per capita income is measured in log scale as the distribution of income has a high positive skewness. This is addressed by doing a log transformation of the original variable. The log transformation is the most suitable transformation as shown by the GLADDER technique. Nine possible transformations have been shown in Fig. 8.1 where the log transformation looks closest to the normal distribution.

The above figure shows that per capita income transforms towards normal distribution when a log transformation is carried out. The variable in its original form (identity) does not follow normal distribution as seen from the diagram.

8.5 Results

8.5.1 Descriptive Analysis

Table 8.2 shows that more than 57% women who use dirty fuel in the population of the category considered here do have no education. Only 1.49% of dirty fuel users are educated over higher secondary level. Dirty fuel is used mostly by people with no education and those who received more than primary and up to secondary level. Clean fuels are mostly used by women who have received up to secondary level of education. The Kruskal-Wallis equality-of-population rank test suggests that the differences are significant at less than 1% level. However, the cross tabulation does not produce a picture that reflects clear inverse relation between women's education and choice of clean fuel, as within the dirty fuel user's percentage of women with education up to secondary level is higher than those with lesser education, namely up to primary level.

The education of the woman's spouse also matters in the fuel choice in the household. The following table (Table 8.3) reveals the variation of use of clean fuel across the education of the spouse.

The percentage of women's spouse with no education and education up to primary level are higher for dirty fuel users than the clean fuel users. The reverse happens for those with education up to secondary and higher secondary and above level. The differences are statistically significant. However, in both fuel types, the highest portion is constituted by spouse with education up to secondary level. This is

Table 8.2 Use of clean fuel across the education of woman (%)

	Use of clean fuel (%)		
Education of woman	No	Yes	Total
No education	57.03	30.41	49.33
Up to primary level	8.29	6.96	7.90
Up to secondary level	30.47	47.38	35.36
Up to higher secondary level	2.73	9.20	4.60
More than higher secondary	1.49	6.04	2.81
Total	100	100	100

Source: Author's calculation

Table 8.3 Use of clean fuel across the education of woman's spouse (%)

	Use of clean fuel (%)		
Education of woman	No	Yes	Total
No education	29.78	14.01	25.22
Up to primary level	10.50	6.88	9.46
Up to secondary level	42.47	48.21	44.12
Up to higher secondary level	6.08	12.37	7.90
More than higher secondary	11.17	18.53	13.30
Total	100	100	100

Source: Author's calculation

Table 8.4 Use of clean fuel and poverty

Expenditure/capita < Tendulkar's Poverty line				
		Use of clean fuel		
		No	Yes	Total
Nonpoor	Row (%)	66.44	33.56	100
	Column (%)	73.05	90.75	78.17
Poor	Row (%)	87.75	12.25	100
	Column (%)	26.95	9.25	21.83
Total	Row (%)	71.09	28.91	100
	Column (%)	100	100	100

Source: Author's calculation

followed by spouse with no education for dirty fuels and with above higher secondary education for the clean fuels. However, within a group of fuel users no distinct pattern is found across spouse's education group. These call for a regression model to be run.

In Table 8.4, the use of clean fuel across poor and nonpoor group (as per Tendulkar's poverty line income, 2012) is shown. Among those who are nonpoor 33.56% use clean fuel. 87.75% of the poor use dirty fuel as they cannot afford clean fuels. But, surprisingly 66.44% of the nonpoor also use dirty fuel. So, being just nonpoor according to Tendulkar's poverty line definition, 2012 does not provide enough affordability required for switching to cleaner fuels. Moreover, there are factors like lack of awareness, cultural belief, tradition of family, etc. that stop them to use modern fuels even when they have the needed capability to buy those. 33.56% nonpoor use clean fuels. On the other hand, 90.75% of the clean fuel users and 73.05% of the dirty fuel users are nonpoor. The differences are significant with less than 1% level. The lack of one-to-one correspondence between the status of being poor/nonpoor and the type of fuel used calls for a regression analysis to understand the causality between income and the choice of fuel.

8.5.2 Structural Equation Analysis (Path Analysis)

The hypothesis is that expenditure on clean fuel depends upon how empowered the women of the household are, their educational attainment, their spouses' education, per capita income, number of meals cooked per day and the hours for which stove burns per day. As mentioned before, the women empowerment is measured by structural equation modelling (SEM). Women Empowerment Index (WEI) is constructed considering five indicators, namely WEIF, WEIO, WEIM, WEIP and WEIW. The indicators have been defined earlier. The weights of the indicators in the formation of WEI is determined by the SEM technique. In addition, the study also hypothesizes that there is an interdependence between women empowerment and the arrangement in which cooking is done (denoted as *cooking*). The cooking arrangement is dependent on three exogenous indictors. They are SK, V and CH as explained before. The latent structure of *WEI* and *Cooking* are captured by the SEM technique. Moreover, the type of cooking arrangement depends on the woman's voice in household decision, i.e. *WEI* and on the other way, opportunity to cook in a better arrangement adds to the empowerment as it reflects better affordability and awareness. So, *WEI and Cooking* are related and that is taken care of by the technique applied here. Two measurement models are used here that construct *WEI and Cooking*. The coefficients are standardized.

In the structural model, expenditure on clean fuel (EXCF) depends on LNPCI, EW, ES, MC and SB. The variables are described before. The path analysis also considers the interrelation between the independent variables in the model. The per capita income of the woman depends on her education level. Education level of spouse also affects the per capita income as it is obtained by dividing total income of the household, which includes income of the spouse, by the household size. Education of spouse as well as the woman herself impact total income of the household. Hence, they are related. Education of both woman and spouse are again related between themselves as one's education enhances the inspiration of others to enhance and get higher level education. In the process, overall awareness of the family increases which has an influence on the fuel choice. The mutual dependence of woman and spouse's education has been addressed in the model. The education of the couple, again has an impact on the number of meals cooked in the household. This may have an implication that education increases the probability of getting job. This, in turn, leads to less time spent by the woman and the spouse inside the house, and ideally less meal should be required. Same explanation applies for the number of hours stove burns per day. The number of meals cooked in a household obviously increases the burning time of the stoves. So, relation between MC and SB is also anticipated.

The measurement models and the structural models are illustrated in the path diagram (Fig. 8.2). Boxes contain the variables which are observed in the data and the circles contain the unobserved or latent variables. The path coefficients are shown along the arrows. Here, all standardized path coefficients are taken.

The above figure corresponds to the following equations:

$x_i = \alpha_i + \beta_i X + e.\ x_i$, where x_i's are WEIF, WEIO, WEIM, WEIP, WEIW; X is WEI.

$z_i = \gamma_i + \delta_i Z + e.\ z_i$, where z_i's are SK, V, CH; Z is *cooking*.

$y = \theta + \lambda X + e.\ y$; y is EXCF

$$y = \varphi + \pi_1 \text{LNPCI} + \pi_2 \text{EW} + \pi_3 ES + \pi_4 \text{MC} + \pi_5 \text{SB};$$

$$\text{LNPCI} = \mu_1 \text{ES} + \mu_2 \text{EW} + e.\text{LNPCI};$$

$$\text{SB} = \rho.\text{MC} + e.\text{SB}$$

The result of the path analysis is shown in the following table (Table 8.5).

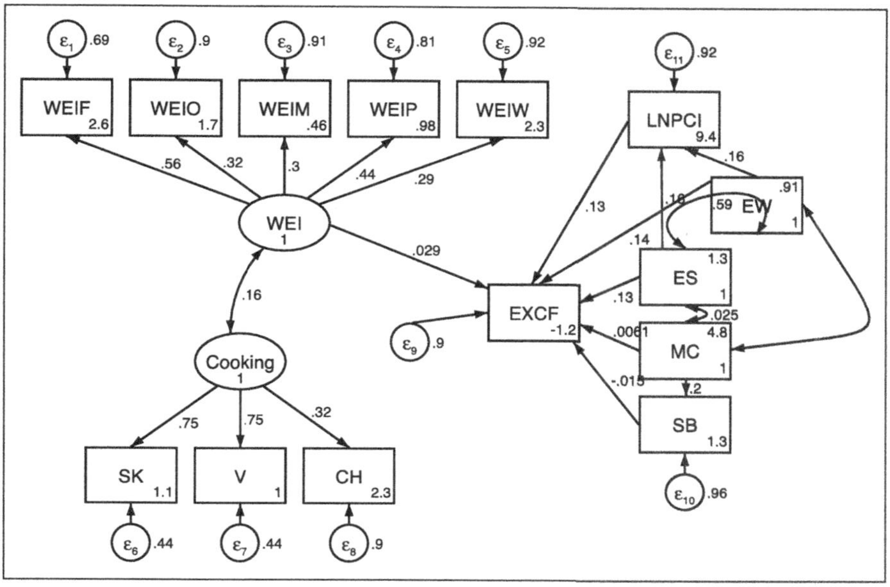

Fig. 8.2 Path diagram

Table 8.5 depicts the result of both measurement models and structural models. The measurement models are presented in the upper panel and the structural model in the lower panel.

8.5.2.1 Measurement Model

Two measurement models have been estimated. The latent variables determined are the *WE*I and *cooking*. The coefficients are all significant.

For *WEI,* the coefficient of WEIF is the highest followed by WEIP. The other observed variables, WEIO, WEIM and WEIW have more or less equal weightage in the formation of WEI. The participation of woman in the financial decision (WEIF) leaves the maximum impact on empowerment. Possession of assets (WEIP) also play an important role in raising the position of the woman within the household and thereby empowering her. Freedom to go outside (WEIO), membership in various associations, groups and bodies (WEIM) and participation in work and related decision (WEIW) also leave significant contribution in making the woman empowered. Significance of the coefficients reflect that the latent structure of the WEI is explained well through these five indicators.

For *cooking*, existence of separate kitchen in the house and presence of ventilation in the cooking area have significant impact on the determination of the latent variable '*cooking*', that stands for cooking arrangement. The use of clean chulha also plays significant role. The hypothesis that *WEI* and *cooking* are mutually dependent

Table 8.5 Result of structural equation analysis

Measurement models—standardized coefficients

Observed variables	Latent variable (*WEI*)	*P* value	Observed variables	Latent variable (*Cooking*)	*P* value
WEIF	0.56	0.00	SK	0.75	0.00
WEIO	0.32	0.00	V	0.75	0.00
WEIM	0.30	0.00	CH	0.32	0.00
WEIP	0.44	0.00			
WEIW	0.29	0.00			

Structural model—standardized coefficients

Explanatory variable	Coefficient (dependent variable-*EXCF*)	*P* value	Interdependent paths					
			Exogenous variables	Coefficient (dependent variable-*LNPCI*)	*P* value	Exogenous variables	Coefficient (dependent variable-*SB*)	*P* value
LNPCI	0.13	0.00	EW	0.16	0.00	MC	0.20	0.00
EW	0.14	0.00	ES	0.16	0.00			
ES	0.13	0.00	Covariances					
WEI	0.03	0.00	Interdependence	Value	*P* value			
			Cov (EW, ES)	0.59	0.00			
MC	0.07	0.30	Cov (EW, MC)	0.10	0.00			
SB	−0.01	0.02	Cov (ES, MC)	0.02	0.00			
Constant	−1.16	0.00	Cov (WEI, cooking)	0.16	0.00			

Source: Author's calculation
Number of observations: 25,663 (missing values are treated by the model)
Root mean squared error of approximation (RMSEA): 0.08
P value: 0.00

is strengthened by the significance of the covariance obtained between the two variables (shown in the last row of the Table 8.5).

8.5.2.2 Structural Models

The lower panel of the Table 8.5 presents the structural model. The model has been explained before. The dependent variable is expenditure on clean fuel (EXCF). The explanatory variables identified for the model are hypothesized to explain the expenditure on clean cooking. The result shows that income (LNPCI), education of woman (EW) and her spouse (ES) and the empowerment of woman (WEI) affect the expenditure on clean cooking positively. All these indicators are significant. As a person earns more, he/she climbs in the energy ladder moving towards the cleaner energy choice from the dirty option. This happens because cleaner energy is dearer than the dirtier ones and as income increases, affordability increases and the person goes for cleaner fuel. The positive coefficient of LNPCI signifies that phenomenon. Moreover, higher income ideally accompanies higher awareness through better education opportunity. This is shown by the structural model involving LNPCI, EW and ES. EW and ES both have positive significant impact on LNPCI. This awareness also makes the case for choice in favour of clean fuel. Education of woman and her spouse is important in this context as it implies enhanced awareness in both. Positive and significant coefficients of EW and ES in explaining EXCF provides evidence for that. The number of meals cooked per day (MC) does not affect EXCF significantly. It may be because that households maintain a portfolio of fuels, and they may choose dirty fuel or a mixed bag if the number of meals increases. The number of hours stove burns for cooking, heating, etc. has a negative impact on EXCF implying again that the longer the stove burns the more households go for dirty fuel as this is cheaper than cleaner option. More use compels households to choose dirty fuel.

When all the above-mentioned variables are controlled, the incremental contribution of women empowerment can be estimated. This is coming out to be positive and significant. This implies that woman, if empowered, can take decisions regarding the household expenditure and becomes aware about the adverse effects of dirty fuel. A sufficiently empowered woman can have voice in household decisions and can also influence the household purchase that includes fuel. In addition, as the children under 5 years are majorly carried by their mothers or grandmothers during cooking, and the children more than 5 years of age more or less roam around their mothers, it is justified that an empowered mother would take care of her child's health and will make a choice of fuel that would affect her child least. So, empowerment makes the woman confident, aware, conscious and strong enough to make the choice in favour of clean fuel that would protect the health of her children and other household members. On the other hand, lack of empowerment and awareness prevents woman to make proper voice and remain to continue with the dirty fuel with traditional cooking arrangement making her own children's and others health in a serious hazard, if her male counterpart does not pay enough attention to the matter.

Table 8.6 Fit statistics for original model

Fit statistic	Value description
RMSEA (Root mean square error of approximation)	0.081
Comparative fit index (CFI)	0.64
Tucker-Lewis index (TLI)	0.54

Source: Author's calculation

This may happen even when the household can afford clean fuel and availability of that does not put a constraint. Woman empowerment and awareness are very crucial for making the clean fuel choice within the household and thereby reducing the hazardous health effect of traditional fuels which is a serious concern of policy makers in most of the developing countries including India.

8.5.3 Model Fit (Original Model)

Few statistical tests are applied here to fit the model. They are chi square, RMSEA (root mean square error of approximation), comparative fit index (CFI), and Tucker–Lewis index (TLI). The chi square value with the present sample size is coming significant rejecting the model. In Table 8.6 different fit statistics for the model is reported.

The Comparative Fit Index (CFI) and the Tucker-Lewis Index (TLI) have values 0.64 and 0.54 respectively. These values are also suggesting that the model is not acceptable as the rule of thumb is a value of at least 0.95 is required to accept the model. The root mean square error of approximation (RMSEA) takes a value 0.081 and typically RMSEA of 0.05 is required for good approximation. It also rejects the model.

8.5.4 Modification of the Model

As the existing path analysis is not explaining the structure of the relationship among the variable well, a modification of the model has been tried. The modification includes covariances between the error structure of the following variables: WEIF & WEIO; WEIF & WEIM; WEIF & WEIP; WEIF & EXCF; WEIF & SK; WEIF & CH; WEIF & LNPCI; WEIO & WEIM; WEIO & WEIP; WEIO & WEIW; WEIW & LNPCI; EXCF & SK; EXCF & CH; SK & V; SK & LNPCI; V & LNPCI, CH & SB; EW & *cooking;* ES & *cooking*. The modifications have been included keeping the theoretical justification in view. Women's freedom to take decisions in financial matters (WEIF) makes the woman stronger in expressing views and hence she enjoys more freedom in going outside home (WEIO). Also, WEIF impacts the women's participation in associations as members (WEIM). Women's possession

(WEIP) is likely to enhance WEIF and WEIF also helps woman to take decisions regarding expenditure on the clean fuel spent by the household (EXCF). WEIF influences the decisions of the household whether to have separate kitchen (SK), ventilation in the cooking area (V) and the type of chulha (CH) the household is using. WEIF also depends on the per capita income of the household. The freedom of the woman to go outside home (WEIO) has connections with whether she belongs to any association as a member (WEIM), and also with the property possessed by her (WEIP). Women's participation in work (WEIW) has obvious connection with WEIO. WEIW is likely to impact the per capita income of the household (LNPCI). EXCF is related to SK and CH. Having separate kitchen (SK) and the chulha type (CH) have connections. The per capita income of the household defines the financial position of the household and therefore the kitchen type and presence of ventilator in the kitchen area are influenced by the affordability and therefore by LNPCI. The hours of stove burns (SB) depends on the chulha type. Finally, the entire cooking arrangement depends on the educational attainment of the woman and her spouse. The Incorporating these modifications, the model has been estimated again and the result is shown in Table 8.7.

In the modified model, the weightage of *women's participation in associations as members (WEIM)* has increased in women empowerment and that of *WEIO* and *WEIP* have gone down. Participation in association exposes the woman to outside world and people from different stratum of the society. This empowers woman. The loadings of WEIO and WEIP have gone down. Simply possessing the property or freedom to go outside always do not lead to empowerment, power to take decisions have large contributions in empowerment that possibly come as a fall out of membership in associations. Both in original and modified model *women's freedom to take decisions in financial matters (WEIF*) plays a vital role in empowering the women. In the latent structure of *cooking,* the coefficients of SK and V have gone down and that of chulha type (CH) have gone up. The loading of WEI has increased in the modified model implying women empowerment plays more important role in determining the expenditure in clean fuel in the revised model. It strengthens the claim that demand for clean fuel depends on, among other factors, on the empowerment of women inside the household as that helps them to reveal the demand for clean fuel. All other interpretations remain same in the modified model as in the original model.

8.5.5 Model Fit (Modified Model)

The goodness of fit indices have improved manifold indicating that the modified model is an acceptable model. The new fit measures are shown in the following table (Table 8.8).

The rule of thumb for all the three indices mentioned in Table 8.8 indicate that the model can be grossly accepted in the modified form.

Table 8.7 Results of modified model

Measurement models—standardized coefficients

Observed variables	Latent variable (*WEI*)	*P* value	Observed variables	Latent variable (*Cooking*)	*P* value
WEIF	0.63	0.00	SK	0.47	0.00
WEIO	0.04	0.00	V	0.43	0.00
WEIM	0.50	0.00	CH	0.49	0.00
WEIP	0.34	0.00			
WEIW	0.18	0.00			

Structural model—Standardized coefficients

			Interdependent paths					
Explanatory variable	Coefficient (dependent variable-*EXCF*)	*P* value	Exogenous variables	Coefficient (dependent variable-*LNPCI*)	*P* value	Exogenous variables	Coefficient (dependent variable-*SB*)	*P* value
LNPCI	0.13	0.00	EW	0.16	0.00	MC	0.20	0.00
EW	0.14	0.00	ES	0.16	0.00			
ES	0.13	0.00						
WEI	0.13	0.00						
MC	−0.003	0.50						
SB	−0.01	0.03						
Constant	−1.10	0.00						

Source: Author's calculation

Number of observations:25,663 (missing values are treated by the model)

Table 8.8 Fit statistics for modified model

Fit statistic	Value description
RMSEA (Root mean square error of approximation)	0.047
Comparative fit index (CFI)	0.91
Tucker–Lewis index (TLI)	0.85

Source: Author's calculation

8.6 Conclusion

This chapter tries to estimate the impact of women empowerment on the household fuel choice. This is an important policy matter because indoor pollution is one of the most important risk factors in the developing world (World Bank 2009). The direct factors that affect the indoor smoke are the type of fuel household is using and the cooking arrangement. The fuel choice is an endogenous decision for the household, influenced by the affordability and awareness of the person who makes the purchase decision. The affordability factor may generally be taken care of by the supply of cleaner fuels at a subsidized rate on the part of the government. The subsidized supply of fuel is a necessary condition for altering the fuel choice, but it is in general, not sufficient. This is because, even when the household is sufficiently able in the economic side, clean fuel does not enter their decision set due to lack of awareness. The utility function, in this case, does not contain the clean fuel when they make the choice for optimum bundle of goods. As the main user of fuel is generally the woman of the house, their perception is very important. The voice of woman is essential when the fuel is purchased for the household use. This is possible when the woman is empowered, and she possesses sufficient awareness regarding the adverse effects of pollution created out of dirty fuels. This work finds women empowerment affects the expenditure of the household on clean fuel significantly. An empowered woman makes choice in favour of clean fuels. She and her husband's awareness also play a crucial role. So, for a clean indoor environment the supply of cleaner fuel is important and would have the maximum favourable outcome in terms of clean choice of fuel when woman can take the decision regarding the matter. This is possible when they are empowered and enlightened enough. So, policy should target at raising the awareness of the women through providing proper education to the woman, through creating awareness for her family members, through raising job opportunities and financial inclusion of the woman and creating an environment that would enable them to make larger participation in the society as well as to make them confident to take part in household decision.

References

Cecelski, E. (2003). *Enabling equitable access to rural electrification: Current thinking on energy, poverty and gender*. Washington, DC: The World Bank/ASTAE.

Clancy, J. S., Skutsch, M. M., & Batchelor S. (2003). The gender – energy – poverty nexus: Finding the energy to address gender concerns in development. In *Paper prepared for the UK Department for International Development (DFID)*, London.

Desai, S., Reeve, V., & National Council of Applied Economic Research, New Delhi. (2011). *India Human Development Survey-II (IHDS-II), 2011–2012. ICPSR36151-v2*. Ann Arbor, MI: Inter-university Consortium for Political and Social Research [distributor]. https://doi.org/10.3886/ICPSR36151.v2.

ESMAP Report. (2004). *The impact of energy on Women's lives in rural India*. Washington, DC: The World Bank.

Groot, N., Mohlakoana, N., Knox, A., & Bressers, H. (2017). Fuelling women's empowerment? An exploration of the linkages between gender, entrepreneurship and access to energy in the informal food sector. *Energy Research & Social Science, 28*, 86–97.

Human Development Report, UNDP (2011).

Muchiri, L. (2008). Gender and equity in bioenergy access and delivery in Kenya. In *Practical action Eastern Africa*.

Reddy, A. K. N. (2000). *Energy and social issues*. UNPD, New York: World Energy Assessment. ISBN 92-1-126-126-0.

Reddy, B. S., & Nathan, H. S. K. (2012). *Energy in the development strategy of Indian households – The missing half*. Mumbai: Indira Gandhi Institute of Development Research.

Skutch, M. M. (2005). Gender analysis for energy projects and programmes. *Energy for Development, 9*(1), 37–52.

World Bank (2009). *Indoor air pollution: Sustainable rural and urban development*. Retrieved October, 2019 from http://web.worldbank.org/archive/website01100/Program/WEB/0__C-133.HTM.

Chapter 9
Smart City and Urban Poor: Can They Coexist?

Bishnu Prasad Mishra

9.1 Introduction

The Smart City, as a concept, is a new government initiative in India since last 5 years. The way the initiatives are going around in identified cities of India are widely seen as localities that actively embrace new technologies to achieve desired outcome. However, the way the concept of smart cities being implemented in India has three dimensions: the heavy techno centricity, highly complex and interconnected projects, and the ad hoc conceptualization of projects. As a result, the legitimacy is questioned, confidences of citizens in the initiatives are low and issues of financing, regulation and governance exists to a large extent.

Urbanization has become an integral part of the socio-economic growth of developing countries including India (Mohanty, 2019). Cities are home to knowledge externalities and which along with agglomeration externalities act as a powerful driver of growth. The levels of urbanization vary across countries and continents, but population growth is much faster in cities than in rural areas of India due to both higher natural increases and net migration net migration (Adikalam 2010, HPEC 2011, MUD & McKenzie 2010). Cities tend to be the focal points of economic activity and as cities develop, they are likely to act as magnets for investments, industrial production and other economic activities. Urban lifestyles are much more similar across countries and continents (Hoelscher & Aijaz 2016).

In India, 31% (337 million) of the total population live in urban areas. Within this, 42.6% live in 53 cities with more than one million population/urban agglomeration (Census of India 2011). The urban population in India is likely to increase to 50% by

B. P. Mishra (✉)
XIMB, Xavier University, Bhubaneswar, Odisha, India
e-mail: bishnu@ximb.ac.in

A. K. Mishra et al. (eds.), *Critical Perspectives on Emerging Economies*,
Contributions to Economics, https://doi.org/10.1007/978-3-030-59781-8_9

2050 (UN DESA 2014), and it is expected that by then most of the people living in India will reside in urban areas, of which 138 of them will have population above 500,000 people (World Urbanization Prospects). Great cities of the world are products of not only market forces but also policies and actions by governments that magnified the beneficial effects of externalities while minimizing their negative consequences (Mohanty 2014).

The "Smart City Mission in India" aims at robust and implementable models of urban planning based on smart plans, projects, processes and solutions (Bhole 2017). The idea is to invest Rs 100 crore annually over a 5-year period at least equally matched with resources by urban local bodies of the states to implement "Area based or Pan City" programmes. Area-based models include city improvement or retrofitting, or city renewal or redevelopment and city extension or green field development. Pan-city model includes projects having citywide implications.

A focus on cities almost inevitably brings with it the recognition of the existence of multiple social groups, neighbourhoods, contestations, claims and inequalities (Sassen 2019). We need to enter the diverse worlds of work and social contexts in the urban space and we need to understand whether and how they are connected. The "Urban Poor" issues are being closely discussed as we are heading towards the implementation of "Smart City" projects in the most part of India. In the process of implementation, the Urban Poor settlements are constantly relocated to the city fringes (Mathur 2011, Sharma 2014). There are cases when the relocation is voluntary, but most of the cases involve forceful evacuation to cleanse an area in the garb of development of city infrastructure—a pattern observed and usually referred to as "Involuntary Resettlement". (Kumari et al., 2008 & Modi 2009a, b, c).

Legally in India, the Disaster Management Act 2005 refers to R&R as "rehabilitation and reconstruction"; resettlement does not figure in this regime or in the accompanying frameworks. On the other hand, the Land Acquisition Rehabilitation and Resettlement Bill 2011 frame looks at R&R as "rehabilitation and resettlement". This is a crucial distinction. Earlier "relief and rehabilitation" as R&R was also used in the context of disasters, but recently "reconstruction" is added to the mix. Relocation does not figure in either the land or the disaster legal frameworks.

Voluntary R&R could mean people doing it of their own will, self-motivated or in agreement with the institutional aspirations. Involuntary R&R is often seen as evictions, or forced moves to locations without choice. Often these kinds of movements are forced by either the government, or natural circumstances that leave people with no choice to stay in the existing place of habitation. "Resettlement is a complex social process; at its best it should support and nourish the coping and adaptation processes that enable a population to regain the functionality and coherence of a viable community, resilient enough to deal with social and environmental stressors. Central to these tasks are the issues of rights, poverty, vulnerability and other forms of social marginality that are intrinsically linked to displacement." (Oliver-Smith and de Sherbinin, 2014).

The article is divided into four parts: The Bhubaneswar city in the state of Odisha and its demographic profile followed by the Smart City initiatives currently being implemented resulting in relocation. Next, the available literature review on relocation and objective of the study, methodology of survey and important finding with limitations. Finally, in the conclusion, the policy options/interventions required to improve the current position are highlighted.

9.2 Odisha: Demographic Profile

Odisha is a coastal state of India on the eastern side. It comprises 30 districts and covers an area of 1.56 lakh square kilometres. It has abundant natural and mineral resources—coal, iron, bauxite, chromium and manganese. 24% of India's coal deposits, 54% of bauxite, 30% of Iron ore, 95% of chromite and 40% of manganese are found in Odisha (Directorate of Economics and Statistics, Government of Odisha). From governance perspective, Odisha is divided into 317 tehsils and 314 community development blocks. There are 107 urban local bodies, 6236 gram panchayats and 47,258 villages. Odisha has an overall population of 4.20 crores, out of which 2.12 crores are males and 2.08 are females. The decadal population growth has been 14%. The population density is 270 per square kilometre as against 382 per sq. km of India. The gender ratio is 979 against 1000 males. The decadal growth in urban and rural population have experienced positive growth; rural population grew from 3.13 crores to 3.50 crores and city population grew from 55.17 lakhs to 70.03 lakhs. In percentage, rural population grew by 11.77% and urban population by 26.94% during the decade.

9.2.1 Local Governance Structure of Bhubaneswar City

Bhubaneswar is the capital city of Orissa. It is one of the first planned cities of India and has become prominent due to economic and religious importance. It is called temple city of India due to large number of beautiful temples and architectural heritages. Bhubaneswar Municipal Corporation (BMC) is the principal provider of civic services to the residents of Bhubaneswar, the capital. The entity started as a notified area committee in 1948 and became a municipality in 1979. As the city grew, the entity was upgraded as Municipal Corporation in 1994. BMC covers an area of 135 sq. km and provides service to 8.41 lakh people. BMC area has 377 slums where 3.09 lakh people live in 60,126 slum households. 37% of Bhubaneswar population lives in slums. BMC comprises 67 wards and 46 revenue villages. There are 60,126 slum houses in Bhubaneswar. Out of which 38.05% is considered good, 54.02% is liveable and 7.93% is dilapidated. 63.19% slum households live in their own homes, 22.30% households live in rented homes and rest 14.51% live in other forms of home. Households having number of dwelling rooms: 1.63% households have no exclusive rooms, 39.30% households have one dwelling room, 34.09% households have two dwelling rooms and 24.98% households live in three and above rooms.

Table 9.1 Expenses budgeted by BMC for the Urban Poor (in Rs. Million)

Year	Total expenses budget	Amount allocated for Urban Poor	Percentage
2013–2014	4259	1221	28.68
2014–2015	4150	622	14.98
2015–2016	4501	1099	24.42
2016–2017	2812	800	28.45
2017–2018	3290	357	10.84

Source: Author's Estimation from BMC budget document (http://www.bmc.gov.in)

As per the available data in respect of the budgetary allocation for expenses for Urban Poor in Bhubaneswar city, the following table details the rate of allocation over the period of 5 years starting from the Year 2013 to 2018. In the year 2017–2018, the percentage allocation is the least as the work of Smart City progressed (Table 9.1).

9.2.2 *Migration*

Migration is becoming a serious issue for cities like Bhubaneswar which can be seen from the decadal city growth and large slum population. Growing urbanization and employment opportunities have attracted majority of the people away from their home to earn basic livelihood. 67% among the Bhubaneswar slum dwellers are migrants. The demographics show that intercity migration is 98%. Migration from other districts of Odisha to Bhubaneswar is very high. Interstate migration is only 2%. 95% Migration has been from rural to urban. Only 62% of the migrant households have migrated more than 5 years and 65% of migration is permanent in nature. The reasons of migration are primarily for employment opportunities.

9.2.3 *Making of Smart City Bhubaneswar*

Bhubaneswar was accorded the Smart City tag on January 28, 2016 in the first list of 20 cities released by the centre. It got the first place because of the blueprint of development which are as follows:

Bhubaneswar, through participatory decision-making, responsible governance and open access to information and technology, to be a:

- Transit oriented city with a compact urban form that promotes active, connected and sustainable mobility choices.
- Liveable city providing diverse range of housing, educational and recreational opportunities; while enhancing its heritage, arts and traditional communities.
- Child-friendly city providing accessible, safe, inclusive and vibrant public places.

- Eco-city coexisting in harmony with nature for nurturing a resilient, clean, green, and healthy environment.
- Regional economic centre attracting knowledge-based enterprises and sustainable tourism activities by leveraging and empowering its institutions, local businesses and informal workforce.

Bhubaneswar's proposal envisions retrofitting and redeveloping 985-acres cantered around main railway station in the heart of the city to a vibrant 24 × 7 destination—the Bhubaneswar Town Centre District (BTCD). Bhubaneswar's state-of-the-art Intelligent City Operations and Management Centre (ICOMC) is at the core of its pan-city proposal. Hence, in true sense may well be called a model "Smart Part-city". The capital city will see a major change after the development of the Bhubaneswar Town Centre District, which is a 985-acre demarcated area from Bapuji Nagar to Sahid Nagar. The BTCD area has a lot of slums which was cleared/ forcefully cleansed for almost 26 projects implementation. These households partly got officially relocated to the fringes of the city where a few got allotted alternate housing facility.

The Bhubaneswar Smart City Project Status up to March, 2019 indicates the tardy progress made for implantation and as the identified area for Smart City does not cover slum, the expenditure for Urban Poor is observed to be minimal.

1. Total number of projects tendered/cost incurred—16
2. Cost discovered in case of tender done—Rs. 9543.4 million
3. Cost incurred till date of SCM fund—Rs. 2353.4 million
4. Total funds released to Bhubaneswar Smart City Ltd. (BSCL)—Rs. 1960 million (during 2019–2020)

9.3 Social Vulnerability: Literature Review on Relocation

There seems to be a persistence of poverty and inequality in urban areas, particularly seen through the lens of slums and unemployment (Baker 2004, Dupont 2008). Although the proportion of the poor in the total population is falling both in urban and rural areas, the absolute number of Urban Poor is increasing (Chen and Raveendran 2012).

Million plus cities are indeed home to 40% of the slum population. However, the majority of the poor are, in fact, concentrated in medium and small towns—80% of the Urban Poor reside in cities with populations less than one million (Revi et al., 2008). In terms of employment, the extent of informality in urban employment is high at around 70%. It has remained largely unchanged over the course of the past decade. Almost 60% of the total urban employed are wage workers, and 67% of this category are informal wage workers. The remaining are largely the urban self-employed, which includes own account workers, employers and contributing family workers (Chen and Raveendran 2012, Revi 2008, Revi et a.l, 2014).

9.3.1 Gaps

Some of the gaps found in the reviewed literature were as follows: There is not one national database for past, ongoing and planned relocations including scale, reasons, impacts, etc. and also best practices for governments and organizations to learn and implement in their context.

Relocation has been attempted in many cities across India; however, either most of them did not involve long-term follow-up of the displaced people or if they did, there is no information on these issues found from the literature. There are reviewed articles which give us an idea about the number of people/communities that were displaced, reasons for displacement, but there very little information on the experiences of displaced families.

There is limited understanding on the types of housing and other facilities provided to people post displacement (Jain et al. 2016).

9.3.2 The Primary Issues of the Survey

- Are these newly developed localities, does help the Urban Poor in meeting their basic needs?
- In a planned (so-called) localities on the city fringes, are these people not segregated to a world thrust upon them?
- What are the support systems provided to continue with the same lifestyle enjoyed by them earlier?
- In respect of people forcefully uprooted, is there life for rebuilding?

These are few questions which were the subject matter of a survey in the city of Bhubaneswar. We have covered the two important clusters of Ghatikia and Bharatpur area of Bhubaneswar, Odisha, where there is presumably higher concentration of relocated/resettled families sheltered.

9.3.3 Methodology Used for the Survey

A month-long outreach survey was undertaken, through document analysis and a self-reported questionnaire (Copy enclosed as Annexure-1) was filled out by the interviewers.

Research Sample Sample consists of 2065 respondents from two identified slums, Ghatikia and Bharatpur, in the fringes of the city of Bhubaneswar, which consists of 10,000 (approx.) household units.

Research Questions The study is divided into four parts. A pilot study was done to improve the reliability and validity of the questionnaire used for the main study.

Part 1 consists of general information regarding the respondents which includes demographics (e.g. age, gender, monthly income of the household). Then personal information is about the main source of income, monthly household income, economic status, any photo ID card, bank account in their name, mobile number, type of house, etc.

Part 2 of the survey is about the details of new location among the participants. For example, the details of new relocated/settled location, available facilities in respect of living condition and the approximate time spent in commuting to the work place, primary source for provision of health, education, etc., their availability and access for usage.

Part 3 of the survey is all about the details of livelihood options in new relocated location and the time to travel to work in old places in continuing employment. If new work is opted under changed circumstances or a new business, what is the facilitation processes coming from the new location and other members of the family are evidenced.

Part 4 consists of information on both physical and financial vulnerability and the coping behaviour for crisis management. There is also information solicited on source and methods to cope in a crisis, what are the contributions from the government schemes, whether the assistance is in form of Cash or Kind and the sources of information for the availability of such assistance.

9.4 Survey Findings

Part 1 of the survey covers the general information about the participants; we found out of 2076 participants: number of males is 16,019 (which is 78.46% of the respondents) and 446 females (which is 21.54% of the total samples). There are 17 missing cases. The average age of the participants is 42 (Table 9.2).

The majority of the respondents are from general categories and out of that 15.6% lives in pucca houses (allotted by BMC), 72.4% lives in semi-pucca and rest 3% lives in kutcha houses (Table 9.3).

More than 75% of the respondents were not having any type of card where they will get social benefit as a citizen. The ration card holders are more than the BPL card

Table 9.2 Social status of the participants

Social status	No. of participants
SC	363
ST	242
OBC	486
General	858
Minority	127

Table 9.3 Economic status of the respondents

Economic status	Number of participants	Percentages of participants
APL	13	0.63
BPL	138	6.65
Ration card	241	11.60
Antodaya	56	2.70
Others	3	0.15
Not having any card	1625	78.27

Table 9.4 Percentage of valid photo ID card

Photo ID card	Number of participants	Percentages of participants
Voter ID	855	41.3
Aadhaar card	1073	51.7
Employment guarantee card	5	0.2
Others	21	1.0
Not having any above-mentioned cards	124	4.2

Note: the above-mentioned number of participants were those who was able to produce the card to the interviewer

Table 9.5 Basic facilities currently being used

Facilities	Available (%)	Not available (%)
Water	46	54
Electric	61	39
Latrine	71	29
Health	17	83
Primary education	12	88
Earlier facilities comparison	11	89

holders. To understand the economic status in a better way, we have asked the respondents about the monthly household income. 10.7% of the participants earn more than 2000 rupees per month, 54.3% of the respondents earn more than 5000 rupees per month and less than 10,000 rupees. 29% of the respondents earn more than 10,000 rupees per month. When it comes to having a bank account in their name or one of the family members name, 1681 (81%) of the respondents replied that they have and 301 (14.5%) of the respondents were not having any bank account. Rest of the 94 (3%) of the respondents were not ready to disclose it (Table 9.4).

Part 2 of the survey is about the acceptance level of living conditions in the new location where they have got relocated. Respondents were asked about the approximate distance over which they have shifted where majority of them (more than 94%) moved beyond 10 km and more from the old place of in the relocated area, 39% of occupants were allotted alternative by Bhubaneswar Municipal Corporation (BMC). Asked about the available living conditions currently they are using, the response is summarized in Table 9.5.

Table 9.6 Approximate time in spent in travelling to work per day

Travel time (in minutes)	% of participants
15	Nil
30	12
60	27
90	51
>90	1
Not sure about it	9

Table 9.7 Coping with vulnerability

Vulnerability	Redressal source (%)			
Physical sickness-neighbourly help	Yes	91	No	9
(Reliability)	Yes	89	No	11
(Willingness)	Voluntary	87	Coerced	13
Financial help-	Neighbour	26	Members back home	47
Strength of social network for assistance	High	90.1	Medium	8.7

From Table 9.4, it is clear that 46% of the participants are getting water facility from tap, 61% electricity and latrine facility 71% (due to availability of community latrine under Swacch Bharat initiative). Availability of health facility is minimal at 17% and the most deficient is the primary education at 12%. In comparison to the facilities they were enjoying in the previous place and now, the response was in mostly negative (around 38%-none and 48%-minimum). Only 14% of respondents categorized the current facilities as medium in context of level of planning and provision of services.

Part 3 is related to the livelihood options available for post relocation and if the old occupations are pursued, then what are the differences being faced particularly in respect of travel to work place (Table 9.6).

Majority of people have to travel to work (71% of the respondents) beyond 1 h and the cost involved up to rupees 25–30 per day for majority of them. Around 14% of people have changed to small services and shops in and around the locality. They are supported in their ventures by other family members. (Partly-36%, Fully-16%). As the mode of travel to work 26% use public transport and 17% only use their own conveyance (semi-skilled category). However, the bulk of the daily wage labourers are being taken by contractors, at their own cost, to the place of work as reported.

Part 4 elaborates the respondent analysis regarding crisis management and coping behaviour in case vulnerability in terms of help, both physical and financial, the source of help extended and level of assurances. The extent of government support extended in relocation and otherwise post-settlement, the nature of support and source of the information about support is outlined (Table 9.7).

Among the total number of participants, it appears that the element of mutual help in physical distress is relatively high in relation to financial emergencies. The measurement of social collateral among the respondent group is relatively high as 90% of respondents admitted being helped in case of need by the neighbours in the

Table 9.8 Status of government intervention benefits (%)

Knowledge of government schemes	yes	38	No	62
Source of knowledge	Neighbour	22	Others (NGO)	78
Benefits availed	Yes	47	No	53
Benefits received in kind	Ration	11.6	Gas	35.8
Benefits received in cash	Yes	33	No	67

locality. But for emergency, financial support is still forthcoming from back home linkages to the extent of 47% which implies that the people have still maintain relationship to the original home land for coping mechanism.

As regards, government support to these sample localities, the assistance has come both in kind and cash. The availability of benefits from the government schemes are skewed because of ignorance coupled with lack of verifiable documents. These findings can be inferred from the following Table 9.8.

9.4.1 Findings of the Study

In short, the data revealed spectacular findings in respect of Urban Poor which stands contrary to the general belief.

- It is a common thinking that the Urban Poor are less enterprising in nature.
- They subject to high vulnerability in case of relocation as their lives get started afresh without ecological support in a new environment.
- They are usually crushed under the burden of re-adjustment.
- Their social collateral is poor because of lack of cohesion, conflict and disparate background in a new setting.

9.4.2 Limitations of the Study

1. The number of samples being limited, as usual, it may be subject to sampling bias, how much may be the rigour in selection of respondents.
2. Some parameters are qualitative in nature, which may be affected by the judgement as perceived by the interviewer. Hence, observations are quite subjective.
3. Taking the period of survey, it may not be unusual for the respondents to answer the questions depending on the most recent experiences which may differ over a periodic enquiry.

9.4.3 Policy Actions

- The government should facilitate the identification of settled inhabitants as legitimate citizens of the city. The necessary identity papers for the households are to be quickly arranged, if required, with the help of the NGOs.
- The common living conditions of the locality have to be improved substantially to make the area liveable and conducive to basic hygiene and safety.
- The informal structure of the group has to be recognized and to be strengthened with necessary back up of required formality without distinction of groups, caste and religion. The people should not be only recognized as a vote base at the time of election when a lot of promises are made by the candidates, but seldom translated to effective implementation.
- The basic necessities like health, education and nutrition under various government schemes at par with other developed localities have to be delivered to instil confidence among the relocated ones that they are not discriminated.
- The social exclusion and deprivation which are currently observed have to be removed with better governance standard of ground level operating functionaries of the BMC. These parts of the city are still considered fringes with regard to public service provisions made available to the city residents, for example, transport, roads and drain infrastructure, and night patrolling.
- Lastly, the fact that these people are integral to the city and immensely contributing to city's growth has to be recognized. The planning should be made, keeping in mind, the granular layers of assessment of the locality needs so as not to convert these areas to Ghettos in future.

9.5 Conclusion

Urban systems, particularly from the perspective of informal economy and settlements, go relatively unrecognized in the context of cities. However, such systems support an important aspect of economic and non-economic activities in cities. There is a need to understand such informal systems, activities and settlements, institutional architecture—particularly informal grouping of people, informal processes, rules, norms and conventions (that supports the existence of the Urban Poor) which needs to be understood and assessed.

While cities agglomerate risk, create risk and often serve as respondents to risk experienced on forceful eviction, they also offer transformational opportunity to address these risks building on the established institutional and financial capacities of the cities as well as their limited numbers. Social capital (including community cohesion and social fabric); whether it gets disturbed post-resettlement or whether it gets strengthened and contributes to building resilient communities/individuals is an important area. Certain direct impacts (of varying kinds) on the people and the impact on the extant cultural heritage also need to be assessed.

The processes of urbanization (particularly in developing a Smart City) have unleashed an outcome that is riding on the incidence of huge development deficits within groups that are most exposed to physical risks. These risks get exacerbated through inadequate provision of services, lack of institutional support mechanisms and (state) non-recognition of informality. The most vulnerable are therefore underwritten through informal support structures (service and institutions), which go unreported and get unrecognized. Multiple risks intensify vulnerabilities and therefore, propel the poor and vulnerable groups to co-create *juggad* safety nets. The scale and intensity of support systems are however inadequate. But, nevertheless, they enable the relocated household to certain extent to survive with a semblance of dignity.

Annexure-I

1.Name	:					
2.Sex	:	Male		Female		
3.Age	:					
4.Social Status	:	SC	ST	OBC	Gen	Minority
5.Address	:	Present		Permanent		
Village/Hamlet/Street/Area	:					
Gram Panchayat/Ward	:					
Block/NAC/Municipality	:					
District	:					
6.Do you have any address proof	:	Electricity bill	Municipal Receipt	Any other documents		
7.Tel/Mobile No.	:					
8.Type of House	:	Pucca	Semi-Pucca	Kutcha		
9.No. of Persons in the family	:	Adult		Children		Total
10.Occupation/Main source of Income	:					
11.Monthly Income (INR)of household	:	>2000 PM	>5000 PM	>10,000/<10,000 PM		
12.Economic Status	:	APL	BPL	Ration Card	Antodaya	Others
13.Do you have any card mentioned above	:	Yes		No		
14.If Yes, Mention the card type and Number	:					
15.Do you have any Photo ID Card	:	Voter ID	Aadhaar Card	Employment Guarantee Card	Others	
15.If Yes, Mention the Card type and Number	:					
16.Any member of the family holds a Bank Account	:	Yes		No		
17.Name of the Bank Account holder	:					
18.If Yes, Mention the Bank/Branch name/ Bank Account Number	:	Bank Name	Branch name	Bank Ac Number/ Bank IFSC code		

Part-2 New Location

1.Type of Urban form	:	Cluster		Dispersed	
2.Distance between the old and new location	:	3km	5km	10km	>10km
3.Is the house allotted by BMC	:	Yes		No	
4.Land tenure status in new location	:	Rented	Owned	Encroached	
5.Size of the House	:	Medium	Small	Bare minimum	
6.Whether the basic facility like water Latrine Facility & electricity available	:	Yes		No	

7.Any school is available nearby	:	Yes		No	
8.Any primary Health Care available	:	Yes		No	
9.Do you enjoy convenience of earlier place	:	Yes		No	
10.Level of planning and provision	:	Good	Medium	Minimum	None

Part-3 Livelihood options

1.How do you earn your income	:	Daily wage	Support service	Semi-skilled	
2. Have you changed your occupation because of Relocation		Fully	Partially	NO	
3.How much you have to travel daily to work	:	15 m	30 m	60 m	90 m
4.What is the mode of transport	:	Personal		Public	
5.What is the approx. cost of travel to work (to & fro per day)	:	10 Rs	25 Rs	30 Rs	50 Rs
6.If not is category 1, Are you running your own business	:	Yes		No	
7.what is the involvement in the business of other family members	:	Nil	Partly	Fully	

Part-4 Crisis management & Coping Vulnerability

1.If you have any physical help (in case of sickness) can you rely on your neighbors	:	Yes	No		
2.Are they helpful and come forward to assist	:	Yes	No		
3.If you have any financial need, you depend on	:	Members back home	Neighbor	Friends in the same locality	
4.If their help is forth coming	:	Voluntarily	Non-voluntary		
5.Strength of social networking in case of emergency	:	High	Medium	Low	
6. Are you aware of the different benefits from Govt. Scheme?	:	Yes	No		
7. How do you know about the schemes?		From Neighbor	From others		
8. Have you benefited from any Government Scheme?		Yes	No		
9. What is the Benefits Received in kind?		Ration	Gas	Construction material	Any other
10. Have you received any Money?		Yes	No		

Thanks for providing the valuable information

Date: Signature of the Respondent

References

Adaikalam, V. F. (2010). Eviction, housing and livelihood in Chennai. *Refugee Watch, 36*, 31–52.

Baker, J. (2004). *Analysing urban poverty, a summary of methods and approaches* (Vol. 3399). Washington, DC: World Bank Publications.

Bholey, M. (2017). Smart cities and sustainable urbanism: A study from policy and design perspective. *Scholedge International Journal of Multidisciplinary & Allied Studies, 4*(6), 36–49.

Census (2011). GOI.

Chen, M. A., & Raveendran, G. (2012). Urban employment in India: Recent trends and patterns. Margin. *The Journal of Applied Economic Research, 6*(2), 159–179.

Dupont, V. (2008). Slum demolitions in Delhi since the 1990s: An appraisal. *Economic and Political Weekly*, 79–87.

High Powered Expert Committee (HPEC). (2011). *Report on Indian urban infrastructure and services*. Government of India: Urban Development Ministry.

Hoelscher, K., & Aijaz, R. (2016). Challenges and opportunities in an urbanizing India. *International Area Studies Review, 19*(1), 3–11.

Indian Institute for Human Settlements, Bangalore (2014). Locating the debate - poverty and vulnerability in Urban India. IIHS–RF paper on Urban Poverty.

Jain, G., et al. (2016). *Reducing relocation risk in urban areas - a diagnostic report*. Bangalore: Indian Institute for Human Settlement.

Kumari, A., Banerjee, J., Nanbetiya, K. K., Sinha, V. K., Kumar, V., Prakash, A., & Chaurasia, R. (2008). Development, displacement, resettlement and rehabilitation in India - an overview. In *National Seminar on Policies, Statutes & Legislation in Mines*.

Mathur, H. M. (2011). *Resettling displaced people. Policy and practice in India*. London: Taylor & Francis Ltd.

Ministry of Urban Development, McKenzie (2010). Resurgent analysis. Government of India.

Modi, R. (2009a). *Beyond relocation: The imperative of sustainable resettlement*. New Delhi: SAGE Publications.

Modi, R. (2009b). *Resettlement and rehabilitation in urban Centres*. New Delhi: SAGE Publication.

Modi, R. (2009c). Resettlement and rehabilitation in urban centres. *Economic and Political Weekly*, 20–22.

Mohanty, P. K. (2014). *Cities and public policy- an urban agenda for India*. New Delhi: SAGE Publication.

Mohanty, P. K. (2019). *Planning and economics of cities*. New Delhi: SAGE Publication.

Revi, A., et al. (2014). Indian urban poverty strategy (2013–17). In *United nations development Programme*. Bangalore: Indian Institute for Human Settlements.

Revi, A. (2008). Climate change risk: An adaptation and mitigation agenda for Indian cities. *Environment and Urbanization, 20*(1), 207–229. https://doi.org/10.1177/0956247808089157.

Sassen, S. (2019). *Cities in a world economy* (5th ed.). Thousand Oaks, CA: SAGE Publications.

Sharma, P. (2014). Serving the cities: An Indian scenario. *IOSR Journal of Humanities and Social Science (IOSR-JHSS), 19*(1), 15–22. Ver. X.

Index

A. K. Mishra et al. (eds.), *Critical Perspectives on Emerging Economies*, Contributions to Economics, https://doi.org/10.1007/978-3-030-59781-8

The manufacturer's authorised representative in the EU is Springer
Nature Customer Service Centre GmbH, Europaplatz 3, 69115 Heidelberg,
Germany. If you have any concerns regarding our products, please
contact ProductSafety@springernature.com

Printed and bound by CPI Group (UK) Ltd, Croydon, CR0 4YY
28/09/2026
02224086-0019